The Foreign Policy of Saudi Arabia

Harvard Middle Eastern Studies, 19

Published in cooperation with the Dayan Center for Middle Eastern and African Studies, Tel-Aviv University

THE FOREIGN POLICY OF SAUDI ARABIA

The Formative Years, 1902–1918

Jacob Goldberg

Harvard University Press
Cambridge, Massachusetts, and London, England   1986

Library of Congress Cataloging-in-Publication Data

Goldberg, Jacob.
  The foreign policy of Saudi Arabia.
  (Harvard Middle Eastern studies ; 19)
  Bibliography: p.
  Includes index.
  1. Saudi Arabia—Foreign relations.
2. Ibn Saud, King of Saudi Arabia, 1880–1953.
I. Title.   II. Series.
DS227.G65   1986   327.53'8   85-24838
ISBN 0-674-30880-8

To the Memory of My Parents, David and Chana

Preface

WITH the oil boom of the 1970s, Saudi Arabia gained considerable prominence in the economics and politics of the Middle East. What had hitherto been a relatively obscure area became suddenly the focus of interest, both popular and scholarly. Yet according to J. B. Kelly, the books on Saudi Arabia have thus far in general been "long on rhetoric and short on factual accuracy," so that "there remains both room and need for studies of Saudi Arabia which will conform to the scholarly standards expected of historians" (Review, *Commentary*, May 1982, p. 88).

This book attempts to fill the void in one of the most intriguing areas of twentieth-century Saudi Arabia: the foreign policy of the kingdom.

The foundations of Saudi foreign policy were not laid in the period beginning in the second half of the 1920s, when the kingdom became unified and practically independent. Rather, the roots of Saudi foreign policy developed in an earlier period, the last decade of the nineteenth century and the beginning of the twentieth. It is this period which provides the time frame for the book.

During the research for the study I was fortunate to draw on the talents and expertise of a wide range of scholars. I am deeply in their debt, but there is not enough space to mention every one of them by name. I will single out only a few. Nadav Safran of Harvard University gave me more advice than he himself realized. It is a pleasant duty to thank the Dayan (Shiloah) Center for Middle Eastern Studies at Tel-Aviv University, particularly its director, Itamar Rabinovich, for the assistance they provided me throughout the preparation of the manuscript. I am indebted to my former teachers, now colleagues, Shimon Shamir, Haim Shaked, and Uriel Dann for their guidance and advice throughout my years as a student at Tel-Aviv University. My gratitude also goes to Iris and George Goodman and Miriam and Jerome Katzin for defraying the cost of typing the final manuscript. Lucy Goldman has consistently been a source of help in many ways, for which I shall always be grateful.

Finally, I owe my wife, Chaya, more than I can possibly express for bearing the strains and inconveniences caused by this book. Her unlimited devotion and perseverance made the work a shared endeavor. The book is dedicated to the memory of my parents, who emerged from the horrors and ashes of Europe determined to bring to this world a new generation, but who, alas, did not live to see it come to fruition.

Contents

Introduction   1

1. The Former Saudi States   6

2. The Molding of a Statesman   30

3. Recognition of Ottoman Sovereignty, 1902–1912   44

4. Saudi-Ottoman-British Ambiguities, 1913–1914   81

5. Independence and British Protection, 1914–1915   112

6. Between the Hammer and the Anvil, 1916–1918   136

7. Patterns of Saudi Foreign Policy   165

Appendix A   Treaty Between Ibn Saud and the Turks   191
Appendix B   Drafts of the Anglo-Saudi Treaty   193
Appendix C   The Anglo-Saudi Treaty, December 1915   196
Bibliography   199
Notes   207
Index   225

The Foreign Policy of Saudi Arabia

Introduction

Ibn Saud under feelings of hostility to the Turks speaks friendly and
would welcome a British Political Agent, but remove the Turkish
pressure and he would want to sweep away Muscat and rule to the
sea.

W. Lee-Warner, India Office

The first rock on which we shall split with Ibn Saud will be in his
annexation of Qatar; and from Qatar to the Trucial Coast is but a
step.

S. G. Knox, Officiating Resident, Persian Gulf

SAUDI ARABIA's foreign policy has received surprisingly little attention. Moreover, the evolution of Saudi foreign policy has been
viewed from a distinctly British historical perspective or from a
general Middle Eastern one, not from a Saudi vantage point.[1] This
book attempts to fill the gap by treating Saudi foreign policy from
a Saudi perspective.

Furthermore, it contests the conventional view that the establishment of the third Saudi state in 1902, after eleven years of Saudi
exile, signified in all respects a continuation of the first two Saudi
states of the eighteenth and nineteenth centuries and thus a revival
of their traditional pattern of political conduct. According to that
view, Ibn Saud, the founder of the third Saudi state and the head
of Wahhabism, a militant fundamentalist Islamic reform movement, turned the Saudi-Wahhabi theocracy into "a powerful means
for expansion" and thereby "imposed his will" on Arabia. As a
result, "the first decisive act of revived Wahhabism under Ibn Saud"
was the Saudi conquest of Hasa from the Ottomans in 1913.[2]

This book disproves a corollary view about a characteristic feature of the traditional Wahhabi-Saudi conduct, territorial expansion. Until the 1930s, it was assumed as a matter of course that

Ibn Saud would follow in the footsteps of his predecessors and continually extend Saudi-Wahhabi rule. The twentieth-century Saudi state was expected to be based on unlimited expansion, a principle inherent in the tenets of the fundamentalist Wahhabi doctrine. The unqualified use of such expressions as "the Wahhabis," "the Wahhabi theocracy," "revived Wahhabism," and "the Wahhabi leader" to denote the third Saudi state and Ibn Saud in the first three decades of the century illustrated the tendency to see that state only in terms of continuity with its two predecessors. After Ibn Saud's incorporation of the Hejaz, the western part of the Arabian Peninsula, into Saudi dominions in 1926, it was therefore predicted that he would turn to the east and extend his rule over the Persian Gulf principalities of Bahrain, Qatar, and Abu Dhabi. Then the Saudis would invade Iraq and Transjordan and reach the gates of the Syrian desert.

Such views and interpretations were expounded by British officials who for many years had been in close contact with Ibn Saud. Sir Percy Cox, described as "the oldest and closest of the Englishmen who knew Ibn Saud," stated in 1927: "Practically Ibn Saud thinks that he is justified in principle in regaining any territory that his forefathers had a century ago, whether as territory or as a sphere of influence. Oman was in their sphere of influence. As long as we paid him a subsidy he kept his hands off the Hejaz, since it ceased he has extended his authority over that country, and I have little doubt but that in the course of time he will seek to extend his authority over the interior of Oman."[3]

A year earlier St. John Philby, who had known Ibn Saud personally for thirty-five years and had written no less than a dozen books on Arabia, expressed confidence that "Ibn Saud is by no means at the end of his expansionist tether. The new dispensation will yet extend over a greater area than it covers at present and the unification of Arabia in the wider sense of the term will increase its prospects of permanence. I do not see how even Yemen can long remain in detachment from the union." Philby thought that the small Persian Gulf entities would eventually cease to exist as independent principalities and would be absorbed into the vast Saudi state. David Hogarth, one of the central figures at the Arab Bureau in Cairo, enthusiastically shared the view that "Ibn Saud would perpetually find new lands to conquer." Hogarth even suggested that the Saudis "must mop up the countries of Southern Arabia— Yemen, Hadramawt and Oman."⁴

Even those who perceived a shift in twentieth-century Saudi foreign policy viewed such a change as having occurred only in the 1930s, when it became apparent that Ibn Saud was no longer expanding territorially. This new perception was reflected in the gradual disappearance of the term "Wahhabi" and its replacement by "Saudi" to designate the state, its ruler, and its policies, high- lighted by the new name of the kingdom, "Saudi Arabia," intro- duced only in 1932. But there was still no doubt that in the first three decades of the century the state had been a Wahhabi one whose foreign policy was governed and guided by Wahhabi prin- ciples.

The history of Saudi political conduct toward Great Britain and the Ottoman Empire in the period 1902–1918, however, does not tally with these conventional views. In the field of foreign policy, rather than being a continuation, the twentieth-century Saudi state marked a sharp break with the previous pattern of Wahhabi-Saudi conduct and constituted a turning point in Saudi history. Fur- thermore, the shift did not occur in the 1930s but was inherent in the Saudi state from its very inception in 1902. As a result of this change, Saudi territorial expansion, which had characterized the two previous Wahhabi-Saudi states, came to an end in the late 1920s. The shift thus accounted in part for the ability of twentieth- century Saudi Arabia to survive.

'Abd al-'Aziz Ibn Saud started to pursue a "new," non-Wahhabi Saudi foreign policy immediately upon reconquering Riyadh and establishing the third Saudi state in 1902. The basic features of modern Saudi foreign policy, which has outlived Ibn Saud, are rooted in the formative years of the state between 1902 and 1918. Thus, twentieth-century Saudi foreign policy cannot be understood without an understanding of this formative period.

Ibn Saud, the man and the statesman, both embodied and de- termined the direction of Saudi foreign policy. Certain events in his personal history prompted him to steer a hitherto uncharted course for his newly established state. The key to Ibn Saud's con- duct lay in the years of exile that he had spent in Kuwait from 1893 to 1901, during the most impressionable and formative stage of his life, between the ages of thirteen and twenty-one. The period he stayed there, under the tutelage of Kuwait's ruler, Mubarak, constituted a political apprenticeship and a schooling in realpolitik. In Kuwait, which was the cosmopolitan and commercial hub of the Persian Gulf, Ibn Saud became the first Saudi ruler to be exposed to non-Wahhabi, if not anti-Wahhabi, influences. And he was a spectator to scenes of international politics and intrigue expertly manipulated by Mubarak. Ibn Saud's education in Kuwait laid the groundwork for the new foreign policy he was to pursue after re-establishing the Saudi state in 1902.

The term "foreign policy" is not used here in its standard contemporary meaning, owing to the subject and the period under consideration. The Saudis had a patriarchal society and a highly personalized way of decision-making. Though the term is modern, the Saudi usage is highly traditional. "Foreign policy" retains its central reference to the necessity imposed upon any leadership at one stage or another to make decisions and take steps regarding its foreign relations. But it excludes other components inherent in the modern meaning, such as decision-making processes, state institutions, and bureaucracy. This is not to say that Ibn Saud's foreign policy lacked domestic foundations. On the contrary, the Saudi ruler operated under certain constraints, and there were checks on his power and freedom of action. He was involved in confrontations over foreign policy issues with other groups in the society, such as the ulama or religious scholars, tribal leaders, and merchants. However, these checks and constraints were of minimal significance, and they did not prevent him from successfully steering his own policies. Thus, Saudi foreign policy in the 1902–1918 period and to a large extent in the next three decades was essentially the product of one man's thoughts and acts—Ibn Saud's.

Modern Saudi diplomatic history is delineated by three major milestones: the collapse of the second Saudi state in 1891 and the subsequent Saudi exile in Kuwait; the Saudi return to Riyadh in 1902, initiating Ibn Saud's efforts to devise a strategy for obtaining independence from the Ottomans; and the final disappearance of the Ottomans from Arabia in 1918, allowing the emergence of the Hashemite family of the Hejaz as the major adversary of the house of Saud. In a broader sense, these events marked the evolution of the Saudi state from a small entity living under the shadow of the sultan to an independent state completely and finally relieved of the historical threat posed by the Ottoman Empire. The framework for this narrative, as well as the basis for the analysis, is provided by the trilateral system of relations between Ibn Saud, the Ottomans, and the British. In this sense the study sheds light on the international relations of the early twentieth century and on the process that precipitated the disintegration of the Ottoman Empire in its Arab territories.

Ibn Saud's political sophistication was evidenced by his maintenance of a delicate balance of power with the British and the Ottomans, his masterly use of the carrot-and-stick approach, and his ability to separate temporal, diplomatic questions from the traditionally pervasive religious Wahhabi framework. No attempt is made here, however, to account for or analyze the internal developments of the Saudi community in the early twentieth century, such as the position of Wahhabism and the Ikhwan organization in Saudi society or the significance of the division of authority between Ibn Saud and his father, 'Abd al-Rahman, whereby the son assumed political leadership while the father remained the imam of the community. In fact, because of the inaccessibility of the Saudi archives and the paucity of available material, such a study can probably not be conducted. Nevertheless, internal factors are treated if they elucidated or had an impact on Ibn Saud's foreign policy.

To appreciate the full scope and magnitude of the twentieth-century shift in Saudi policies requires an understanding of the origins and evolution of the Wahhabi-Saudi alliance. That alliance, which was concluded in 1745 between the Saudi family and the founder of the Wahhabi ideology, led to the creation of the first Saudi state and thus shaped the modern history of Arabia. The eighteenth- and nineteenth-century Saudi states constitute the basis from which Ibn Saud's policies in the twentieth century diverged.

1

The Former Saudi States

I entered Mecca . . . I destroyed all things that were idolatrously worshipped.

Saud to Sultan Selim

You are instructed to expel the Wahhabi invaders from the Hejaz.

Sultan Mahmud II to Muhammad 'Ali

My dependencies extend from Kuwait to Oman over which you should exercise no control.

Faisal to British Resident

We recognized the independence of Bahrain and the other Sheikhdoms and will permit no Saudi interference in their affairs.

British Resident to Faisal

WITH THE OTTOMAN CONQUEST of Egypt in 1517, the sultan, Selim I, assumed the title Khadim al-Haramayn al-Sharifayn (Servant of the Two Holy Shrines—Mecca and Medina), as the Hejaz was usually appended to Egypt in medieval times. During the reign of his successor, Suleiman the Magnificent (1520–1566), Ottoman power extended itself farther in the Arabian Peninsula, encompassing Hasa and Bahrain, and for a short time even Muscat, in the Persian Gulf region. During Suleiman's reign Yemen also came under Ottoman control, and thereafter the areas along the Red Sea coast became part of the Ottoman Empire. But Ottoman control of eastern Arabia was never more than precarious and nominal. On the western side of the peninsula, the Hejaz and Yemen were in reality autonomous provinces except where Ottoman garrisons were stationed. Although the Ottomans claimed sovereignty over the whole of the peninsula, their control over central Arabia was sporadic and practically nonexistent. Handicapped by long lines of communication and administrative decay, the Ottomans had rarely, even in their heyday, done more in the interior of the peninsula than to play off the major tribes against each other. The affairs of the desert were scarcely worth the attention of the Sublime Porte (the Ottoman sultan) in Constantinople.[1]

Such a state of affairs left ample freedom for local elements to assert their control over various parts of the peninsula. Out of the rivalries among these local elements, numerous small emirates emerged in the vast area between the Hejaz in the west and the Persian Gulf in the east. This area, known geographically as Nejd but also referred to as "the heart of the peninsula," "the interior," and "central Arabia," bordered on the eastern foothills of the Hejaz in the west, the Persian Gulf coast of Hasa in the east, and two major sandy deserts—the Great Nafud in the north and al-Rub' al-Khali (the Empty Quarter) in the south. These emirates were in theory part of the Ottoman Empire, but in practice they were independent. One such entity was Dar'iyya and its vicinity, north of Riyadh, where in the beginning of the eighteenth century Sa'ud Ibn Muhammad, the eponymous founder of the Saudi dynasty, became the emir. In 1726, his son Muhammad assumed control over the emirate.[2]

By the beginning of the eighteenth century, Arabia had practically reverted to its pre-Islamic period known as al-Jahiliyya (the Era of Ignorance). Observance of the prescribed rites of Islam was lax, and superstitious beliefs were widespread. It was not surprising that a second prophet arose to protest against the misconduct of the people. That missionary was a Nejdi religious scholar by the name of Muhammad Ibn 'Abd al-Wahhab (1703–1792). Although strict observers of Islam generally chose to ignore the transgressions and treat the transgressors with pity, Ibn 'Abd al-Wahhab was determined to fight them. Inspired by the teachings of Ibn Taymiyya, a Syrian theologian and follower of the Hanbali legal school, he preached a return to classical Islam and the rejection of all innovations, such as saint worship, vows, and pilgrimages to shrines. The central theme of his doctrine was the principle of the unity, oneness, and incomparability of God. Anyone who deviated from the doctrine's tenets was ipso facto a non-Muslim.[3]

Regarding himself as an apostle of moral and spiritual regeneration, Ibn 'Abd al-Wahhab sought a force capable of propagating and imposing his ideas on the people. After the ruler of 'Ayaina abandoned him, Ibn 'Abd al-Wahhab finally received the permission of Muhammad Ibn Saud, the emir of Dar'iyya, to settle in his town.[4] Muhammad was the first Saudi ruler to adopt what became known as the Wahhabi doctrine (see table). The term "Wahhabism" was coined pejoratively by the opponents of the movement. Ibn 'Abd al-Wahhab's adherents referred to themselves as Muwahhidun (Unitarians) and to their new doctrine as Din al-Tawhid (Religion of Unity). With the Saudi embrace of Wahhabism the present era of Arabian history begins.

The First Saudi State

In 1745 an alliance was forged between the priest, Ibn 'Abd al-Wahhab, and the prince, Muhammad Ibn Saud, establishing a new order. Its main tenets were the commendation of virtue and the

Rulers of the House of Saud

Ruler	Period
First Saudi State	
Muhammad ibn Sa'ud	1745–1765
'Abd al-'Aziz ibn Muhammad	1765–1803
Sa'ud ibn 'Abd al-'Aziz	1803–1814
'Abdallah ibn Sa'ud	1814–1818
Second Saudi State	
Turki ibn 'Abdallah ibn Muhammad	1824–1834
Faisal ibn Turki	1834–1838
Khalid ibn Sa'ud	1838–1842
'Abdallah ibn Thunain	1842–1843
Faisal ibn Turki	1843–1865
'Abdallah ibn Faisal	1866–1870
Sa'ud ibn Faisal	1870–1875
'Abdallah ibn Faisal	1875–1889
'Abd al-Rahman ibn Faisal	1889–1891
Third Saudi State	
'Abd al-'Aziz ibn 'Abd al-Rahman	1902–1953

condemnation of vice. This alliance between the temporal power of the house of Saud and the unitarian Wahhabi doctrine has largely determined the course of events in Arabia since then.

Of the two components of this alliance, the religious Wahhabi factor served as the cohesive force of the community, while the power of the house of Saud served as the means for disseminating the religious doctrine by force.[5] The community was essentially a religious-military confederacy, whose principal object was proselytism, conquest, and the establishment of an empire. The new movement declared the lives and property of its antagonists to be forfeited by their religious heresy and applied itself to executing the sentence. The punishment of the infidels was rendered lawful and even obligatory. Aside from proselytism, pillage and plunder therefore became the principal objects of the new community, which was based on constant expansion and aggression at the expense of those who did not share its ideas.

During the second half of Muhammad Ibn Saud's long rein (1726–1765), most of Nejd was unified under Saudi-Wahhabi rule. Under his successor, 'Abd al-'Aziz (1765–1803), the community, zealous to impose its doctrines, extended its operations beyond the confines of Nejd. Toward the end of the 1780s, the Wahhabis succeeded in extending their control over most of central Arabia. Throughout the peninsula the Hejaz and Hasa remained the only two focal points of adversity. In 1792 Hasa was reduced for the first time, and in 1795 it was finally conquered. It came to form a base in eastern Arabia for the wider extension of Wahhabi influence.[6]

The Ottoman government cared little about the activities of the Wahhabis as long as the extension of their control was confined to central Arabia. But the situation changed once villages and towns on the western borders of Iraq were subjected to Wahhabi depredations. As early as 1784 the Wahhabi menace began to alarm the Ottoman authorities in Iraq. The occupation of Hasa in 1795 further enhanced and facilitated Wahhabi attacks on Iraq, especially in the vicinity of Basra. Consequently, the Porte recognized the necessity of countering Wahhabi aggression.

In 1798 the governor of Baghdad, Suleiman Pasha, raised a force of 5000 troops, to which he later added a contingent of twice that strength drawn from the local tribes. The objective of the force was the Wahhabi capital Dar'iyya. But failing to occupy the Wahhabi stronghold of Hufuf in Hasa, the force was obliged to conclude a truce with the Wahhabis and return to Basra.[7]

The Ottoman reaction should have taught the Wahhabis that henceforth their proceedings would be a matter of concern to the Porte. The Ottoman expedition should have conveyed to them that the freedom of action they enjoyed in their operations in Nejd would no longer exist if they tried to expand beyond its confines. Instead, they drew a lesson only from the failure of the expedition, disregarding the causes that had compelled the Ottomans to dispatch it. Thus, the ill-managed expedition inspired the Wahhabis with contempt for Ottoman troops, and soon thereafter, Iraqi locations were again subjected to pillage and plunder.

Wahhabi attacks on Iraq culminated on April 20, 1801, when a force of 10,000 troops appeared at the gates of Karbala, a town sacred to the Shi'ites, whose holy shrines were anathema to Wahhabi doctrines. The Wahhabis considered an attack on the city to be a service to the true faith against saint-worshipers whom they regarded as the incarnation of infidelity. The invaders took only eight hours to massacre more than 5000 people, demolish the domes of various tombs, including that of the Prophet's grandson Husain, and plunder the whole city. The atrocities perpetrated in Karbala shocked the Muslim world far beyond the limits of the Shi'a persuasion, but there was unreserved joy in Dar'iyya.[8]

The Ottoman government was wholly occupied with affairs in Europe and Egypt, where its position steadily declined. Consequently, it could not divert any resources at that time to Iraq and Arabia, even in the face of such a challenge as Karbala. It remained for Suleiman Pasha to form another force on his own, largely tribal in composition, and march on Nejd in 1802. The expedition ended in disaster. At one of its halts, the commander was murdered, and upon the approach of the Wahhabis the whole force dispersed in confusion.

That the conduct of the Wahhabis at Karbala was not an isolated incident became evident only a year later by its repetition in the holy cities of the Hejaz. In 1792 hostilities had already broken out between the Wahhabis and the sharif of Mecca, whose religious practices, such as building of and pilgrimage to shrines, were irreconcilable with Wahhabi doctrines. But it was not until the first decade of the nineteenth century that the Wahhabis extended their control over the Hejaz. In 1802 they conquered Taif, east of Mecca, killing all the inhabitants, including children. In 1803 Mecca, too, fell. Tombs that served as the objects of Muslim pilgrimage were razed, and a Wahhabi reformation was instituted. A year later, Medina succumbed to a blockade, its governor was expelled, and all the Ottoman troops were removed to Jidda. The qadi, the superintendent of the Prophet's mosque, was dismissed and replaced by a Wahhabi. The treasures of the tomb of the Prophet were appropriated by the Wahhabis, who attempted to destroy the dome of the building itself. Earlier in 1803, the pilgrimage traffic to the Hejaz from Syria, Egypt, and Persia was discontinued, except for people who accepted the Wahhabi tenets.[9] The Wahhabis forbade all public prayers for the sultan and insisted that the holy cities were their responsibility and not the Porte's.

The desecration of the Prophet's tomb and the atrocities committed in the cities of the Hejaz horrified a Muslim world already estranged from the Wahhabis by the Karbala affair, and it alienated all Sunnis, mainstream Muslims, not only Shi'ites, from the Wahhabis. Far more important was the reaction of the Ottoman government to this challenge. For the sultan to be deprived of the title "Servant of the Two Holy Shrines," with all the prestige it embodied in the Muslim world, constituted a severe blow to his prestige. But the Wahhabis did not contemplate an Ottoman reaction. Displaying a complete lack of interest in the Porte's attitude toward their proceedings, they did not try to evaluate the comparative forces held by them and the Ottomans and assess the consequences of a possible confrontation. Such calculations appeared irrelevant in the context of their mission, the propagation of the real tenets of Islam, which in their minds did not admit of any compromise.

This Wahhabi attitude toward the Ottomans is illustrated by a letter sent from the Wahhabi leader, Saud, to the Ottoman sultan. Its brevity recalls Caesar's "Veni, vidi, vici," and Saud's assumption of a place of equality with the sultan is remarkable:

Saud to Selim—I entered Mecca on the fourth day of Muharram in the 1218th year of the Hijra. I kept peace toward the inhabitants. I destroyed all the things that were idolatrously worshipped. I abolished all taxes except those that were required by the law. I confirmed the Qadi whom you had appointed, agreeably to the commands of the prophet of God. I desire that you will give orders to the rulers of Damascus and Cairo not to come up to the sacred city with the Mahmal and with trumpet and drums. Religion is not profitted by these things. May the peace and blessing of God be with you.[10]

There is a complete absence of any titles or salutations and of any reference to Selim as the sultan or head of the Islamic community. The letter constitutes an outright challenge.

After 'Abd al-'Aziz was stabbed to death by a Shi'ite, in revenge for the death of his family in the 1801 Karbala massacre, his successor, Saud the Great (1803–1814), continued the Wahhabis' encroachments on the Ottoman provinces of Iraq and Syria. In 1803 Wahhabi raiders plundered the area of Najaf, and in the next year a Wahhabi force overran the neighborhood of Zubair and Basra. In 1806 Najaf and Samawa were attacked, and in 1810 a plundering raid penetrated to within a short distance of Baghdad. But the Wahhabis were not content with border raids on Iraq, sometimes extending across the Euphrates, and in about 1806 they started to raid in the direction of Syria. In a sudden foray into the Hauran district, they struck terror into the heart of Syria. In the space of three days they sacked no less than thirty-five villages, leaving nothing between them and Damascus.[11]

At the turn of the nineteenth century, the Wahhabis moved to extend their authority in a new direction—the southeastern part of the peninsula—instigating conflicts with Oman, Muscat, and the Pirate Coast sheikhdoms. In 1800 they made their first appearance east of the Jafurah Desert, south of Hasa, and in the spring of that year Buraimi was seized. For the next eighteen years, this important oasis served the Wahhabis as a base from which to plunder Oman and exact tribute from its sultans. In the east, Wahhabi encroachments on Qatar and Bahrain culminated in 1810 with the appointment of a Saudi governor over these two sheikhdoms.[12] But in attempting to assert their control in the Persian Gulf area, the Wahhabis had to contend with a new power, Great Britain.

Britain's overriding interest since the early eighteenth century had been to maintain control over the sea route to India, the jewel in the British Empire's crown. When their commercial interests extended into Persia and the Persian Gulf, the British established a permanent presence in the area by creating in 1769 the position of the political resident in the Persian Gulf, who was based at Bushire, on the Persian shore of the gulf. It was clear, however, that the Persian Gulf was of vital importance to Great Britain, primarily in the context of India. British policy in the gulf centered on two main objectives: suppressing Arab piracy so as to maintain a "maritime peace," and resisting rival imperial challenges by other European powers. To achieve these ends, in a series of bilateral agreements the British compelled the various gulf sheikhs to pay due regard to Britain's interest in maritime peace on pain of punitive naval actions or even deposition. It was up to the Royal Navy, supreme in the gulf, to ensure that no rival power challenged Britain's hegemony. In 1820, the chiefs of the Omani Coast were induced to sign a General Treaty of Peace with Britain, by which the government of India was granted the right to police the waters in the Persian Gulf. Legally, this right was confined to suppressing piracy; practically, it was applied to all political relations. In 1835, the Maritime Truce was signed between the sheikhs of the Pirate Coast and the British. These agreements turned the area into the Trucial Coast and made Britain the predominant power in the gulf. But beyond the gulf coast, the British remained utterly indifferent to, indeed were eager to stay out of, the interior of Arabia.

The Wahhabi drive for influence along the gulf coast brought them for the first time into contact with British power. They were suspected of instigating the piracies of the Qawasim, who inhabited the ports of Sharja and Ras al-Khaima, and of attempting to destroy the independence of Muscat, which the British government desired to maintain. At the close of 1809, India dispatched an expedition to the Pirate Coast to destroy the Qasimi war fleet and to render whatever aid it could to the sultan of Muscat to protect Oman from Wahhabi conquest. In 1810, at Shinas on the coast of the Gulf of Oman, the British had their first brush with the Wahhabis when they stormed and took a fort seized earlier by the Qawasim with Wahhabi backing. At the conclusion of the campaign, the British addressed a letter to the Wahhabi ruler requiring him to restrain those under his influence from committing piracy. Saud replied that he had no quarrel with Christians, but he seemed unimpressed by the British operations on the coast. As a result, the British had three more encounters with the Wahhabi pirates.[13]

By the end of the first decade of the nineteenth century, the Wahhabi empire was at its height, extending from the gates of Damascus and Baghdad in the north to Yemen and Hadramawt in the south, and from the Red Sea in the west to the Persian Gulf in the east. Above all, it held indisputable control of the two holiest cities of Islam, Mecca and Medina. Within sixty years the Wahhabi-Saudi alliance had won control of most of Arabia in a jihad that echoed the achievements of the first Muslim conquerors.

The Sublime Porte could not tolerate a situation whereby heretics, as the Wahhabis were considered to be, stripped the holy cities of Ottoman rule. The Wahhabis' menace was all the more dangerous as they did not seem content with the Hejaz and continued to harass the gates of Syria and Iraq. Accordingly, Sultan Mahmud II requested Muhammad 'Ali, the newly rising viceroy of Egypt, to undertake the expulsion of the Wahhabi invaders from the Hejaz. The first expedition left Egypt for Arabia in 1811 under the command of Tusun, Muhammad 'Ali's son. In October 1812 the Egyptian force astonished the Wahhabis by conquering Medina and killing more than 1500 people. Three months later, Mecca, Jidda, and Taif were also recovered, and for the first time in ten years, the general pilgrimage to the holy cities was resumed.

But neither Muhammad 'Ali nor the Porte was content with the expulsion of the Wahhabis from the Hejaz, and late in 1813 the Egyptian viceroy was ordered to proceed in person to Arabia. For a year the Egyptian forces were occupied in battles along the Red Sea coast, in Asir and Yemen, but toward the end of 1814 they resumed the vigorous struggle against the Wahhabis. In the battle of Bisal, between Taif and Kulakh, which erupted in January 1815, the Wahhabis were decisively defeated, losing more than 5000 troops. Following the battle, Muhammad 'Ali addressed a letter to the new Saudi ruler, 'Abdallah (1814–1818), demanding his submission.[14] Nejd was temporarily saved from the Egyptian onslaught only because of developments in Egypt, which necessitated Muhammad 'Ali's return. In May 1815 a Saudi-Egyptian agreement was reached by which the Wahhabis abandoned any claims to the holy cities and recognized the sultan as their overlord.

The Ottomans, however, discontent with this agreement, ordered the Egyptian viceroy in 1816 to resume the struggle against

the Wahhabis, and an Egyptian expedition commanded by Muhammad 'Ali's son, Ibrahim, left for Arabia. By the end of 1817 the
whole of Qasim submitted to the expedition, and in March 1818
the Egyptians faced the Saudi capital of Dar'iyya. After a six-month
siege the Wahhabis surrendered, and the power of their community
as an organized state was broken. 'Abdallah, the last Saudi ruler,
was sent to Constantinople and there beheaded. In order to eliminate the Wahhabi menace once and for all, on orders from Constantinople, Dar'iyya was razed and the fortifications of every town
and village in Nejd were destroyed. The members of the Saudi
family were exiled to Egypt, where they were promptly impris-
oned.[15] Only eight years after the Wahhabi empire had reached its
zenith, it seemed irrevocably destroyed.

This sudden and swift reversal of fortunes has been ascribed to
the fact that the Wahhabi state was "too far extended to defend
itself successfully against a determined foreign invader." St. John
Philby, for instance, asserted that the empire "had reached out
beyond the possible limits of effective conquest" and failed "to
hold together its vast dominions." Another writer argued that "the
success of the Wahhabi-Saudi alliance was also its downfall. Partly,
its conquests fell apart because the original religious impulse began
to fade and was replaced by sheer force, xenophobia and self-
aggrandizement."[16]

Such explanations, however, fail to point out the decisive factor
that caused the destruction of the Saudi state. For one thing, the
Ottoman government, which brought about the destruction of the
state, could and did tolerate the extension of Saudi control over
the whole of central, eastern, and southeastern Arabia to the shores
of the Indian Ocean. For another, the Wahhabis never asserted
over the territories north of Nejd the kind of control that they
enjoyed in central and eastern Arabia. Although these territories
lived under the constant fear of Wahhabi raids, they were hardly
under Saudi rule. Moreover, it was not the extension of Saudi rule
per se which rendered the state incapable of defending itself against
a foreign invader. Had the Wahhabi dominions encompassed merely
Nejd and the Hejaz, without Hasa, the coast, and northern Arabia,
"the foreign invader" would still have been provoked to intervene.
For the Ottoman reaction was triggered neither by the vast occupations in the east and south or by the raids in the north but by

the conquest of the Hejaz, which deprived the sultan of the justification for his title, the caliph, or Muhammad's successor. Equally,
had the Wahhabis' authority been confined merely to Nejd and the
Hejaz, they would still have been incapable of defending themselves against the invaders. For it was not the vastness of their
territories which rendered them vulnerable to a foreign reaction,
but the relative strength of the Wahhabis and their invaders.

In essence, there were two major reasons for the destruction of
the Saudi state, both of which originated in the state's pattern of
political conduct toward foreign powers. First, the Wahhabis never
realized that upon emerging from central Arabia, they ceased to
operate in a vacuum of unlimited freedom of action. Their fallacy
was perhaps inescapable, because the cohesive force of their community was the dissemination of a religious doctrine, and the Wahhabis conceived of this mission as limitless. Consequently, the
consideration of existing political realities had no place in Wahhabi
activities, since they were to alter these realities and create new
ones. The Wahhabis treated all territories as equal objects of expansion, without distinguishing between areas whose occupation
did not affect other powers and regions where the Wahhabis' expansion was intolerable and bound to elicit foreign reaction. As a
result, they embarked on a policy of unlimited, indiscriminate expansion.

The second reason for the destruction of the Saudi state was the
Wahhabis' failure to mobilize the services of another power in
order to deter and counter the invaders, which was another con-
sequence of their policy of disregarding political realities. They did
not anticipate that, with the kind of aggressive policies they were
pursuing against the Porte, they would find themselves one day in
need of the support of another power. They were already aware of
the growing British interest in the Persian Gulf coast, but they did
not try to court the British or harmonize their activities with British interests. Although it is questionable whether the British, at
that time in alliance with the Porte, would have helped the Saudis,
the Saudis, who were not aware of the alliance, did not try to
mobilize British support. Instead, their policy alienated them from
the British, who as a result welcomed the Egyptian drive to crush
the Wahhabis. Accordingly, when Captain Sadlier was dispatched
to meet Ibrahim Pasha, he was instructed to make arrangements

with the Egyptians "with a view to the complete reduction of the Wahhabi power." He was further ordered to offer "the aid of the British naval and military forces" to facilitate the expedition's operations.[17] Thus, instead of having one power as a counterpoise to the other, the Wahhabis committed the worst possible political mistake: they alienated both the Ottomans and the British.

Furthermore, the Wahhabis never tried to evaluate their own power and assess the prospects for unlimited expansion, nor did they attempt to evaluate their main adversary's power. They did not envisage a situation whereby they might be defeated by superior forces which would not only check their expansion but also bring their very existence as a state to an end. When they finally did realize that they were weaker than the Egyptian invaders and, consequently, were ready to recognize the sovereignty of the Ottoman infidels, it was too late. By then the Porte was determined to eliminate the Wahhabi threat once and for all. Had the Saudis abstained from occupying the Hejaz and menacing Baghdad and Damascus, their vast state, encompassing central, eastern, and southeastern Arabia, might well have continued to exist.

The Second Saudi State

The Egyptian presence in Nejd proved to be a short-lived phenomenon, for the expedition soon realized that a complete occupation of the Wahhabi dominions could not be maintained. Around June 1819 the Egyptians withdrew from Hasa and installed the sheikhs of the Bani Khalid tribe as the representatives of the Ottoman government. In November, Ibrahim Pasha, with the bulk of the Egyptian forces, finally withdrew from Arabia, leaving only small detachments in Qasim, Dar'iyya, and Riyadh.[18] The departure of the Egyptian expedition proved once again that conquering central Arabia was one thing and maintaining effective control was quite another. At the same time, it provided the Saudis with an opportunity to reassert themselves in their previous dominions and begin a fresh campaign of Wahhabi conquest and conversion.

The founder of the second Saudi state was Turki Ibn 'Abdallah (1824–1834), grandson of the first Saudi ruler, Muhammad Ibn Saud.[19] Following the pattern of his predecessors, Turki first strove to consolidate his position in Nejd and established Riyadh as the new capital of the Saudi state. Next, Turki proceeded to reassert the Wahhabi positions in eastern Arabia, and in 1830 he recovered Hasa. The conquest of this important province gave impetus to further Wahhabi expansion along the coast, and the Wahhabis turned their attention toward Bahrain, Qatar, and Oman. As a preparatory move in this direction, Turki in 1831 approached the British through the sheikh of 'Ajman, expressing his desire to renew the "treaty which was made by you and the Imam Saud."[20] The British could locate no such treaty, and a noncommital but friendly answer was transmitted to Turki.

Saudi pressure on the coast focused at first on Bahrain, whose ruler, fearing a Saudi onslaught on the island, agreed in 1831 to pay an annual tribute. In 1832 the Saudis launched a full-scale invasion of the Omani coast, and early in 1833 they recovered the important oasis of Buraimi. In order to prevent an overt military confrontation, the sultan of Muscat found himself obliged to pay a M.T. 5000 annual tribute (the Maria Theresa silver thaler or M.T., once the standard currency of the Austro-Hungarian Empire, remained until recently a favorite coin in parts of Arabia). By the end of 1833, the whole coast of the Persian Gulf acknowledged Saudi rule and paid tribute, but this acknowledgment was only temporary. In 1833 the ruler of Bahrain repudiated his agreement to pay tribute, and in 1834 he annexed the island of Tarut.

The Saudi pressure along the coast had by 1825 prompted the sheikh of Sharja to solicit a promise of British assistance. He renewed his appeal in 1831, following Hasa's occupation, but in both instances no British assurances were given. The Saudis enjoyed freedom of action on the coast because of India's policy of abstaining "from any interference in any wars not arising from piratical causes." Indeed, in 1834 India was even ready to let Muscat fall into Saudi hands, since there was no indication that they would indulge in piracy.[21]

In May 1834, Turki was assassinated and his son Faisal (1834–1838, 1843–1865) acceded to the throne. Faisal had great difficulties making his authority felt in Nejd and, more particularly, in Hasa. As a result, it was not until 1836 that he moved to attack Bahrain by first seeking the support of the sultan of Muscat. But the sultan conditioned his agreement on the consent of the British government, and consequently the project came to naught.[22] Before

Faisal had another opportunity to focus on the coast, an imminent danger re-appeared from the west.

Muhammad 'Ali, the viceroy in Egypt, had gradually established himself as a regional power similar, if not superior, to the Porte. His defeat of the Saudis in 1818 and in particular his recovery of the holy cities had endowed him with great prestige in the Muslim world at large. After the Ottoman sultan grudgingly conceded the provinces of Syria and Adana to him in 1833, Muhammad 'Ali gave several indications that his next target was Baghdad. But in order to clear the approaches to Baghdad, he had to reduce the Saudis once more and assume effective control over Nejd.[23]

His first step was the appointment in 1835 of a Bahraini merchant as customs supervisor at the Saudi port of Qatif, by order of Ahmed Pasha, governor of the Hejaz. But this act was frustrated by Faisal's refusal to accept the Egyptian nominee, who was then forced to depart from Qatif. Faisal further demonstrated his disregard of the Egyptians a year later, when he rejected Muhammad 'Ali's demand that he join him in the campaign against Asir, the coastal province adjacent to the Red Sea, between the Hejaz in the north and Yemen in the south.

In view of the traumatic Saudi experience with the Egyptian forces only twenty years earlier, Faisal might have been expected to be more forthcoming in his dealings with Muhammad 'Ali. After all, the seven-year Saudi-Egyptian struggle should have impressed upon Faisal the reality of the Egyptian superiority and the disastrous consequences of questioning this superiority. The memory of the Egyptian invasion and the knowledge of the overwhelming firepower, especially artillery, that the Egyptians could bring to bear if necessary, all should have made Faisal aware of the real balance of forces. The Saudi community under his rule was by no means stronger than that crushed in 1818 by the Egyptian expedition. Nevertheless, Faisal chose to defy the Egyptians, risking their retaliation and its possible consequences.

Muhammad 'Ali was accordingly determined to replace Faisal by a more subservient ruler, and to that end he released Khalid Ibn Saud, the pretender to the Nejdi throne, from prison in Cairo. Khalid left for Arabia accompanied by an Egyptian force, intending to make good his claims. Only then did Faisal become aware of the danger, whereupon he sent messengers and submissive letters to Muhammad 'Ali. But it was too late. The whole affair resembled the previous Egyptian-Saudi confrontation in that the Saudis failed to act on the basis of their relative weakness vis-à-vis their opponents. In both instances, their final readiness to draw the necessary conclusions from these relative forces came too late.

In 1837 the Egyptian expedition occupied Qasim and defeated Faisal in the neighborhood of Riyadh. In 1838 the Egyptians launched their final attack on the district of Kharj, to which Faisal had retreated. Realizing that resistance would be useless, Faisal surrendered and was deported to Egypt in December.

The imprudent Saudi political conduct found expression in the repetition of a tactical error that they had committed in the earlier conflict. Facing the menace of a hostile power, the Saudis failed even to contemplate the possibility of approaching another power with a view to countering that pressure. They did not consider that Britain, the dominant power in the Persian Gulf, could view Egyptian designs in Arabia as detrimental to British interests and might therefore collaborate with them in thwarting the Egyptian attempt. The Saudi failure to recognize the potential convergence of Saudi and British interests regarding Egyptian designs seems all the more fatal in view of the subsequent British actions against the Egyptians, which make it reasonable to assume that a Saudi overture to the British would have elicited a positive response. London was seriously alarmed by Muhammad 'Ali's attempt to extend his authority over such distant regions as Iraq. Foreign Secretary Palmerston instructed the British consul-general in Cairo to convey to Muhammad 'Ali the warning that Her Majesty's government "would not view with indifference Egyptian schemes in the Persian Gulf." The uncompromising opposition of the British government to Muhammad 'Ali's ambitious designs eventually forced him to reverse his plan and recall his troops.[24] Thus, an early Saudi overture, which could have elicited a prompt British reaction, might have pre-empted the Egyptian expedition and thus saved Nejd from the second Egyptian occupation.

The Egyptian conquest of 1838 marked the end of the first period in the history of the second Saudi state, during which independence within more modest boundaries was regained, maintained, and then temporarily lost. Five years would pass before the last vestiges of the Egyptian presence were removed. The Egyptians installed

Khalid Ibn Saud (1838–1842) as emir in Riyadh and considered him their puppet. In 1840 he addressed a letter to the British representative at Bahrain expressing his desire to renew "the amicable relations which had existed between Saud and the British Government."[25] But in practice he failed to live up to his desire, and his designs against the sheikhdoms constantly worried India. At one point, India instructed its resident in the gulf to keep a watch on Khalid's movements and warn him, if necessary, that the British government would resist any attempt on his part to invade Oman.

Khalid's successor, 'Abdallah Ibn Thunain (1842–1843), did not effect any change in this respect, for his designs along the coast immediately alarmed the chiefs, who sought the support of the British. The resident remonstrated with 'Abdallah, claiming that Saudi influence on the coast had always been conducive to piracy and had necessitated British reaction. 'Abdallah, while promising to cooperate in the suppression of piracy, nevertheless maintained that the people of Oman were his subjects.[26]

In 1843 Faisal managed to escape from prison in Egypt, with the help of Egyptian collaborators, and his return home and accession to the throne marked the beginning of the second period or golden era of the second Saudi state.[27] Soon after his return, Faisal made it clear that he intended to reimpose his rule wherever it had existed before. Indeed, under Faisal's second rule the Saudis endeavored to assert or reassert their power at various times in Bahrain, Qatar, the Trucial Coast, and northern Oman.

Within a month of his return, Faisal informed the Trucial chiefs, who were in alliance with Britain, that he was sending a deputy to their region. The chiefs interpreted the letter as the beginning of Saudi pressure and in November 1843 requested the British resident to support them "in order to repel the invaders." But they were informed that Britain had no desire to interfere in the internal politics of Arabia further than was necessary to maintain the peace of the gulf. In early 1845, however, after the returning Saudis had committed atrocities in Oman, the British did intervene, warning the Saudis to abstain from further attacks upon Oman. Saudi pressure did not cease, and Muscat finally agreed to pay an annual tribute of M.T. 5000 to Riyadh. In 1853 the Saudis resumed their pressure on Oman, demanding a greatly increased tribute. The Saudis undertook an invasion of Batina, whereupon the British intervened and forced the Saudis to abandon their intentions.[28]

Saudi designs on Bahrain brought them into an even more serious collision with Britain. Following four Saudi attempts to invade the island during the period 1845–1847, its ruler, weakened by consistent Saudi encroachments, agreed to pay an annual tribute of M.T. 4000. In 1850 relations between Faisal and Bahrain became strained again, and at the end of the year Faisal arrived at the base of Qatar with a large force, intending to invade Bahrain. After the Saudi preparations had assumed formidable proportions, the British resident informed Faisal that Britain did not recognize Saudi authority over either Bahrain or any other maritime states, "which had been dealt with as independent Sheikhdoms for over thirty years." The appearance of a British squadron finally convinced Faisal of the seriousness with which Britain regarded the matter, and he called off the expedition. A settlement was reached in 1851, whereby Bahrain agreed to pay once more a M.T. 4000 annual tribute.[29]

Three years later the sheikh discontinued the payment, alleging that Faisal was intriguing to gain possession of Bahrain by supporting rival members of his family. As a result, Faisal moved to attack the island, but once again the British resident intervened under India's instructions, warning Faisal that no interference with Bahrain would be permitted. This communication caused Faisal "intense irritation and dissatisfaction," and in September 1854 he protested to the resident. Affecting not to understand why the British government was opposed to his invading Bahrain, Faisal argued that "an understanding has long existed between me and Britain regarding my dependencies extending from Oman to Kuwait over which you should exercise no control nor should you interfere in any way in their affairs." The resident was quick to dispel any misconceptions Faisal might have entertained, asserting that Britain recognized "no authority between itself and the Trucial Chiefs," who were independent and "with whom Britain had contracted treaties of upwards of thirty years' standing." The resident added that the British government recognized Bahrain "as an independent chiefship" which it would defend against all comers. But Faisal refused to give up and replied that he still regarded himself as "having authority over all the Arabs." This led the resident, Captain Jones, to inform his superiors that "we had borne too long with Feysal, who, while giving us fair words, still falsified all he said by steadily pursuing his fixed object of universal dominion along the coast."[30]

In 1859 Faisal renewed his attempts to invade Bahrain, disregarding the resident's previous warning and the presence of a British corvette off his coast. A British squadron was promptly dispatched to threaten Dammam, and the Saudi attempt collapsed. It was obvious that, without the vigilance with which Britain watched the independence of Bahrain, the island might have become attached to the Saudi province of Hasa.[31]

In February 1865 Colonel Lewis Pelly, the British resident, undertook an adventurous journey to the Saudi capital. The principal object of the visit was to remove the animosity against Britain which the British frustration of Saudi designs on the coast was believed to have excited in Faisal, and to warn him against any fresh attacks on the sheikhs. In the three interviews that Pelly had with Faisal, the emir assured the resident of his cooperation in suppressing piracy. He claimed, however, to have sovereignty over all eastern Arabia, from Kuwait to Ras al-Hadd, the southeasternmost tip of the Arab littoral of the gulf, "and beyond, which God has given unto us," and concluded that, "be Arabia what it may, it is all ours." Pelly found Faisal to be blind and frail with age, "surrounded by stern Wahhabi zealots who deeply resented the presence in their midst of the representative of an infidel Power."[32] In the face of their disapproval, Pelly retreated, determined to maintain Britain's guard in the gulf against further renewal of Saudi incursions there. Pelly's visit was of little or no political benefit, for only five months later the British and the Saudis were once again on a collision course.

In August 1865 a revolt broke out in Oman against the sultan. Faisal strove immediately to take advantage of the situation by sending a force from Buraimi to ravage eastern Oman. The force plundered the coastal town of Sur, murdered one British Indian subject, and wounded another. The British promptly demanded reparations, and in November Riyadh responded that all British subjects taken prisoners at Sur would be released and their property restored. But the Indian authorities had already determined to embark upon a more resolute and vigorous policy against the Saudis. Accordingly, they encouraged the sultan of Muscat to stage a more active resistance to Saudi encroachments and offered him money, munitions, and, if necessary, British naval support. Concomitantly, they informed Riyadh that the sultan was a friend and ally of the British government, which could not regard an encroachment on Oman without grave concern.

Meanwhile the sultan of Muscat and the Trucial chiefs, encouraged by the British decisiveness, arranged for a fleet to blockade the Saudi ports of Qatif and Uqair. In December a British warship, carrying 18-pound guns with ammunition for the sultan, disembarked on the Omani coast. At this juncture a Saudi force attacked a coastal town in Batina, and the British Indian traders residing there were driven into the sea, where one drowned. In January 1866 Colonel Pelly addressed a letter to Riyadh, demanding a written apology, assurance that such outrages would not be repeated, and payment of compensation in the amount of M.T. 27,000. The resident further warned that if in seventeen days from the delivery of the letter his demands were not met, Saudi forts on the seaboard would be destroyed.[33]

In the meantime Faisal had died in Riyadh in December, and his son 'Abdallah (1866–1870, 1875–1889) succeeded him.[34] The new ruler apparently had more pressing problems to solve than the British ultimatum, so he deferred a response. When no answer to the ultimatum was received and the period of grace expired, the British proceeded to carry out their threats by sending armed boats to Qatif. These demolished the island fort of Abu-Lif and destroyed a Saudi vessel in the harbor but failed to destroy the Dammam fort. At the end of February the resident finally received the Saudi reply to his ultimatum, in which 'Abdallah stated that he desired a consultation and would send an emissary. Soon afterward, a Saudi envoy arrived at the British residency at Bushire, and on April 21 he had an interview with Pelly, in the course of which he submitted the written declaration:

> I am authorized by Imam Abdallah bin Faisal to request the Sahib, the Resident in the Persian Gulf, to become the medium of friendship between Imam Abdallah and the British Government.
>
> Secondly—I assure the Resident on the part of Imam Abdallah that he will not oppose or injure British subjects residing in territories under the authority of Abdallah, and Thirdly—I assure the

resident on the part of Imam Abdallah that he will not injure or attack the territories of the Arab tribes in alliance with the British Government, specially the Kingdom of Muscat, further than in receiving the zukat that has been customary of old.[35]

Thus, it took an unequivocal military demonstration to convince the Saudis of Britain's supremacy in the Persian Gulf and its determination to defend its interests. It was the Saudis themselves who caused India, in 1845, to modify its existing policy of reserve and nonintervention, when it became evident that Faisal's designs were not compatible with the integrity of Bahrain and Muscat.[36]

At the time of Faisal's death, the second Saudi state had reached its height. The accession of 'Abdallah to the throne in 1866 marked the beginning of the third and last period in the history of the state. 'Abdallah's position in Riyadh was extremely precarious from the very inception of his rule, and it was constantly weakened by the rivalry and personal enmity of his brother Saud. In 1870, Saud finally broke into open rebellion and rallied his allies for a decisive battle against his brother. In the encounter 'Abdallah was defeated and fled to Jabal Shammar, while Saud (1870–1875) entered Riyadh as the new ruler.[37]

At this juncture 'Abdallah demonstrated his political imprudence by invoking the support of the Ottoman authorities in Baghdad against his brother, the usurper. The Ottomans, who prior to 1871 had exercised hardly any effective control or jurisdiction in central Arabia, accepted 'Abdallah's invitation with unconcealed jubilation. By the late 1860s the Porte had started to pursue a vigorous policy of expansion and consolidation in the Arabic-speaking provinces of the empire.[38] 'Abdallah's proposition, therefore, provided the Ottomans with a unique opportunity to extend their control to central Arabia, relying on the explicit request of the legitimate ruler whose authority they aimed to restore.

By July 1871 an Ottoman expedition from Baghdad had completed the occupation of Hasa but found it impossible to advance across the desert to Riyadh.[39] Belatedly, 'Abdallah discovered that the Ottoman objective was hardly that of restoring him to power. By November Midhat Pasha, the wali of Baghdad, announced that Saudi rule in Nejd was at an end and that the administration of the country had been assumed by the Ottomans.

The occupation of Hasa seriously impaired the position of the Saudi state. For one thing, the fall of Hasa caused the Saudis to lose all their positions in eastern and southeastern Arabia, which had been precarious since Faisal's death in 1865. For another, by removing the Saudis from the seashore, the Ottomans obtained a powerful hold upon Nejd and all the routes leading to central Arabia. But even in the face of a common enemy, 'Abdallah and Saud could not reach a reconciliation and instead sapped their energy by petty intertribal fighting. As a last resort, Saud invoked the support of Great Britain against the Ottomans, whose occupation of Hasa "by maritime aggression" contradicted the traditional British policy of preventing maritime landings upon the coast. But in view of previous Saudi behavior along the coast and the trouble it had caused the British authorities, Britain had no interest in supporting the Saudis, and no assistance was offered.[40]

Meanwhile, major changes occurred in the northern part of Nejd, in the district of Jabal Shammar. The district had been under the governorship of the Rashidi family since 1835 when a certain 'Abdallah Ibn Rashid, "noble, brave and forebearing," had taken over the capital of the district, Hail. Informing the Saudi ruler, Faisal, of his action, 'Abdallah Ibn Rashid recognized Saudi suzerainty and welcomed a Wahhabi qadi to Hail. Thus, 'Abdallah became the founder of the Rashidi dynasty, which served its Saudi masters faithfully until the early 1870s. It became independent before the end of the nineteenth century and eventually eclipsed the Saudi dynasty, surviving until 1921 (see table).[41]

The Ottoman occupation of Hasa in 1871 coincided with a major development in Jabal Shammar, the accession in 1872 of Muhammad Ibn Rashid to the governorship of the district. With the constant decline of the Saudis in the 1870s, precipitated by internal dissensions and the conquest of Hasa, the new Rashidi ruler began to impinge on the dominions of his nominal Saudi suzerain. In 1877 the Rashidis openly challenged the authority of the Saudis, and for the next ten years a contest for the supremacy in Nejd was in full swing. In 1887 Ibn Rashid managed to take Riyadh, and in 1891 he decisively defeated the Saudi family, whose members fled to the coast seeking refuge.[42] With the Rashidi takeover of Nejd and the Saudi family in exile, the second Saudi state came to an end.

Rashidi Rulers of Jabal Shammar

Ruler	Period
'Abdallah ibn 'Ali ibn Rashid	1835–1848
Tallal ibn 'Abdallah	1848–1868
Mut'ib ibn 'Abdallah	1868–1869
Bandar ibn Tallal	1869–1872
Muhammad ibn 'Abdallah	1872–1897
'Abd al-'Aziz ibn Mut'ib	1897–1906
Mut'ib ibn 'Abd al-'Aziz	1906–1907
Sultan ibn Hamud	1907–
Sa'ud ibn Hamud	1907–1908
Sa'ud ibn 'Abd al-'Aziz	1908–1919
'Abdallah ibn Mut'ib	1919–1920
Muhammad ibn Tallal	1920–1921

Unlike its predecessor, the second state was destroyed not by an external power but by internal disintegration. Nevertheless, its pattern of conduct in the sphere of foreign relations, especially with Great Britain, demonstrated that the shortcomings which had characterized the first Saudi state persisted into the second. A glance at the state of affairs in the Persian Gulf area should have made the Saudis cognizant of a number of factors: that Great Britain was the predominant power in the region; that British policy focused on the desire to maintain maritime peace; that in view of Britain's clear supremacy, the Saudis should strive to concert their schemes with British interests or should at least not contradict these interests; and that the constant threat posed by the Egyptians and the Ottomans, manifested in 1838 and 1871, provided an additional reason for not alienating Britain and for retaining her goodwill. Instead, Saudi designs along the coast throughout the period were basically incompatible with British interests. Britain's presence in the gulf did not act as a constraint on the direction of Saudi policy, nor did it restrain or modify their ambitions. Indeed, the British factor was not a consideration at all, whereas it should have played a primary role in Saudi thinking. Furthermore, although the first Saudi state perhaps lacked the basic information about Ottoman and Egyptian power to enable it to evaluate the relative forces, both Turki and Faisal were clearly aware of British power. As early as 1819, after a British expedition had launched a major assault on Ras al-Khaima, the Wahhabis became familiar with "the awesome arms of the Christians who came in great ships with dreadful weapons, innumerable soldiers, and awe-filling stratagems."[43] Turki and Faisal refused to draw the necessary conclusions from such British superiority. In 1837, Faisal similarly failed to reach an accommodation with Muhammad 'Ali, although the Egyptian military superiority had been devastatingly demonstrated just two decades earlier.

Because the Saudis failed to abstain from alienating the British, they could not muster Britain's support as a counterweight to the Ottoman and Egyptian invaders. The Saudi failure to cultivate friendly relations with the British and to mobilize their support contrasts with the initial British goodwill toward both Turki and Faisal and the British policy in the gulf. The British at first expressed "friendly feelings and amity" toward Turki, impressed with his "good sense and talents for government" and thinking that there was "no cause for regretting the ascendancy of the Wahhabis in Eastern Arabia." Furthermore, in view of Britain's attempts to establish relations with all gulf rulers and to absorb their entities into its gulf treaties network, Britain would very likely have embraced the Saudis as well, by virtue of their being rulers of a considerable part of the gulf coast. The rationale underlying Pelly's visit to Riyadh substantiated Britain's desire to reach an accommodation and understanding with Faisal. Indeed, had the Saudis acted in line with British interests and favorably responded to Pelly in 1865, six years later Britain might have come to their support against the Ottoman occupation of Hasa. It was the Saudis themselves who, by pursuing an anti-British policy along the gulf coast, prompted Britain to reverse both her favorable attitude and her reluctance "to intervene in Arabian affairs," and who, by disregarding the balance of forces between the two, placed the two countries on a collision course. That even Faisal did not comprehend the nature of British policy was further demonstrated by his occasional requests to Britain in 1848 and 1850 to support the extension of Saudi rule to Oman and Bahrain.[44]

The only discernible change in the foreign policy of the Saudi state occurred in the context of Saudi-Ottoman relations, when the Saudis abstained from raiding Syria and Iraq or occupying the

Hejaz. It is doubtful whether this represented a deliberate and calculated change in the substance of Saudi policy, amounting to a new and consistent pattern of political conduct. The Saudis' abstention from attacking Syria, Iraq, and the Hejaz was motivated primarily by their military incapacity to embark on such ambitious designs, caused by domestic weakness, rather than by their apprehension that such attacks might trigger an Ottoman retaliation. In two of the three periods of its history, the second Saudi state suffered from an inherent weakness, caused in the first period by the Egyptian invasion and in the last period by internal struggles, which fundamentally curbed its ability to expand. Even in its heyday under Faisal, the state's control of the Nejdi districts, Qasim and Shammar, was less firm than in the earlier era, and its fluctuant position along the coast was precarious. Under such circumstances the Saudis were too preoccupied with difficulties in Nejd and along the coast to contemplate further expansion in the direction of the Hejaz. Faisal's own experience of Egyptian power could have taught him how much stronger the Egyptians and the Ottomans were than the Nejdis. But the lessons he derived, if any, were confined merely to a change in his relations with the Porte. Had the change been motivated by a new understanding of political realities, it would have manifested itself first and foremost in the Saudis' policies vis-à-vis the British, with whom they were in close contact. Instead, the history of Anglo-Saudi relations was a story of incompatible interests in almost constant collision.

A considerable number of differences existed between the first and second Saudi states, affecting the degree of cohesiveness in the society, the relationship between the Saudi and Wahhabi components of the community, the magnitude of religious fervor, and the reasons for the state's ultimate destruction. Some change was also discernible in the second Saudi state's policies toward the Ottomans, which were predicated on more rational calculations. Such a change, however, attributable to domestic troubles and military weakness, did not amount to a consistent and systematic pattern of foreign policy. Thus, the common denominator in the foreign policies of both Saudi states lay in the Saudis' failure to consider existing political realities in their calculations. In other words, both Saudi states pursued a policy that was totally, if not diametrically, opposed to the notion of realpolitik.

2

The Molding of a Statesman

Mubarak treated Ibn Saud as a son. He took him to his audiences and conferences where Ibn Saud met representatives of the French, British, Russian, and German Governments. He saw how Mubarak handled them and how the problems of the outside world affected him.

'Abd al-Latif Ibn 'Abd al-Majid

Ibn Saud's sojourn in Kuwait was his best teacher because it provided him with the necessary preparations for the great day.

Fuad Hamza

AMONG THOSE WHO FLED from Riyadh in 1891 was the eleven-year-old 'Abd al-'Aziz (hereafter Ibn Saud), Faisal's grandson and the fourth child of 'Abd al-Rahman. After wandering for two years between the gulf coast and the Rub' al-Khali, the al-Saud, or Saudi family, were finally permitted to settle in Kuwait.[1] The nine years spent in Kuwait proved to be a crucial factor in the reestablishment and final success of the third Saudi state. This was the site where Ibn Saud, the founder and then king of the third Saudi state, spent his formative years, and where his views, weltanschauung, and character were formed. Most important, his proximity to the center of political activity in Kuwait not only shaped his political outlook but also molded him into a political animal. Last but not least, this foreign experience distinguished Ibn Saud from all previous Saudi rulers, whose experience of the world at large did not exceed the limits of desert Arabia or Egyptian prisons. It was of great significance that Ibn Saud experienced the Kuwaiti period while still in his formative years, from the age of thirteen to twenty-one, when he was open to all sorts of influence and his character had not yet become permeated by the Wahhabi education.

Before being exposed to life in Kuwait, Ibn Saud's education did not differ from that of any other devout Wahhabi. He learned to recite the Koran, studied the ethics of Islam, attended all religious services, accompanied his father five times a day to the mosque, and scrupulously observed the fasts. While the family was in Kuwait, his father hired a Wahhabi scholar from Qasim to teach him the Wahhabi principles and laws.[2] In short, the stern tenets of the Wahhabi faith were the only item in Ibn Saud's educational curriculum.

Life in Kuwait was very different from that in Nejd. Detached from their natural environment in central Arabia, the Saudis found it impossible to live in a closed island of Wahhabi austerity, let alone isolate their children from the immediate neighborhood. For Ibn Saud, who had hitherto known only Riyadh and the desert, Kuwait was full of new experiences. It was the "Marseilles" of the Persian Gulf. Since it was the outlet from the north to the gulf and, hence, to India, merchants from Bombay and Tehran, Arabs from Aleppo and Damascus, Armenians, Turks, and Jews, traders from the East, and even Europeans came to Kuwait. In such a place, "Ibn Saud lived the ordinary life of an Arab youth. He loafed in the harbor and listened to the sailors. He sat on the edge of the cafés and sucked in the talk of the traders and the travellers and picked up the news of Baghdad, Damascus and Constantinople."[3]

Meanwhile, the Ottomans were hardly satisfied with the total Saudi defeat. Their policy in Arabia was based on maintaining a balance of power among the various tribes and preventing any single element from acquiring a predominant position. The elimination of the Saudis from central Arabia and the emerging hegemony of Ibn Rashid were hardly in line with the Ottoman strategy. As a result, the Ottomans offered to install the Saudis back in Riyadh with the help of Ottoman troops and arms on the condition that they accept an Ottoman garrison in Riyadh, acknowledge Ottoman sovereignty, and pay an annual tribute. But 'Abd al-Rahman refused. Nevertheless, from 1893 the Ottomans provided the exiled Saudi family with a monthly pension of M.T. 58.[4]

Since the Ottoman occupation of Hasa in 1871, Kuwait had been under close Ottoman surveillance. In that year the Kuwaiti ruler, 'Abdallah al-Sabah, accepted from the Porte the title qa'im-maqam, or governor of a sub-district, which he retained until his death in 1892 (see table). The Ottoman administration was organized from

Rulers of Kuwait

Ruler	Period
Muhammad ibn 'Abdallah al-Sabah	1892–1896
Mubarak ibn 'Abdallah al-Sabah	1896–1915
Jabir ibn Mubarak al-Sabah	1915–1917
Salim ibn Mubarak al-Sabah	1917–1921

the smallest unit, a nahiya under a mudir, to a qadha under a qa'im-maqam, to a sanjaq under a mutessarif, to the highest unit, a wilaya under a wali. 'Abdallah's successor, Muhammad al-Sabah was unwilling to oppose the Ottomans and handed over real control of his principality to a pro-Ottoman Iraqi by the name of Yusuf al-Ibrahim.[5]

The turning point in Kuwaiti history occurred in May 1896, when the ruler and his brother were assassinated by their half-brother Mubarak, who subsequently proclaimed himself the new sheikh of Kuwait.[6] Yusuf al-Ibrahim, who was one of the objects of the coup, managed to escape to Basra. The assassination was the result of an interfamily struggle as much as it was an anti-Ottoman move. Mubarak had always resented the loss of Kuwait's former independence and viewed with alarm the growing degree of Ottoman control. That a member of his family had relinquished the effective rulership and handed it over to a foreigner with obvious aspirations to replace the al-Sabah presented an even greater challenge to Mubarak.

With Mubarak's accession to power, a new chapter began in the life of Ibn Saud as well. Prior to his coup, Mubarak had come to know the fifteen-year-old Ibn Saud, and "he took a great liking to him." Mubarak treated Ibn Saud "as a son, invited him often to his house, talked much to him and taught him much worldly wisdom during these years of exile. He took him with him in his work, his audiences and his conferences, and for Ibn Saud it was a fine schooling. Here with Mubarak, Ibn Saud was surrounded by new ideas, new people, novel customs and ways of thought, many of which were unknown and forbidden in Riyadh." According to one of Ibn Saud's playmates of the Kuwaiti days, he attended Mubarak's majlis, or public assembly, faithfully from his school days onward. By another account, Mubarak even taught him history, geography, mathematics, and a little English, and later offered him work as his secretary.[7]

The emerging distinction between Ibn Saud and his predecessors first manifested itself in the different way in which he and his father, 'Abd al-Rahman, treated Mubarak. Whereas Ibn Saud admired his mentor, 'Abd al-Rahman disapproved of Mubarak and resented the lax, immoral, and unorthodox life he led. The fine silk clothes, tobacco smoking, and dancing girls for which Mubarak became known were all anathema to the strict and zealous Wahhabi. He refrained from visiting Mubarak and disapproved of his son's liaison with him. But Ibn Saud was too fascinated by the new world revolving around Mubarak to follow his father's advice.[8]

With the coup in Kuwait and Mubarak's assumption of power, even broader horizons opened up to Ibn Saud. Through Mubarak, Ibn Saud caught a glimpse of international politics and intrigue on a far larger and more complex scale than that of the intertribal rivalries to which he had previously been exposed. Ibn Saud could not have found a shrewder actor in all Arabia under whom to serve his political apprenticeship. Mubarak was a born politician, wise in the wiles of his own Arabian milieu and also in those of the world beyond, where the great powers were coming to eye Kuwait as a strategic asset at the head of the Persian Gulf.

In the last two decades of the nineteenth century, Europe's imperial struggles had multiplied. In Africa, France, Germany, and Britain had just carved up a continent among themselves. In Asia, Russia was steadily expanding her power and influence—eastward to Vladivostok and the China Sea, southward to the interior of Afghanistan and Persia—while both France and Germany were attempting to obtain from the Ottoman Empire a privileged status in its Arabic-speaking provinces. These conflicting interests came to a head in the Persian Gulf in the 1890s, endangering the paramount position Britain had enjoyed for the better part of the nineteenth century, which had in effect turned the gulf into a British lake.

The Russians, having already established an informal protectorate with Britain over the shah of Persia, proceeded to install a consul at Bushire, alongside the British political resident. In addition, they strove to obtain from Kuwait a concession to build a new railway from the Persian Gulf to Tripoli on the Mediterranean coast, to circumvent the British-controlled Suez Canal in the passage from Europe to the Orient. On top of this, they started a heavily subsidized shipping line from Odessa to Kuwait.[9]

The first French attempt to probe Britain's grip on the Persian Gulf was made in Muscat in the 1890s, when a new French consul there tried to lure the sultan away from his British protectors by political intrigue and offers of trade. In 1899 the French attempted to establish a coaling station in Muscat, and they granted French flags to Omani vessels. France also became involved in the arms trade in the gulf, viewed by Britain as illicit. The Germans soon entered the fray with a rival railway scheme. Viewing the decline of the Ottoman Empire as a golden opportunity for commercial expansion, providing new markets for its growing industries, the German government launched a *Drang nach Osten* (drive to the East) which was a conscious effort to turn the Ottoman provinces into a German economic preserve. At its core was the plan for a Berlin-Baghdad railway extending to Basra, with Kuwait as its terminus, which would tie half of the Middle East to Germany and open the possibility of a formal alliance with the Ottomans that would challenge Britain's hegemony in the Middle East.[10]

The Ottomans strove to reinforce their hold on whatever territories they had not yet lost to the other powers. During the reign of Sultan Abdul Hamid (1876–1909), the Porte began to pursue a policy of consolidation and expansion in the Arabic-speaking parts of the Ottoman Empire, even as far away as Kuwait and along the Arab littoral of the gulf. Moreover, claiming sovereignty over all Arabia, the Ottomans were determined to consolidate their position in the interior of the peninsula. Indeed, their reoccupation of Hasa in 1871 had provided them with a base in the region from which they could carry out their policies.

Viewed from London, the conflicting aspirations of the various powers had one common denominator: they all threatened Britain's paramount position in the gulf and endangered not only the security of the land and sea routes to India but also the British rule over India itself. The Russian danger, with its eastern expansion, pressure on Persia, and quest for a warm-water port, alarmed the British most of all. In attempting to counter these threats, the British had to walk a tightrope between their desire to consolidate their positions along the Arab coast of the gulf, on the one hand,

and their reluctance to be drawn into peninsular politics and further alienate the Ottomans, on the other. During the 1890s the two goals became gradually irreconcilable. By 1892, primarily in reaction to Ottoman pressure, Britain had added nonalienation bonds to her original treaties with the Trucial sheikhdoms, Bahrain and Muscat. These bonds obliged the respective rulers not to enter into an agreement or correspondence with any power other than Britain—a stipulation that included the Porte, their nominal sovereign! In 1893, the British notified the Porte that they recognized Ottoman sovereignty as extending from Basra to Qatif, a town in Hasa, but that the coast south of this point was "debatable land."[11] Thus, having previously adhered to the principle of "maintaining the integrity of the Ottoman Empire," Britain began gradually to realize that adherence to such a principle was unfeasible and to contemplate other approaches.

British policy was soon put to the test in Kuwait. In the late 1890s, Kuwait was a microcosm of the conflicting aspirations of all the powers. Caught in the center of these conflicting designs was Mubarak, who sought most of all to detach Kuwait from the Ottomans and gain an independent status for his principality. Mubarak's court thus became the center of diplomatic activity on an international scale. For the eighteen-year-old Ibn Saud, this was a unique and extraordinary experience. He "met foreigners of all sorts, traders, merchants, travellers, representatives of the French, British, Russian and German Governments. He saw how Mubarak handled them and how the problems of the outside world affected him. At audiences and conferences, Ibn Saud would sit in a corner, his feet curled up under him, watching always, alert, absorbing all that happened, learning always."[12]

The political lessons Ibn Saud derived from the five-year period he spent at Mubarak's court were invaluable for the ultimate success of the third Saudi state. At Mubarak's feet he learned the complexities of the art of statecraft. Ibn Saud was fortunate that Kuwait and the al-Saud coincidentally shared a major common problem, how to carve an independent status for themselves in the face of the Porte's desire to bring them under direct control. It was by no means fortuitous that Ibn Saud's strategy in the period 1902–1915 resembled the policy pursued by Mubarak in 1897–1901. Mubarak provided a working model for Ibn Saud.

Mubarak adopted a meticulous policy in order to obtain practical, if not formal, independence from the Porte. Promptly after assuming the rulership of Kuwait, Mubarak hastened to profess loyalty to the sultan, and he hoisted the Ottoman flag in the Kuwaiti harbor. By doing so, he hoped to preempt the Porte's possible interpretation of his coup as anti-Ottoman and hence to prevent Ottoman retaliation. Early in 1897 the Ottomans sought to reassert their direct control over Kuwait, of which they had been deprived by the removal of Yusuf al-Ibrahim, by sending a quarantine official to reside in Kuwait. Alarmed at the perceived Ottoman threat, Mubarak indicated to J. F. Whyte, the British consul at Basra, that he might desire some sort of protectorate relationship with Great Britain. But the British showed little interest in Mubarak's overture.[13]

On June 30, 1897, an expedition led by Yusuf al-Ibrahim sailed down from Basra to Kuwait but was repulsed by Mubarak's adherents. Mubarak interpreted the move as a further indication of Ottoman designs and requested a meeting with a British official. On the basis of the British government's authorization, J. Gaskin, an assistant to the resident, arrived at Kuwait on September 5. Because Mubarak refused to go on board the British ship *Lawrence* lest he offend the Ottomans, the interviews were conducted on shore.

Mubarak explained that he and his people feared that the Ottomans were contemplating the annexation of Kuwait. In order to circumvent such a contingency, he desired to be taken under British protection in the same manner as the sheikhs of Bahrain and Trucial Oman. In exchange, he promised to assist the British government in maintaining law and order in his part of the gulf. The overture was rejected by the British government, which decided not to bring Kuwait under its protection or to interfere more than was necessary for the maintenance of general peace in the Persian Gulf.

In late October 1897, Yusuf al-Ibrahim organized another expedition from Basra to Kuwait. The British political resident in the gulf suggested that a gunboat be sent to Kuwaiti waters "to observe," and London approved the proposal. Although the expedition did not materialize, the gunboat's presence suggested to Mubarak that this time the British might be responsive to his overture. In November he repeated his request for British protection, but he was rejected once again.

Meanwhile the Ottomans seemed to accept the fait accompli, because in December 1897 they appointed Mubarak by imperial decree as the qa'im-maqam of Kuwait. But they soon proved that, by appointing Mubarak, they sought merely to demonstrate that he was an Ottoman vassal. Renewing their pressure on Kuwait, they appointed a commission to investigate complaints against Mubarak, and subsequently they concentrated in Basra a force of six battalions totaling 6000 men, whose objective was presumably the conquest of Kuwait. Mubarak quickly appealed for British help, but the British were still reluctant to intervene. The Ottoman threat against Kuwait was eclipsed by the probable damage to British-Ottoman and British-Russian relations if the British Government decided to interfere in Kuwaiti affairs.[14]

The British position changed radically in 1898. At the beginning of the year the British found that the Russians were striving to establish a coaling station in Kuwait. In August they learned that a Russian count, Kapnist, was attempting to obtain from the Porte a concession for the construction of a railway from the Mediterranean to the Persian Gulf at Kuwait. The British feared that, in the absence of any British agreement with Mubarak, the Russian scheme might result in the creation of Russian territorial rights in Kuwait.

When in early 1899 the British learned that the Russian government had given its support to the Kapnist scheme, the British government reacted promptly. It did not approve a declaration of a protectorate over Kuwait, for all that was needed at the moment was "a bond to guard against any Russian territorial claims." As one official explained, "we don't want Kuwait, but we don't want anyone else to have it." On January 23, the political resident in the gulf, Colonel Meade, and Mubarak signed an agreement whereby the sheikh of Kuwait "does pledge and bind himself, his heirs and successors not to receive the Representative of any Power at Kuwait, without the previous sanction of the British Government; and he further binds himself, his heirs and successors not to cede, sell, lease, mortgage, or give for occupation or for any other purpose any portion of his territory to the Government or subjects of any other Power without the previous consent of His Majesty's Government for these purposes." In exchange for Mubarak's obligations, Colonel Meade presented him with a letter assuring him, on behalf of the British government, "of the good offices of His Majesty's Government towards you, your heirs and successors as long as you, your heirs and successors scrupulously and faithfully observe the conditions of the bond."[15]

The next few months witnessed strenuous efforts by the Ottomans to restore Kuwait to the fold of the Porte's suzerainty. Mubarak on his part, encouraged by the British commitment, showed a new intractability in his dealings with the Ottoman authorities. In February 1899 the British apprehended an Ottoman movement against Kuwait by sea and were forced to consider the question of protective measures. In March the situation seemed so serious that the Indian government instructed the H.M.S. *Lapwig* to be stationed in the neighborhood of Kuwait. The Ottoman attack did not materialize.

Shielded by the British presence, Mubarak decided to demonstrate further his autonomous status. In May 1899 he established regular customs at Kuwait and began to levy a 5 percent duty on all imports, including those from Ottoman areas. The Ottomans could not acquiesce in such a flagrant challenge to their authority, and in September they sent a harbor master and five soldiers to take charge of the port of Kuwait. Mubarak resisted the effort, and the Ottomans were obliged to return to Basra.

In view of the Ottoman attempts to reassert their presence in Kuwait, coupled with rumors of a forthcoming Ottoman military movement against the principality, the British government decided to react officially in order to dissuade the Porte from any unilateral steps. An official communication warned the Ottomans that Britain had friendly relations with Mubarak and that, if any attempt were made to establish Ottoman authority at Kuwait without previous agreement with the British government, "a very inconvenient and disagreeable question would be raised."[16] In response, the Porte assured the British that no military expedition was contemplated and that the establishment of a harbor master would be pressed no further.

Confident of British protection against the Ottomans, Mubarak moved to mend his relations with the Porte. In November 1900 he went to Basra in response to an Ottoman request that he make an official visit to the town. The Ottomans conferred upon him an honorary title, the Order of Mejdieh (Glory) of the second class, and Mubarak in return promised to abstain from relations with foreign powers.[17]

But relations with the Ottomans quickly deteriorated. In February 1901, the joint Kuwaiti-Saudi forces launched an attack on Ibn Rashid, and they suffered a severe setback in the battle of Sarif.[18] The Ottomans sought to exploit Mubarak's defeat in May by pressing on him the acceptance of an Ottoman military garrison at Kuwait. Mubarak interpreted the Ottoman move as an attempt to force him to surrender his independence, and five days later he approached the British with a request that they assume a permanent protectorate over Kuwait. The Ottomans further challenged Mubarak's position when they assembled a considerable military force on the Euphrates and the sultan instructed that a customhouse and telegraph office be established in Kuwait as tangible proofs of Ottoman authority.

The British, though reluctant to accept the idea of a protectorate, decided to meet the Ottoman threat with resolve. In August 1901 the British government authorized the gunboat *Perseus* to prevent, by force if necessary, the landing of Ottoman troops at Kuwait. On August 24 the Ottoman warship *Zuhaf* entered Kuwait harbor, and its commander had a meeting with Mubarak in which the sheikh was pressed, in vain, to recognize Ottoman sovereignty. At this juncture the commander of the British ship conveyed his government's warning to the Ottomans, whereupon the Ottoman ship left Kuwait. Protests were soon dispatched from Constantinople to London, but the British government remained as firm as ever, and the Ottomans had to abandon the issue.

The Porte again strove to take advantage of Mubarak's defeat at the Rashidi hands. On December 1, 1901, two Ottoman officials arrived in Kuwait on board the *Zuhaf* and presented Mubarak with a telegram from the sultan, containing an ultimatum: either he would receive an Ottoman military detachment, or he would have to leave Kuwait and retire to Constantinople. On December 6, Mubarak received assurances that the British government would support him and would not tolerate an attack by Ottoman ships or troops on Kuwait. As a result, Mubarak did not respond to the ultimatum, nor did the Ottomans try to implement it.[19]

This juncture marks the close of the Kuwaiti episode in Ibn Saud's life, for in December 1901 he was already embarked on the adventure that would culminate a month later in the re-establishment of the al-Saud in Riyadh. Yet the political lessons he had derived in Kuwait constituted the basis for his future political conduct.[20] First and foremost, Ibn Saud learned from Mubarak that, in view of the existing forces of the Ottomans, independence from the Porte could not be obtained by a military confrontation but rather through political means. He learned how Kuwait could both achieve practical independence from the Ottomans and avoid a military showdown by securing the protective presence of another power. In addition, Ibn Saud learned that, as long as independence and protection from the Ottomans were not secured, it was necessary to pay lip service to the Porte by professing loyalty to the sultan, recognizing the fiction of Ottoman sovereignty, accepting Ottoman titles, and doing anything else that did not impinge on a reasonable degree of freedom of action. In this context it was important not to undertake anything that might prematurely alienate the Ottomans, such as entering into an overt collusion with foreign powers.

Ibn Saud also became acquainted with Britain's supremacy in the Persian Gulf region, which caused other powers to withdraw whenever they encountered a determined British stand. He witnessed how, in a very gradual process, Mubarak managed to overcome Britain's initial reluctance and embroil it in the conflict as a counterpoise to the Ottoman pressure on Kuwait. He was cognizant of the way in which Mubarak manipulated the Russian card, using it to induce the British to intervene by assuming protection over Mubarak's principality in order to remove the Russian danger. He also learned that Mubarak did not rely on British protection until he possessed the official assurance of the British government in writing. Ibn Saud then observed how the British scrupulously respected their agreement with Mubarak and lived up to their undertaking to provide him with their "good offices" in the face of offensive Ottoman designs. It was not only the swiftness of the British reaction to the Ottoman threats that impressed him, but also the fact that the Porte did not really stand up to the British challenge and instead accepted the fait accompli.[21]

One striking aspect of Mubarak's strategy was the employment of Britain, a Christian power, against his Muslim Ottoman sovereign. That this was conceivable for Mubarak, a man completely detached from Islam, was not surprising. But that Ibn Saud, who remained until the end of his life a disciple of Wahhabi tenets, would pursue the same strategy was inconceivable and unexpected. Yet Ibn Saud did employ a Christian power against his Muslim sovereign, and thus, in the realm of politics, Ibn Saud allowed political considerations to transcend the Wahhabi doctrine.

Ibn Saud also drew an important lesson from the Ottoman attitude toward the Saudis while in exile in Kuwait. He was aware of the Porte's attempts to encourage the Saudis to reoccupy Riyadh with Ottoman support and understood that it was not in the Ottoman interest to eliminate the Saudis from the central Arabian arena. On the contrary, as the Porte sought to check the hegemony of Ibn Rashid, the Saudis were an ideal instrument for that purpose. Ibn Saud concluded that the Ottomans would not view with disfavor a Saudi re-establishment in Nejd, provided Ottoman sovereignty was recognized.

Such political lessons could also have been drawn by Ibn Saud's father, 'Abd al-Rahman, for he himself was also cosmopolitanized while in exile in Kuwait. Though disapproving, on religious grounds, of his son's close relations with Mubarak, 'Abd al-Rahman was not blind and did not remain aloof to all the major political developments he witnessed in Kuwait. After all, it was to him that the Ottomans made their proposal to help reinstall the Saudis in Riyadh, even though such a move was bound to weaken the Ottomans' own ally, Ibn Rashid. 'Abd al-Rahman took note of the struggles and competitions among the various powers and realized the supremacy of Britain in the gulf region. He understood that the rules of the game were based on power and pragmatic considerations of realpolitik and had little or nothing to do with religious beliefs and values. There was, however, a major difference between father and son. Whereas Ibn Saud underwent the Kuwaiti experience while in his formative years, open to all kinds of influences, 'Abd al-Rahman was already in his late forties, possessed of a solid and deep-seated Wahhabi weltanschauung. Nevertheless, the common Kuwaiti chapter enabled 'Abd al-Rahman to become a partner in the policies that his son, Ibn Saud, pursued in subsequent years toward Britain and the Ottomans.

In 1897 the great Muhammad Ibn Rashid, whose personal dynamism had been largely responsible for the successes of his clan and who had brought about the destruction of the second Saudi state, died and was succeeded by 'Abd al-'Aziz Ibn Rashid, "a brave warrior but a poor politician."[22] The great state that the Rashidi ruler had built during his twenty-five years in power was gradually disintegrating. Old loyalties began to dissolve, and unrest was widespread in Nejd. Mubarak sought to exploit the new situation in Nejd and bring about a change in the balance of power in central Arabia that would serve Kuwait's interests. Kuwait was strongest, in Mubarak's eyes, when central Arabia was not dominated by a single power. Since the Rashidis enjoyed virtual hegemony there and entertained hostile designs against Kuwait as well, Mubarak sought to weaken the Rashidis by lending his support to the plans of the al-Saud to recapture Riyadh. The re-establishment of the Saudi entity would restore the Arabian balance of power, enhance the position of Kuwait, and divert the Rashidis' interest from Kuwait to Riyadh. But the decisive defeat of the joint Kuwaiti-Saudi forces at Sarif in 1901 frustrated Mubarak's designs. As a result of the Saudis' defeat, 'Abd al-Rahman turned the reins of Saudi leadership over to his son, Ibn Saud, while he himself continued to retain the title of imam. More than any other factor, this separation of political and religious leadership illustrated the kind of considerations that would guide Ibn Saud in his foreign policy for the next half-century.

The Kuwaiti chapter in Ibn Saud's life provided the source of his policies in subsequent years—his strategies, tactics, and conduct toward Britain and the Ottoman Empire. In addition, it made Ibn Saud's background fundamentally different from that of former Saudi rulers. Faisal's exile in Egypt, which impressed on him the notion of Egyptian superiority, was fundamentally different from Ibn Saud's exile in Kuwait. Whereas Faisal was a prisoner, Ibn Saud was not only a free man but also an enthusiastic student of international diplomacy at Mubarak's court. This difference affected their behavior in the postexile period: Faisal modified his policies only vis-à-vis Egypt and the Porte, but Ibn Saud developed a pragmatic judgment of existing political realities and his cautious conduct amounted to an overall plan of foreign policy.

At the age of twenty-two, Ibn Saud was about to inaugurate the third chapter in modern Saudi history. At this juncture, his worldview had been shaped during his formative years by two major sets of influences: the humiliating flight from Riyadh to exile and the political-diplomatic apprenticeship in Kuwait. The flight from

Riyadh and the elimination of the second Saudi state exacerbated the overall trauma dating back to the destruction of the first Saudi state in 1818. This experience inculcated in Ibn Saud a determination to avoid the repetition of such devastating events by securing independence and protection for his state. The second influence, his apprenticeship in Kuwait, taught Ibn Saud the means, methods, and strategies for obtaining these goals. It was in such a frame of mind that Ibn Saud ventured out of Kuwait in late 1901 on his way to reinstate the house of Saud in Riyadh.

3

Recognition of Ottoman Sovereignty, 1902–1912

May the eyes of the British Government be fixed upon us and may we be considered as your protégés.

Ibn Saud to Kemball

I beg that our tender of loyalty and submission may be accepted.

Ibn Saud to the Sultan

Had the British brought us under their wings, none of our expressions of submission to the Ottomans would have been necessary.

Ibn Saud to Shakespear

THE ARABIA IN WHICH the al-Saud began their third ascent to power in 1902 was little different from that which their ancestors of the eighteenth and nineteenth centuries had known. The revolution in Middle East communications, prompted by the opening of the Suez Canal in 1869, had had very little impact on internal developments in the peninsula, let alone in central Arabia. The discovery of major oil fields under the deserts of Arabia, which would bring about major changes in the Saudi state during the later twentieth century, was not to occur until the 1930s. The seclusion of central Arabia thus remained stark, and much of the peninsula was unknown territory for the West. In the whole of the nineteenth century—an age of European expansion, exploration, and scientific pursuit—only three Europeans succeeded in reaching Riyadh. Unbearable heat, sometimes exceeding 120° F; the absence of land routes, transportation, and communication; the menacing emptiness of the desert; and the frightening accounts of those who did travel to the peninsula—all deterred future travelers and made Arabia as inaccessible as ever.

Commercially, central Arabia had nothing to offer to the mercantile and industrial world. Its natural resources seemed minimal, and the economy was mainly a subsistence one. Its people were few and scattered. In 1900 the peninsula population probably did not exceed three million, and its expansion was constantly curtailed by periodical droughts. The society was tribal in structure and patriarchal in rule. In the severe conditions of the interior, the nomadic pastoral tribes and the oasis dwellers lived in much the same way as they had for millennia. Apart from the holy cities of Mecca and Medina, only the port town of Jidda and the small ports along the gulf coast were of any importance.

Ottoman policy in Arabia was tied into the overall policy of the empire just two decades before its final disintegration. Viewed against the background of the European theater—where relations with Britain, Germany, and Russia were of crucial significance to the survival of the empire—Arabia was of marginal importance. It was only around its shores—the Hejaz, Yemen, and the Arab littoral of the Persian Gulf—that Ottoman interests rested. Nevertheless, the Porte continued to claim sovereignty over the entire peninsula and at various stages sought to give practical demonstration of such claims. After all, these were the days of Sultan Abdul Hamid (1876–1909), in which the Porte tried to pursue assertive and forceful policies of consolidation in the Arabic-speaking provinces of the empire. But these attempts were hampered by both long lines of communication and serious troubles in other parts of the empire. In central Arabia, even the traditional policy of playing one tribe against the other was not very useful, inasmuch as Ibn Rashid became the predominant power in the area, eclipsing and removing the house of Saud altogether from the scene. The main obstacle facing the Ottomans, however, was the British presence in the gulf.

By the turn of the twentieth century, Great Britain was at the peak of its global power. The British had replaced the Ottomans as the dominant power in Egypt, seized Cyprus, and won control of the Suez Canal. In the Persian Gulf, they had evolved a system of treaties with Arabia's coastal rulers that ensured their virtually unbroken control of the seas from Aden to the northern head of the Persian Gulf, Kuwait. But they still refrained from intervening in the politics of the interior of the peninsula as long as no rival power threatened their predominant position in the region. The

British foreign secretary, Lord Lansdowne, made it abundantly clear that Britain would regard the establishment of any base in the gulf by any other power as "a very grave menace to British interests and we should certainly resist it with all means at our disposal."[1] During the first decade of the twentieth century, Britain's position in the gulf improved considerably. The entente cordiale that London reached with France in 1904 and the agreement that it signed with Russia in 1907 virtually eliminated these two powers as serious threats to Britain in the gulf. Furthermore, the Young Turk revolution in 1908 and subsequent developments in both Constantinople and the Ottoman provinces of North Africa and the Balkans diverted Ottoman attention away from the gulf. Thus, from 1904 until just before the outbreak of World War I, Britain was not seriously challenged in the gulf.

To monitor the situation in the gulf and keep the area under close surveillance, the British had devised an elaborate administrative system which reflected both the hierarchy and lines of authority within the British administration as well as the role the Persian Gulf played in the overall context of Britain's foreign policy. The system was based on British political agents who were stationed in the various gulf sheikhdoms, such as Muscat, Abu Dhabi, Bahrain, and Kuwait. The agents supervised Britain's interests in the gulf region and were responsible to the political resident in the Persian Gulf stationed in Bushire on the Persian coast (see table). The resident in turn reported to the foreign secretary of the government of India and to the viceroy in Delhi. Only then was the accumulated news of Arabia and the gulf transmitted to the British government at home, first to the India Office and finally to the Foreign Office. Thus, communications concerning Ibn Saud usually began their way in Bahrain, the British agency closest to Ibn Saud, then proceeded via the resident in Bushire to the government of India in Delhi, and moved on to the India Office and, finally, the Foreign Office in London. The introduction of the telegraph, which linked Europe and India from the mid-1860s, facilitated communication among these authorities.

Formally Saudi-British relations were within the jurisdiction of the Indian government. As of the last decade of the nineteenth century, however, with the growing importance of the Persian Gulf for overall British foreign policy, the Foreign Office came gradually

British Officials in the Persian Gulf

Official	Period
Political Resident in the Persian Gulf	
C. A. Kemball	1900–1904
Percy Cox	1904–1913
J. G. Lorimer	1913–1914
S. G. Knox	March–Nov. 1914
Percy Cox	1914–1920
Political Agent, Kuwait	
S. G. Knox	1904–1909
W. H. I. Shakespear	1909–1914
William Grey	1914–1917
R. E. A. Hamilton	1917–1919
Political Agent, Bahrain	
John Gaskin	1902?–1906?
Francis Prideaux	1906?–1909?
Arthur Trevor	1912–1914
A. J. Keyes	1914–1916

to dominate the decision-making process in the context of Saudi-British relations. Indeed, the Foreign Office made all the crucial decisions regarding the Saudi issue starting in 1904, blocked all attempts by British officials in the gulf and India to change Britain's attitude toward Ibn Saud, and finally approved a reversal in British policy after 1913. It ensured that the "local" and "regional" interests of the Indian government and its officials in the gulf were subordinated to the "global" perspective of the imperial government in London. Despite this clear hierarchy, the formation and execution of British policy were not devoid of problems. Personality clashes, interoffice rivalries, overlapping administrative responsibilities, elongated command chains and communications between London and Arabia, all came to characterize British policy toward the Saudis. In the final analysis, however, the Foreign Office was in firm command of the making and execution of Britain's policy toward Ibn Saud. The Foreign Office's views prevailed even when the issues at stake were not major policy questions but rather such problems as meetings, contacts, and communications with Ibn Saud, despite the obvious resentment of the Indian government, which was supposed to have jurisdiction in this kind of matter.[2]

In central Arabia, the turn of the century witnessed the beginning of the decline of the Rashidi dynasty, which had been paramount in the region for three decades. Though there was a strong Wahhabi community in Jabal Shammar, religion was a less important element in the Rashidi state than in the Saudi community. Tribal consciousness, not Wahhabi belief, was the basic cement unifying all the people of Jabal Shammar. The Rashidi administration, albeit religious, was more of an example of extended tribalism, whereas the Saudi-Wahhabi state had been a theocratic community that overrode tribal loyalties. The result was the creation of a looser political organization in Hail.[3] Under the leadership of two great rulers, Tallal Ibn 'Abdallah (1848–1868) and Muhammad Ibn 'Abdallah, the Rashidis managed to overcome these inherent weaknesses. But they never really recuperated from the death of Muhammad, who was largely responsible for their success in overwhelming the Saudis and reigning exclusively over central Arabia. Muhammad even managed to convince members of the al-Sheikh—the family of the founder of Wahhabism, Muhammad Ibn 'Abd al-Wahhab—to stay on in Riyadh after the expulsion of the Saudi family in 1891 and collaborate with the Rashidis. This not only drove a wedge between the two pillars of the Saudi-Wahhabi state but also conferred on the Rashidi dynasty a semblance of legitimacy it had previously lacked. After Muhammad Ibn Rashid's death, however, the Rashidis started to lose their grip on their territories, and their state entered a process of slow disintegration. It was at this juncture that the young 'Abd al-'Aziz Ibn Saud made an entrance by restoring the house of Saud to the central Arabian equation.

The capture of Riyadh by Ibn Saud on the night of January 15, 1902, was an almost unprecedented military adventure. The military act was immediately followed by a political move of no less significance. Lest the Ottoman Empire interpret the re-establishment of the Saudis in Riyadh as a direct challenge, Ibn Saud notified the Porte through the wali of Basra that his activities were aimed at retrieving his ancestors' dominions from the Rashidi usurpers and not at ousting the Ottoman government. He assured the sultan that he would rule the recovered country as his loyal subject.[4]

In view of both the deep-seated, century-old enmity of the Saudis toward the liquidators of their previous state and their perception of the Ottomans as infidels, this act was remarkable. Rarely in Saudi history had a Saudi ruler so explicitly acknowledged Ottoman sovereignty over Nejd. That such a recognition was conveyed following a Saudi victory, not a defeat, rendered it all the more exceptional. The communication was reminiscent of Mubarak hoisting the Ottoman flag immediately after assuming the rulership of Kuwait. It became a paradigm of the policies Ibn Saud would pursue in future years.

Ibn Rashid wished to obtain precisely what Ibn Saud sought to avoid: the intervention of the Porte in order to nullify the Saudi achievement. Accordingly, he wrote to the grand vezir, requesting Ottoman aid to suppress "the revolt in Nejd." He accused the British of seeking "to establish themselves in portions of Arabia which dominate the Ottoman possessions of Hasa and Qatif by means of Mubarak and Ibn Saud," and he warned against the consequences of this British intrigue.[5] The Rashidi ruler was justifiably apprehensive that the Porte might not be alarmed by a mere Saudi success and hence resorted to the "British connection," which was bound to arouse Ottoman suspicions.

The Ottomans, for their part, had good reasons to be suspicious of British intentions in the area, given the blow they had suffered by the extension of British protection over Kuwait, an area admittedly in the sphere of Ottoman sovereignty. But the Saudi recovery of Riyadh was something else, and it was not viewed with disfavor. The Ottomans could hardly have failed to profit by the division of power in central Arabia, which contributed to their policy of divide and rule, so long as the local contenders continued to recognize Ottoman sovereignty. Accordingly, they rejected Ibn Rashid's request for military assistance, and they even resumed the payment of Ibn Saud's father's pension, which had fallen into arrears.[6]

The British concern with Ibn Saud's affairs was confined to the extent that they affected the struggle between Ibn Rashid, backed by the Ottomans, and Mubarak, the ruler of Kuwait and the protégé of His Majesty's government. Their political resident in the Persian Gulf, Kemball, doubted that the Saudi re-establishment would be permanent, and he predicted that "Saudi ultimate defeat by Ibn Rashid would seem to be probable."[7]

Meanwhile, Ibn Saud set out to organize his forces against the Rashidi, his local rival. But he must have realized, and his letter to the sultan was evidence of such understanding, that in the long run it was the Ottomans with whom he would have to reckon. For his ultimate goals, the restoration of all the previous dominions of the house of Saud and the achievement of virtual independence from the Ottoman state, entailed an inevitable confrontation with the Porte. Whereas his predecessors sought to build a Saudi-Wahhabi state, disregarding the possible reactions to their acts in Constantinople, Ibn Saud was more than aware of such reactions and strove to find ways to minimize the necessity for an Ottoman response. The lessons he might draw from past Saudi-Ottoman confrontations were highly discouraging.

In order for the Saudis to consolidate their position and successfully embark upon a policy of expansion, it was essential to secure a counterpoise to the Ottoman power, which would deter a possible Ottoman attempt to crush the Saudis. The Kuwaiti model was a case in point, as Mubarak's goal was also to detach himself from the Ottomans and secure independence. The instrument Mubarak employed was the British, whose interests converged with Kuwait's because of their desire to check the Ottomans and the advance of other powers toward the Persian Gulf.

The Saudi hostility toward the Ottomans was of a much more profound nature than Mubarak's, based on both a Saudi dynastic enmity toward those who had brought about the most traumatic experience in Saudi history, the destruction of the Saudi empire in 1818, and a perception of the Ottomans as infidels. No wonder, therefore, that Ibn Saud sought to emulate Mubarak's success by securing British protection over the Saudis vis-à-vis the Ottoman government. To that end, he made no less than eleven overtures to the British in the space of the next twelve years.

The First Overture

Ibn Saud's decision to secure British protection at an early stage in his career became apparent by May 1902, only four months after the recovery of Riyadh. When his father, 'Abd al-Rahman, left Kuwait for Riyadh, Ibn Saud addressed a letter to the British political resident:

> I have no wish to look to any one but yourself because of the favors and protection you extend to all those who place themselves under your eyes. May the eyes of the British Government be fixed upon us. I beg to inform you about the Russian Consul at Bushire, who had come and asked me to write him a letter describing the ill-treatment I have received from the Turks and the help they have given Ibn Rashid against me. I did not see fit to go to other than your Government. I request of your benevolent Government to consider me as one of their protégés.[8]

The Saudi aim was transparent from the terms "protection" and "protégé," and the allusion to the Kuwaiti precedent was unmistakable. A striking similarity exists between this first Saudi overture to the British and Mubarak's opening move in March 1897 asking for the establishment of a British protectorate over Kuwait by employing the Russian card.

For the British, however, there was a fundamental difference between Kuwait and Nejd. Whereas the former was located along the gulf coast, directly within the sphere of British interests, the latter was a central Arabian area beyond the scope of British concern, where an intervention could further strain Ottoman-British relations. Consequently, the Saudi letter was left unanswered, the government of India demanding that no encouragement be given to Ibn Saud. The policy of the British government was "to abstain from connection with the affairs of Nejd and maintain only a watchful, impartial attitude." Not only did the British refuse to come to an understanding with Ibn Saud, but they also urged Mubarak "to abstain from assisting him and encouraging any action" likely to involve Kuwait in difficulties with Nejd or with the Porte.[9] From the British point of view, their rupture with the Ottomans over Kuwait was sufficient reason to avoid an additional rift over an area that lay beyond the sphere of their immediate interests.

Meanwhile, Ibn Saud continued to consolidate his position in Nejd against his Rashidi rival. Occupation of the districts of Hariq and Kharj in 1902 and Sudair in the spring of 1903 considerably improved his position. Even more illustrative of the new balance of forces in Nejd was the battle of Dilam, fought in November 1902. It ended in a complete victory of the Saudis, who inflicted heavy casualties upon the Rashidis.[10]

The Second Overture

In March 1903, Ibn Saud felt confident enough to depart from Nejd for the first time since his recovery of Riyadh, and he traveled to Kuwait. There he was twice visited by the Russian consul to Bushire. The Saudi chief was determined to take advantage of his proximity to British officials in Kuwait and, more particularly, of his meeting with the Russian consul in order to approach the British government again. Ibn Saud later told the commander of the *Sphinx*, Kemp, that the Russians had promised him guns and money and stated that it was necessary for him to have money "to retain the support of the tribes since Ibn Rashid received money and support from the Ottomans."[11] Ibn Saud assumed that the British would dislike a Saudi-Russian deal and would pre-empt it by their own offer along the lines of the Russian proposal. After all, anxiety over Russian intrigues had led the British to accede to the establishment of protection over Kuwait, arguing that "we don't want Kuwait, but we don't want anyone else to have it." In the same vein, Ibn Saud figured, the British might not be interested in Riyadh but would not like others to have it.

Following up Ibn Saud's point, Mubarak sounded out Kemp as to the possibility of the British government's making "an advance of money to Ibn Saud who needed it in order to strengthen his position in Riyadh." This conversation suggested the possibility to Kemball that Ibn Saud had invented the Russian offer, but he himself was inclined to believe that the Russian consul "did make the offer." Lorimer, of the government of India, noted that Ibn Saud's allegation had received some corroboration from "an independent source."[12] But, regardless of whether the Russian offer was made or not, Ibn Saud's decision to use the real or imaginary proposal to induce Britain to enter into relations with him was indicative of his sense of statecraft. It demonstrated his awareness and understanding of the powers' struggle for influence in the Persian Gulf and his readiness to play off one power against the other in order to obtain his goal.

Ibn Saud's decision to reject the Russian offer further reflected his understanding of the balance of forces among the powers in the Persian Gulf. Only Great Britain could serve as a counterpoise to the Ottoman pressure because of its long-established predominant position in the area, and no Russian offers could change that reality. Ibn Saud, who was convinced that he would have to obtain British support in order to gain his independence from the Ottomans, did not wish to act in a way that would certainly alienate the British. This same logic led him to reject the Russian invitation to visit their warship *Boyarim* at Kuwait, which was reminiscent of Mubarak's refusal to go on board the British *Lawrence* in 1897 lest he offend the Ottomans.

The British did not respond to this last overture, except for impressing on Ibn Saud the undesirability of letting "a foreign European country interfere in the affairs of Nejd."[13] But Ibn Saud was determined to enter into an understanding with Great Britain, and eight months later he approached the British once again, this time with a specific proposal.

The Third Overture

The Saudi chief realized that his two previous overtures had expressed his general desire to enter into relations with Britain, but he had offered no tangible gain in return that might induce Britain to entertain the idea. Because he also realized that the Persian Gulf coast alone was of special importance to Britain, he assumed that the removal of the Ottomans from Hasa, the only part of the coast garrisoned by Ottoman troops, would be of great interest to Britain. As Hasa was an integral part of the two previous Saudi states that he intended to restore to the Saudi realm, he further calculated that the British would view his expulsion of the Ottomans from Hasa as a contribution to their interests along the gulf, in exchange for which it would be worthwhile to revise their attitude toward the Saudis.

To sound out the British regarding such a proposal, in November 1903 Ibn Saud sent an emissary to J. Gaskin, the political agent at Bahrain. The Saudi emissary stated that after defeating Ibn Rashid, Ibn Saud would try to eject the Ottomans from Hasa, but that such an expulsion would be a lasting success only if the British government undertook to protect his littoral from an Ottoman invasion. Would His Majesty's government undertake such an obligation?

Although the political agent returned an evasive answer to the Saudi envoy, arguing that "it was inappropriate for the British Government to intrigue with the subjects of a friendly state against their Government," the overture was received with interest in India, eliciting for the first time comments by British officials on the considerations dictating the British attitude toward the Saudis. Louis Dane, the foreign secretary, had already expressed fears in July that, should the Saudis defeat Ibn Rashid, "we may find that, as often happens, we have been backing the wrong horse."[14] Now that the Saudis had made a specific overture, Dane saw an obvious need for political contact with Riyadh, though he still ruled out British protection. The Saudis now controlled the flank of the projected route of the Baghdad Railway, and if they consolidated their position and were alienated by the British, they could menace British interests along the coast.

This apprehension led Curzon, the viceroy, to raise the question of the expediency of sending British officers, in disguise if necessary, on a secret mission to Riyadh. The political resident, Kemball, advised against the move because it would be interpreted by both the Ottomans and the Saudis as an open espousal by Britain of the Saudi cause. London, too, rejected the idea because of its reluctance to deepen the Ottoman suspicions regarding Britain's interests in Arabia, and it vetoed the project.[15]

While the proposal for a mission was not pursued, Ibn Saud's overture did cause a change of mind in India. Its government pointed out that although political contact with the Saudis had abruptly ceased with the Ottoman occupation of Hasa in 1871, the recent Ottoman schemes for trans-Arabian railways, the diminution of Ottoman authority, and the revival of Saudi power had all changed the situation. It was necessary for India to take "a more lively interest in central Arabian affairs," as "the creation of direct relations with Ibn Saud will sooner or later be inevitable." The dispatch went as far as to contemplate the possibility of "reviving the Treaty relations which existed with the Wahhabi Amirs."[16] But Ibn Saud could not have known of such exchanges, and therefore for him the British attitude of indifference remained intact.

Meanwhile, Ibn Saud continued to consolidate his position in Nejd at the expense of the house of Rashid. His military successes in 1904 started with the occupation of the district of Washm in February and culminated in the capture of 'Unaiza on March 11 and Buraida on April 5, bringing the whole of Qasim under his control. Thus, in slightly more than two years, the whole of southern and central Nejd was regained by the house of Saud. Having reached such a position, Ibn Saud assumed the title of "Emir of Nejd," hitherto held by Ibn Rashid.[17]

The Ottomans were naturally alarmed by what they regarded as a disruption of the balance of forces between the local rivals in Nejd. As long as the Saudis were confined to a small part of Nejd and both rivals harassed each other, the Porte could only profit from intertribal fighting. Once the Ottomans perceived that the Saudis had achieved a predominant position in Nejd, their policy was in danger. Furthermore, although Ibn Rashid certainly regarded himself as their vassal, Ibn Saud could only be considered a potential danger if he mirrored past Saudi attitudes, let alone if he allied himself with the British. Besides, the Ottomans faced a recurrent threat to their position in Hasa from disturbances and disorders. Following one such major insurrection in June 1902, the Porte hastened to dispatch reinforcements to the province and nominated the vigorous Sayyid Talib as the new mutessarif or governor of Hasa. Ibn Rashid had been instrumental in Talib's nomination, aiming to divert Ibn Saud's attention from Jabal Shammar to Hasa.[18]

Underlying these immediate dangers to the Ottomans' position in central and eastern Arabia was a far more profound problem related to their position in their Asiatic dominions. A memorandum submitted by Sayyid Talib, now the ex-mutessarif of Hasa, addressed itself directly to that larger problem, offering an insight into Ottoman motivations. He warned that Great Britain had become vitally interested in the Arabian territories bordering on the Persian Gulf, and unless the Ottoman government adopted a more resolute policy, the whole of the region would pass under the protection of England. In addition to Talib's warning, in January 1904 Ibn Rashid resumed his appeals for Ottoman intervention, arguing that Ibn Saud was forming relations with the British.[19]

Talib's memorandum, coupled with Ibn Saud's growing power

and Ibn Rashid's constant appeals for Ottoman intervention, accounted for both the substance and the timing of a new and more vigorous Ottoman policy in April 1904. A general mobilization was declared in Mesopotamia, and by late April eight Ottoman battalions, consisting of some two thousand troops with ten guns, were ready to be sent into Arabia, where the situation of Ibn Rashid had become critical.[20]

The Fourth Overture

The confrontation that Ibn Saud had sought all along to avoid was fast approaching. His previous efforts to mobilize British support having failed, he nevertheless tried once again, assuming that an Ottoman military expedition of such large proportions would induce the reluctant British to abandon their indifferent attitude. After all, it had taken Mubarak almost two years of persistent effort to cause a complete reversal of Britain's policy. There was no reason, therefore, why the British rejectionist attitude should be interpreted as a final stand.

On May 2, 1904, Ibn Saud addressed an urgent letter to the new British resident, Percy Cox, requesting the protection of Great Britain against the "Ottoman invasion." Simultaneously, he addressed a letter to Mubarak, which was immediately transmitted to the resident, reminding him of the Russian offer of protection in March 1903. Ibn Saud indicated that although the offer now recurred to his mind, "it is not palatable," and he preferred to follow Mubarak and ask for British protection.[21] Ibn Saud did not contemplate turning to the Russians even if his overtures to the British were rejected. The remark demonstrated his desire not to alienate the British, as well as a readiness to play the Russian card.

The resident, as well as the Indian government, did not treat the Russian reference as a bluff. India asked London to warn the Porte "not to interfere in Nejd affairs or measures for the protection of British interests may have to be taken," and also suggested that a political agent be posted at Kuwait "to watch events, should the Ottomans persist in their armed intervention." The British ambassador in Constantinople, O'Conor, endeavored to impress on London another necessity, to dissuade Mubarak from assisting Ibn Saud in his "depredations upon the territory of Ibn Rashid."

O'Conor further predicted that the Porte would decline to make any concessions as long as they were "imbued with the idea" that Kuwait was supporting the Saudis.[22]

The Foreign Office accepted the reasoning of India and instructed O'Conor to urge the Porte to abstain from actions likely to exacerbate the tensions in that part of Arabia, "the tranquility of which is a matter of interest" to the British.[23] O'Conor did so on May 15, but he couched his communication in vague language since he did not interpret the Foreign Office's instruction as aimed at "dissuading the Porte from sending assistance to Ibn Rashid." Once the news of the imminent Ottoman expedition reached London, the Foreign Office ordered O'Conor to repeat "in urgent terms" the representation he had made. He was explicitly notified that "to prevent the Ottomans from pursuing the action they contemplate is evidently of great importance."

It was now O'Conor's turn to challenge the whole course of action London was pursuing. He argued that Ibn Saud's "covert threat" to approach the Russians was "an artful and familiar Arab device less calculated to encourage than to alienate support." Moreover, pressing the Porte to refrain from assisting Ibn Rashid on the basis of Saudi appeals, inter alia, would amount to nothing less than an explicit British espousal of the Saudi cause. Finally, there was no ground on which he could request the Porte to abstain from intervention in Arabia, since Ibn Rashid was the party attacked. Nevertheless, on May 23 O'Conor met Tawfiq, the Ottoman foreign minister, and conveyed to him the British government's message. The Indian government felt obliged to refute O'Conor's arguments. Emphasizing that it did not desire to assist Ibn Saud, it nevertheless maintained that an Ottoman expedition of such formidable proportions was bound to diminish British influence in eastern Arabia. Mubarak's position and Britain's influence in Kuwait would be greatly weakened, if not destroyed, were the Ottomans allowed "to absorb Nejd," as they did in 1872, with British acquiescence.[24]

The differences of opinion between the Indian government and O'Conor exposed a much more profound divergence of views between them regarding the nature and significance of the recent re-establishment of the Saudi entity and its relation to British interests, which underlay their respective positions concerning the merit of the British effort to dissuade the Ottomans from dispatching the expedition into Arabia. This divergence had to do with whether the new Saudi entity represented only a continuity vis-à-vis the previous Saudi states or a significant change. O'Conor perceived the Saudi revival only in terms of continuity, asserting that Ibn Saud's object was to re-establish "a Wahhabi dynasty throughout Arabia." As past experience indicated, the maritime principalities under British protection would most probably soon be subjected to increased Saudi pressure. Further Saudi success was therefore "bound to render British influence and authority in Kuwait dangerously precarious." A memorandum composed at the British Embassy in Constantinople also stressed that Ibn Saud would undoubtedly pursue the same ambitions as his predecessors. The position articulated by the Indian government was fundamentally different, as was its evaluation of the impact of further Saudi success on Britain's position in Kuwait. India thought that Ibn Saud represented a change in comparison to the first two Saudi states, in the sense that "the Wahhabi dynasty was now not so much fanatical as territorial." The long-term repercussions of this position were not yet apparent, but one immediate result was that, rather than being imperiled, British influence on Mubarak was increasing with Ibn Saud's success.[25]

Except for producing the dispatch of Knox to Kuwait in August to serve as the first political agent there, the debate within the British government was somewhat academic, as the Ottomans were determined to ignore the British representations. The desire to check further Saudi expansion and "to drive Ibn Saud's Wahhabis out of the Ottoman territory of Qasim" now assumed an obvious priority. Accordingly, on May 28 several Ottoman battalions, ranging from 1500 to 4000 troops and reinforced by twelve guns, left Samawa on the Euphrates on their way to Nejd.[26]

Having heard nothing from the British in response to his appeal, Ibn Saud faced the gravest dilemma since Riyadh's capture in 1902. A Saudi defeat in Qasim could spell the end of Riyadh as well, and a showdown became the lesser of the two evils. A battle ensued on July 14, 1904, at Bukairiyya, halfway between Hail and Buraida, which was a confused affair with no clear victory for either side. Although the Ottomans lost thirteen officers, including the commander of the expedition, they were left in possession of the battlefield. Had they pursued their tactical victory, they might have

won the campaign, because the Saudis suffered enormous casualties, with more than a thousand killed. The Ottomans decided,
however, to reduce some settlements in Qasim first, thus enabling
Ibn Saud to receive reinforcements and face them again. The Ottomans' main miscalculation was their failure to attach due weight
to their chief enemy, the Arabian desert's summer. Unaccustomed
to the desert heat, the Ottoman forces were weakened during the
three-month summer period they were entrenched in Qasim. They
now numbered less than 1000 troops, the remainder having been
killed in the July encounter or having died of hunger and heat.[27]

Throughout the summer Ibn Saud refrained from attacking the
Ottoman force, preferring it to be consumed by heat and hunger
rather than by his own action, which might trigger a large-scale
Ottoman reaction. It was Ibn Rashid who, in breaking up his camp
at Shinana on September 27 and beginning a march, elicited Ibn
Saud's action. The next day the Saudi forces fell upon the combined
Ottoman-Rashidi force near Qasr Ibn Uqail and routed it, killing
550 Ottoman soldiers. Ibn Saud sought to minimize the defeat he
had inflicted on the Ottoman force, and instead of annihilating it,
"he treated the vanquished Ottomans with the utmost clemency
and generosity and allowed them to return to Basra."[28] Nevertheless, the result of the July and September encounters was that the
entire Ottoman force virtually ceased to exist.

Once the news of the Ottoman defeat reached Riyadh, Ibn Saud's
advisers and the Wahhabi leaders assumed a belligerent attitude,
full of boasting and war talk. For them it was now only natural to
use the military momentum to escalate the war against the Ottoman heretics and achieve the ultimate goal of complete independence.[29] Ibn Saud, who had a clearer view, refused to be swayed
by the general enthusiasm. He knew what difficulties he had encountered to defeat a combination of Ibn Rashid and a small Ottoman force. If the Ottoman government took the matter seriously,
the Porte could mass considerable forces against him, and the result would be certain: he would be crushed. Alarmed at the decisiveness of his victory, he approached the Porte so as to minimize
the significance of the recent confrontations and avoid any reference to them as a Saudi challenge to Ottoman authority. This
approach, which illustrated the general Saudi strategy toward the
Ottomans, was embodied in an apologetic letter that his father,

'Abd al-Rahman, addressed to the Acting wali of Basra, Fakhri Pasha:

> My family has of old been known to be loyal to the State and especially to the Commander of the Faithful. But certain intriguing officials, egged on by the tyrant Ibn Rashid, have calumniated us. Ibn Rashid and his following deceived the Government and, contrary to all expectations, brought about the dispatch of Ottoman troops. Subsequently, he and the troops arrived near the village of Bekirie, whereupon all the inhabitants of Nejd and Qasim united and prepared for war against him. Ibn Rashid attacked them. My son 'Abd al-'Aziz urged the tribes to attack Ibn Rashid's band, which fled to the troops and in the ensuing encounter was defeated and routed. The soldiers lost 210 killed, and six guns fell into the hands of the people of Nejd. My son 'Abd al-'Aziz ordered the people to leave them at the village of Bekirie.
>
> Thus, this service proceeded from our affection and loyalty to the State. 'Abd al-'Aziz al-Saud constantly designed to communicate with the Commanders of the troops and ascertain their desires and to telegraph to the Palace, but Ibn Rashid sent out men to apprehend him and seized all the letters and telegrams. After the encounter, we remained expectant. But Ibn Rashid would not rest, marched his following and the troops against the people of Qasim and began to press them hard. He was subsequently attacked, defeated and routed, many of his following being killed, and all his tents, stores and other possessions taken. But my son 'Abd al-'Aziz prevented the Moslem population of Nejd from molesting the troops. I am convinced that their departure is due to the machinations of Ibn Rashid. For neither the Sovereign nor his Ministers would ever allow their subjects to be harassed.
>
> I beg that our tender of loyalty may be accepted as heretofore and that my condition may be reported to His Majesty. I am ready to perform any service to the State and guarantee on oath the security of the roads and pilgrims. I beg that my submission may be accepted and that we may not be left in despair. Despair makes men commit any crime. I repeat my prayer and beg that my pension, some months in arrear, may be paid. The big guns with the soldiers are now with the people of Nejd. They remain in my son's possession. I await your orders.[30]

The Saudi approach articulated in the letter consisted of three main points. While the Sultan was reassured of Saudi submission and loyalty, no concrete acts of surrender or acceptance of sovereignty were offered, except, ironically, for the request that the payment of the pension be renewed. Ibn Rashid and local Ottoman officials, not Ibn Saud, were held responsible for the dispatch of the expedition by deceiving the Ottoman government regarding the real situation in Nejd. Finally, it was not against Ottoman authority but against Ibn Rashid's tyrannical designs that the "inhabitants of Nejd and Qasim" fought, while the Ottoman troops were killed because the Rashidi forces were interspersed within their ranks. On the whole, the letter resembled the one dispatched by Ibn Saud to the sultan following Riyadh's capture, in which Saudi achievements were depicted as aimed against the house of Rashid and not against the Ottoman government. Viewed against the background of past Saudi behavior and the present bellicose state of mind in Riyadh, Ibn Saud's expression of loyalty to the sultan was all the more exceptional.

The Ottoman government could hardly console itself with the rationale offered by Ibn Saud, and it interpreted the recent events in Qasim as a direct challenge. The question at stake now was not the Saudi recognition of Ottoman authority but rather the need to check the continued erosion of Ottoman status and prestige. Consequently, the Porte decided to dispatch a second expedition into Nejd "against Ibn Saud," consisting of twenty-four battalions from Iraq, Syria, and Adana. As a result of the submissive Saudi letter, the Ottoman government also instructed Fakhri to invite Ibn Saud to a meeting in order to settle the affairs of Qasim in a friendly manner.[31] The Ottomans were determined that the expedition demonstrate its presence in Nejd. Were Ibn Saud to come to terms with them, then the objective of the expedition would be conciliatory; otherwise it would be punitive.

Ibn Saud disliked a reference to Qasim in Fakhri's letter of invitation to him since he viewed his authority over that area as nonnegotiable. As yet unaware of the new Ottoman expedition, he felt himself strong enough to start the negotiations from a seemingly uncompromising bargaining position. Accordingly, on November 16, 1904, his father sent a telegram to the sultan and a letter to Mukhlis, the new wali of Basra, professing loyalty to the sultan but claiming ownership of Qasim and requesting them not to dispatch troops into this district because the people "would not tolerate Ibn Rashid and there would be bloodshed."[32] Conspicuously absent was any reference to the Ottoman invitation, for if Qasim were to constitute the topic of the discussion, as stated in Fakhri's letter, there would be no sense in the meeting.

Toward the end of November 1904, the Porte mobilized a 7000-troop expedition, half from Medina and half from Mesopotamia, under the command of Ahmed Faizi Pasha. The magnitude of the expedition, amounting to sixteen battalions, reminded the British of the Egyptian expeditionary force sent to Nejd on behalf of the sultan in the 1810s, which ultimately crushed the first Saudi state. The expedition elicited two diametrically opposed reactions in Riyadh. The Wahhabi ulama, on the one hand, reinforced their bellicose attitude, since they viewed the arrival of the expedition as an opportunity to settle their accounts with the Ottomans. Ibn Saud, on the other hand, modified his previous stand in the opposite direction. After all, the British were not the only ones to recollect the disastrous Egyptian expeditions. In mid-December, Ibn Saud dispatched a message to the sultan: "I have no idea of revolting against the Ottoman Government. As I am the lawful ruler of Nejd and have defeated the usurper Ibn Rashid, I am willing to accept any reasonable terms you impose on me. I am sorry for having fought Ottoman troops in Nejd, but as they were helping my antagonist Ibn Rashid, I was obliged to do so in self-defense."[33]

The Fifth Overture

Ibn Saud was more forthcoming in this message than in the telegram his father sent to the sultan, but his reference to "reasonable terms" was still nebulous, as he did not wish to commit himself to any specific position implying concessions before exhausting his last card. The pattern of May 1904 was repeated once again: faced with an Ottoman expedition, Ibn Saud approached the British through Mubarak. During January 1905, the Kuwaiti ruler repeatedly impressed upon Knox the expediency of extending British protection to Ibn Saud. Mubarak warned that if British support failed to materialize, Ibn Saud would have no alternative but to allow the Ottomans admittance into Nejd. Concerned that a sizable Ottoman force on his western flank would seriously constrain his freedom of action, Mubarak had a personal interest in having London deter the Porte. The British, already accused by the Ottomans of persuading Ibn Saud "to rise in rebellion against the Imperial Government and accept British protection," reasserted their policy of noninterference in the internal affairs of Arabia. In an interview with Mubarak, Knox categorically ruled out British assistance to the Saudis, and he urged Mubarak to refrain from providing any assistance to Ibn Saud. Mubarak, on his part, assured the resident that he would abstain from helping Ibn Saud, though he regarded him as his good friend and wished him success.[34]

Having excluded in advance a confrontation with the Ottoman expedition, Ibn Saud had only one alternative: to come to terms with the Porte even at the price of reversing some of his initial positions. He had reached that conclusion even before the British rejected his overture, and concomitantly with requesting Mubarak to sound out the British, he asked him to arrange a meeting with the Ottomans in case the overture to the British failed.[35] Accordingly, 'Abd al-Rahman requested the wali to meet him at Safwan, and on January 28, 1905, he sent a telegram to the sultan:

My humble petition to be laid before the throne of His Imperial Majesty, our gracious Sovereign, Commander of the Faithful, Caliph of the Prophet of the Lord of all the Worlds:

I am one of the faithful servants of the Shadow of God, whose family, from father to son, has lavished its blood and treasure in the glorious service of the Caliphate. I have no thought or aspiration save that of meriting the approbation of my Sovereign. It is for me a most sacred obligation to contribute the Imperial taxes at their due and proper season and to serve and assist the divinely aided troops of the shadow of God. Only the local authorities, with a view to advancing their personal interests, have misrepresented this weak slave to the Caliph, making him appear a traitor and a rebel. I am submissive to every order and command of the Shadow of God. I neither follow the instigations of any foreigner, nor am I the means of communication with any foreigners. In fact, under the protection of His Imperial Majesty there is no seditious agent or medium of foreigner in all these regions. Ibn Rashid's representatives at the capital naturally strive to provoke the wrath of His Imperial Majesty against me, but His Majesty is the Judge. He does not desire to persecute his most faithful servants.

If the coming Commission of Inquiry does not establish the truth of my assertions, I once more assure His Majesty that I willingly accept the severest penalty that he can impose upon me. Let the Imperial Justice decide.[36]

In order to placate the Porte, the Saudis were even ready to rewrite the history of their own house, claiming to have "lavished" their blood in the service of the sultan, while in fact it was lavished in fighting against the Porte.

While the Ottoman expedition was on its way to Nejd, 'Abd al-Rahman, accompanied by Mubarak, arrived at Safwan, near the Kuwaiti border, where his first meeting with Mukhlis took place on February 8, 1905. The wali proposed that Ottoman civil officials and garrisons be sent into Qasim, which would become a buffer zone between Ibn Saud and Ibn Rashid, and 'Abd al-Rahman agreed, provided the Rashidi did not interfere there in any way. On the whole, 'Abd al-Rahman made humble submission to the sultan in his own name and in that of his son, professing loyalty and devotion to his sovereign and readiness to obey his commands.

In the second meeting on February 13, the wali brought an order from Constantinople, appointing 'Abd al-Rahman qa'im-maqam of the qadha of southern Nejd, which included the areas of Washm and Sudair and of which Riyadh was to be the center, under Saudi control. Qasim was to remain outside the Saudi sphere, ruled and garrisoned directly by the Ottomans, with Salih Ibn Hasan as the qa'im-maqam of Buraida and 'Abd al-'Aziz al-Sulaimi as the mudir of 'Unaiza. Sami Pasha, though remaining at Medina, was appointed military commandant and civil mutessarif of Nejd. Having recognized Ottoman suzerainty and having professed himself the sultan's vassal, 'Abd al-Rahman requested that the allowance of M.T. 58 that he had received from the Porte from 1893 until 1903 be restored. The Ottomans assented, making the payment retroactive to 1903.[37] The Ottomans thus achieved their aims: Ibn Saud made due submission; Qasim was restored to Ottoman rule; neither the Saudis nor the Rashidis would be able to upset the balance of forces, as Qasim would serve as a buffer zone; and finally, since an agreement had been reached, the expedition could avoid fighting and was about to enter Qasim peacefully.

The atmosphere in Riyadh contrasted sharply with that of the Ottomans. The humiliating terms of the agreement centered not merely on the submission to Ottoman authority but also on the status of the Saudi entity. It became a mere qadha in the sanjaq of Nejd in the wilaya of Basra, equal in status to the single town of Buraida. The Saudi ruler was thus two ranks below the wali, not merely an Ottoman vassal but a low-ranking one in addition. The Wahhabi ulama, who were opposed in principle to any agreement with the Ottomans, were even more outraged by the terms of the agreement in which Qasim had been virtually surrendered. Some of them went so far as to accuse Ibn Saud of treason, arguing that submission to Constantinople was unworthy of a Saudi and claiming that "our ancestors would be ashamed of us." In a sense they were correct, for it was inconceivable for the previous Saudi states to have concluded such an agreement.

Ibn Saud, to be sure, disliked the Ottoman presence next door to his capital, though he could take satisfaction in securing for the first time a formal recognition by the Porte of the re-establishment of the Saudis in their former territory. His strategy for coping with the new circumstances was rather different. Instead of forcing a showdown with Ottoman military might, he preferred to let the Ottomans decide on their own to evacuate Nejd with the loss of as little prestige as possible. His policy, consequently, rested on a dual premise: avoiding any public rupture with the Ottomans by coming to terms with them; and making the life of the Ottoman troops in Qasim unbearable without revealing himself to be the cause of their plight, thus forcing them to withdraw. While the February agreement achieved the first objective, the second was realized by what might be called guerrilla tactics.[38]

The expedition entered Qasim in early April, encountering no resistance. The Ottoman flag was hoisted, a salute was fired, prayers for the sultan were read, and administrative posts were established. Ibn Rashid was not present at the ceremonies, indicating that he had no *locus standi* in the affairs of Qasim and satisfying one of the main Saudi demands in the negotiations.[39] Ottoman authority over Nejd was all but fully reasserted. Events soon proved, however, that the Ottoman rejoicing was premature, as Ibn Saud was not content with their presence in Qasim.

Ibn Saud's new strategy is glimpsed in a telegram his father sent to Constantinople concurrently with the occupation of Qasim by Ottoman troops:

> I am the obedient servant of our Lord the Great Caliph, God preserve his throne till the Day of Judgement. I have repeatedly reported to

you about the presumption of Ibn Rashid, his interference in our country and the acts of tyranny, bloodshed and robbery which he continued to commit. Statements have also been presented by the people of 'Unaiza, Buraida and Shaqra. We have been honored with no reply and the evil deeds of Ibn Rashid increase, and all the people of Nejd are disgusted at his violence. When an order came to me from the Vali of Basra to present myself, I came [in February] and showed my submission and obedience. Therefore I beg of you that the favor of our Lord the Caliph may be extended to his servant.[40]

While expressions of loyalty and submission abounded, the Porte was served notice that "the people of 'Unaiza, Buraida and Shaqra" would no longer tolerate "the violence of Ibn Rashid." Inasmuch as the Rashidis were to be excluded from 'Unaiza, Buraida and Shaqra according to the new arrangement, there could have been little doubt as to who was meant by "Ibn Rashid." The communication thus aimed at preparing the ground in Constantinople for the receipt of news regarding the plight of the expedition. At the same time it sought to attribute that plight to popular resentment of Ibn Rashid and not to Saudi machinations against the Porte.

In August 1905, Ibn Saud left Nejd and suddenly appeared at the base of the Qatar Peninsula. Perceiving the Saudi position in Nejd to be sufficiently consolidated, he felt that by now, three and a half years after the Saudis' revival, it was time to display their presence along the coast as well. Not that he neglected the Ottoman troops in Qasim or underestimated the threat they posed to his territories. But having watched them for three months and examined their intentions, he was confident that they would not encroach on his area. Besides, since he wished to avoid being identified as the cause of the Ottoman plight in Qasim, there was no better way to attain this aim than to distance himself as much as possible from the region. Thus, the way was opened for the second stage of the restoration of previous Saudi dominions along the Persian Gulf coast.

Ibn Saud's presence along the coast took the form of four lines of action, all aimed at reasserting Saudi authority over areas and tribes perceived as belonging to the house of Saud. Indeed, while at Qatar, he was quoted as saying, "By God I will explore the country belonging to my father and grandfather from Muscat to Jealan." First, he gathered together the sheikhs of the al-Murra,

Bani Hajir, and 'Ajman tribes, who had been feuding with each other and with the sheikh of Qatar, and effected a reconciliation among them, assuming the role of a sovereign and treating them as subjects. Second, he visited parts of Hasa, avoiding the cities garrisoned by the Ottoman troops, and summoned the inhabitants to issue bills on them. According to an eyewitness, "no one could reject the bills." As a result of these two actions, the position of the Ottomans in Hasa was circumscribed, since they were surrounded by tribes under Ibn Saud's influence, and their garrisons were effectively isolated in the few strongholds they occupied. Third, Ibn Saud appointed three Hasa sheikhs to hear complaints and imprison people, warning that action would be taken against anyone found guilty of committing transgressions.[41]

The last of Ibn Saud's actions, though the least conspicuous, was perceived as the most important by all the parties involved—the coastal sheikhs, the British, and Ibn Saud—triggering both immediate and long-term consequences. On August 22, 1905, Ibn Saud addressed letters to the Trucial chiefs, announcing his visit to Qatar and expressing his intention of visiting the sheikhs' territories in the spring of 1906 "to look into certain affairs."[42] Nothing could have prevented Ibn Saud from making the visit immediately as he was already on the coast, except for one unpredictable factor: the British reaction to such a visit. The letters were thus aimed at testing the British attitude toward a possible extension of Saudi influence over sheikhs with whom Great Britain had treaty relations.

Ibn Khalifa, the chief of Abu Dhabi, understood Ibn Saud's letter well, especially since the Saudi ruler had warned him after the Rashidi defeat that, "Your turn Ibn Khalifa has come now." Ibn Khalifa tried to forge a common front with the sultan of Muscat against the Saudi encroachment on their territories. To that end, he formally requested the Indian government "to take steps to prevent any movement of Ibn Saud towards the Coast."[43]

As for Britain, complete unanimity existed regarding the interpretation and practical significance of Ibn Saud's letters and the British response. All agreed that the issue was Ibn Saud's attempt "to re-establish the old Wahhabi influence his forefathers had formerly acquired in Oman," an attempt that would certainly "cause trouble" and toward which Britain should maintain "a very vigilant attitude." The possibility of Ibn Saud's attacking the coastal chiefs and the sultan of Muscat seemed so real that the Indian government warned against the serious consequences for British prestige and influence and urged preventive measures against such a contingency. As an immediate step, the Indian authorities ordered that Mubarak should be sounded out on the subject with a view to discouraging Ibn Saud from embarking on his project.[44]

The analysis advanced by the Indian government regarding Saudi aspirations along the coast was surprising, to say the least, in view of the fact that this very same government had contested a similar analysis presented by O'Conor on May 16, 1904. Such an obvious discrepancy can be explained only by the different issues at stake in each case. In May 1904, when the problem had centered on India's desire to deter the Ottomans from dispatching a large-scale expedition into Nejd, the Indian authorities tended to underplay the danger the Saudis could pose to the sheikhdoms along the coast. Such an argument was easy to advance, as there were no indications as yet that the Saudis contemplated a move against the coastal chiefs. India was even ready to go so far as to point to a difference in the nature and aspirations of the new Saudi entity in comparison to its predecessors. Now, however, that Ibn Saud had clearly demonstrated that the Saudis entertained designs on the sheikhdoms which were inimical to British interests, India reversed its previous assessment, specifically linking Ibn Saud's aspirations with those of the previous Saudi states.

Interpreting Saudi aspirations and the danger they constituted to British interests was one thing; devising practical measures to pre-empt the Saudi move was something else. For the consensus among British officials regarding the threat was followed by a disagreement over the response. The Indian government suggested that they approach Ibn Saud indirectly, through Mubarak or the sultan of Muscat, so as to ascertain whether he was prepared to stand by "the engagement of his predecessors not to interfere with the Arab tribes in alliance with the British Government." Ibn Saud should be further warned, in the event of his unwillingness to give the necessary assurance, that any attempt on his part to interfere with the chiefs or their subjects would be regarded as "an unfriendly act," and "suitable measures would be taken to frustrate it." In the case of an imminent Saudi attack, India proposed actual armed assistance from British ships to the threatened sheikhs. The India Office, however, questioned the gravity of the situation as described by the Indian government. In view of Britain's desire "to refrain from any entanglements with the rulers of Nejd," the office suggested that no steps be taken in the absence of "any urgent necessity caused by Wahhabi action."[45]

O'Conor rejected both of India's suggestions. Instead, he argued that a direct warning would be more effective and suggested that a British warship should meet Ibn Saud at one of the ports he intended to visit and warn him that "no tampering with the engagements and Conventions of the Trucial Chiefs will be allowed." The Foreign Office accepted O'Conor's view, and accordingly, India was instructed to convey a direct warning to Ibn Saud only in the event of his appearance on the coast.[46]

Meanwhile, Knox complied with India's initial instruction and, on January 19, 1905, sounded out Mubarak concerning Ibn Saud's intentions along the coast. This meeting turned both the debate and the decision of the British government into irrelevant academic exercises. Mubarak dismissed Ibn Saud's letters to the coastal chiefs as "a mere attempt to extort money due to lack of funds." But he promptly conveyed to Ibn Saud the content of the British approach.[47] Learning of the British reaction, Ibn Saud understood the message and relinquished any idea he might have contemplated with regard to the coast. For one thing, he was well aware of his limited power vis-à-vis the British; for another, he needed the British to counterbalance the Ottomans and thus could not afford to alienate them.

Before long, Mubarak informed the British of a letter he had received from Ibn Saud disclaiming all serious designs in the direction of Oman and expressing regret for any accidental remark on his part which might have caused disquiet. The letter was sent to Mubarak but aimed at the British, as is evident by its concluding remark: "We do not know them that we should write to them, and we expect that from you." Ibn Saud wanted the British to know that he was not acting contrary to their interests. The British thus did not have to convey the warning, as Ibn Saud did not embark on his proposed visit.[48]

Ibn Saud's conduct along the coast displayed some of the features that were to characterize his cautious policies in subsequent years. He did not go directly to the coast but rather sought to know beforehand how the British would react to such a Saudi act. Once acquainted with the British position, he drew the appropriate conclusions and abandoned the project.[49] This retreat was an indication of future Saudi behavior toward the gulf principalities as well, for they have all retained their independence until the present day. Ibn Saud's behavior contrasts sharply to the proceedings of his grandfather, Faisal, along the coast in the 1840s and 1850s. The potential British reaction did not figure at all in Faisal's ambitions regarding the principalities. Even when acquainted with Britain's determination to maintain its integrity, he carried on his schemes, insisting on having authority "over my dependencies from Oman to Kuwait."

The Sixth Overture

Toward the end of 1905, the Ottoman expedition had nearly disintegrated as a result of both the Arabian summer and the constant harassment directed against it on behalf of Ibn Saud, though without his active participation. Out of an original force of several thousands, only 750 survived, the rest having died of starvation or having deserted. The Ottoman government did not seem much concerned about the fate of its expedition, partly because its sovereignty was not challenged and partly because it encountered much more serious troubles in the Hejaz, Asir, and Yemen.[50]

Ibn Saud seemed willing to take advantage of this perceived opportunity of Ottoman weakness and of the situation in Hasa, and in early February 1906 he approached the British once more. His emissary, Musa'id Ibn Suwailim, told Prideaux, the political agent at Bahrain, that Ibn Saud felt himself strong enough to turn the Ottomans out of Hasa and Qatif. Ibn Saud wished to enter into treaty relations with Great Britain, allowing Britain to maintain a political agent in Hasa or Qatif in return for its protection against an Ottoman counterattack from the sea.

The fate of this overture was no different from the one made in 1903. Prideaux, while questioning Ibn Saud's capacity to free himself from the Ottomans, refrained from giving the envoy any encouragement.[51] The envoy apparently had additional instructions from Ibn Saud, as he immediately left for Bushire. From there on February 18, 1906, he sent a long telegram to the sultan in Constantinople, which had been signed by Sheikh Qasim al-Thani of Qatar but was evidently sent, as the British recognized, on behalf of Ibn Saud:

> A petition was previously made by this loyal slave, suggesting the undesirability of employing a body of Imperial troops against Ibn Saud—a course for which there was no necessity.
>
> The effect of my advices is now apparent. As Ibn Rashid has caused troubles and disturbances, pious men came forward and solicited Ibn Saud to ward off difficulties. Ibn Saud expelled the evil-doers and wicked persons and secured tranquility to the country and people by his excellent behavior and high character and by his righteous service to the great Lord, the Commander of the Faithful. He still remains ready to render service and protect all the roads, and all the people testify to this. He is beloved by everybody in general. Ibn Saud has indeed repeatedly invoked favor, saying that he is an obedient servant of the Commander of the Faithful, and that he is neither schismatic nor a rebel.[52]

The long-term purpose of the communication was obvious: to affirm Saudi allegiance to the sultan while presenting Saudi activities in Nejd as aimed against the Rashidis. But the immediate causes for its dispatch are more problematic.

One probable explanation is that Ibn Saud was concerned lest the Ottomans become aware of his approach to the British at Bahrain, and therefore he sought to assure the Porte of his loyalty. This would explain his reference to being "neither schismatic nor a rebel." Another explanation relates to the difficulties encountered by the Ottomans in both Qasim and Hasa. The state of their expedition in Qasim was disastrous, while in Hasa Ibn Saud's activities in the summer of 1905 had created serious disturbances throughout the province, causing the authorities there to appeal for the "adoption of the necessary measures" for its defense.[53] Lest the Ottomans attribute their troubles in both regions to his machinations, Ibn Saud sought to placate them with humble statements of submission.

Two other explanations are more likely. First, through the telegram Ibn Saud sought to obtain a peaceful Ottoman withdrawal from Qasim. He regarded such an aim as attainable, because the miserable state of the expedition certainly displeased the Porte. To that end the sultan was reminded that Ibn Saud's previous request that the expedition not be sent had proved justified in view of its apparent failure. To facilitate such a withdrawal and render it more palatable to the Porte, the telegram underscored Ibn Saud's devotion, submission, and obedience to the sultan. He could easily have ejected the small wretched Ottoman force from Qasim, but he would thereby have challenged the Ottomans and perhaps have triggered further expeditions. He preferred, therefore, that the Ottomans depart out of their own "free" will, a face-saving strategem that would not smack of expulsion and humiliation.

Second, the telegram was sent to disarm suspicion preparatory to a further Saudi move. Ibn Saud contemplated a showdown with Ibn Rashid, and he felt the urgency of pre-empting a possible Ottoman interpretation of a Rashidi defeat as a direct challenge to their authority. Hence, the telegram devotes more than one paragraph to degrading Ibn Rashid in Ottoman eyes, depicting him as a ruler capable only of harming Ottoman prestige, whereas Ibn Saud by "his righteous services to the Successor of the Prophet" could only enhance such prestige. Through this argument Ibn Saud sought to impress the sultan with the necessity of switching Ottoman reliance on and alliance with Ibn Rashid to Ibn Saud.

At any rate, the Saudi emissary had no communication with Ibn Saud from the moment he left the agency at Bahrain until he dispatched the telegram to the sultan. One can safely assume, therefore, that the rejection of the Saudi overture by the British had a causal relationship to the Saudi communication to the Porte, and that the envoy was instructed in advance to dispatch the telegram to Constantinople should the British reject the overture. In other words, had the overture elicited an affirmative response, there would have been no need for the telegram, as Ibn Saud would have not only expelled the expedition but also occupied Hasa, unfearful of Ottoman reaction and shielded by British protection. But as the British turned him down, Ibn Saud was reluctant to confront the Ottomans, and instead he reassured them of his submission and loyalty.

The Seventh Overture

Meanwhile, the Saudi-Rashidi rivalry continued unabated, culminating in the battle of Rawdat al-Muhanna on April 11, 1906,
when Ibn Rashid was killed and the whole Rashidi force dispersed.
Ibn Saud hurried to dispatch letters and emissaries to announce
his victory to the sultan, the walis of the Hejaz, Basra, and Baghdad, the grand sharif, and the chiefs of Qatar and Bahrain. Sensing
that the Ottomans remained deeply embroiled in Yemen and realizing that they would not withdraw from Qasim without being
"induced" to do so, Ibn Saud proceeded to take full advantage of
his success. At the end of April 1906 he seized Salih Ibn Hasan, the
appointed qa'im-maqam of Buraida, disregarding both his official
rank and the presence of Ottoman troops in Qasim, and deported
him to Riyadh. Ibn Saud's motive seemed to be that Salih had
taken his position as an Ottoman official too seriously and was
striving to eliminate Saudi influence from Qasim.[54]

At the same time, Ibn Saud sought to make use of Ottoman
weakness in another direction. In May 1906 he resumed his approach to the British, this time through Sheikh Qasim al-Thani of
Qatar. At an interview with Cox, the sheikh repeated the Saudi
proposal of the previous February and suggested that Ibn Saud
should have a meeting with a British officer at some place on the
coast.[55] But British policy had not changed, and Ibn Saud would
not move against Hasa even under the prevailing circumstances
of Ottoman extreme weakness unless assured of British protection.

Instead, Ibn Saud continued to pursue his other objective of
rendering the life of the Ottomans in Qasim unbearable. At the
beginning of June, Ibn Saud ordered all sheikhs and tribes in Nejd
to desist from communicating with the Ottoman officials and troops
and from carrying their mail and supplies. The sheikhs promptly
complied with the instruction. Having learned of the miserable
condition of their expedition, the Ottomans felt all the more obliged
to intervene because of the blow to their prestige from the death
of their protégé, Ibn Rashid. Subsequently, they ordered Sami Pasha
to march with six hundred troops to Qasim and take the necessary
steps to keep the lines of communication open. At the beginning
of July, Sami left Medina, and a month later he reached Qasim.[56]

The Eighth Overture

The arrival of the new expedition was immediately followed by another Saudi overture to the British, this time through Mubarak. Late in August 1906 and again in mid-September, Mubarak endeavored to convince Knox of the desirability of taking Ibn Saud under British protection, especially in the interest of British trade, because of the large number of people residing in Nejd. Knox noticed the close connection between the new Ottoman expedition and the Saudi overture and remarked that it was the expedition which "must have so unusually alarmed both Ibn Saud and Mubarak."[57]

Cox, however, imparted a new long-term perspective to the Saudi overture. He pointed out that a reconsideration of British policy was imperative and set forth the advantages of coming to terms with Ibn Saud: a neglect of Ibn Saud's overtures might make an enemy of him; an understanding with him would relieve the anxieties of the coastal chiefs and improve British relations with them; Ibn Saud would assist in suppressing piracy along the Persian Gulf; and unless he were supported by Great Britain against Ottoman interference, Ibn Saud might approach some other power. The linchpin of Cox's analysis was that a British policy of indifference to events in central Arabia could be pursued only as long as the chiefs there neutralized each other. Once they found a leader, as they had now, the British government would be compelled to enter into relations with that leader. Cox emphasized that he was not demanding outright assumption of a protectorate over Nejd, but rather a change in British policy in favor of an independent central Arabia. But his argument failed to modify London's policy, and India was accordingly instructed that there was to be no alteration in British policy toward the Saudis.[58]

When the British response failed to arrive, Ibn Saud decided once again to negotiate with the Ottomans rather than fight them, and in September 1906 talks began between him and Sami Pasha. Apparently, the chief subject of the discussions was the construction of forts at 'Unaiza and Buraida for the reception of permanent Ottoman garrisons, a point on which Sami insisted in order to prevent the recurrence of the removal of the qa'im-maqam and to render the Ottoman presence more secure. It was precisely this last aim which led Ibn Saud to be adamant in his opposition to the idea.

The negotiations dragged on until the end of October, each side trying to extricate the best possible terms. By this time it had become apparent that, owing to the isolation of the troops in Qasim and the Porte's inability to divert more resources to Nejd, Ibn Saud was in a superior bargaining position. The garrison was in a miserable state of affairs: supplies were scarce, the men were clothed in rags, disease and desertion were rife, and the troops were subjected to frequent harassment by the local population.[59] Realizing that his bargaining power was very limited, Sami was ready to accept a face-saving formula.

According to the arrangement worked out, Ottoman garrisons were to be placed in 'Unaiza and Buraida as nominal recognition of Ottoman suzerainty, provided they did not interfere with the administration of the district. On November 3, 1906, twelve hundred troops with twelve guns withdrew to Medina, and several weeks later an almost equal force retreated to Basra. Only two dozen Ottoman soldiers without officers remained in Qasim. Ibn Saud did not fight and expel the Ottoman forces from Qasim; rather, he caused the majority of them to die in hunger and heat, and the minority to evacuate the area.[60]

The Ninth Overture

The conclusion of the agreement confirmed Ibn Saud's perception of the Ottoman weakness. It made him all the more determined to enforce his supremacy by expelling the Ottomans from Hasa. Hence, on November 17, 1906, he made a new overture to the British, even before the Ottoman withdrawal had begun, through Qasim, the sheikh of Qatar. Ibn Saud's communication, as relayed by Qasim to Prideaux, noted that the resources of Nejd had been exhausted in the wars with Ibn Rashid and that it was essential for Ibn Saud, on economic grounds, to recover Hasa, one of the most productive regions of Arabia, from which he could raise abundant revenues. He therefore proposed a secret understanding with the British government. First, he would apply to the Porte for the governorship of Hasa, and if his application were approved, he would declare himself independent at an opportune moment. If it were rejected, he would invade the province unaided and drive the Ottomans out, provided he knew that he could rely on British naval protection to deter an Ottoman counterattack from the sea. In either case, a public appeal for British protection would be made only after the rupture, and in addition, Ibn Saud would not make his attempt for four or five years. In return, Ibn Saud would enter into a treaty, similar to that contracted by the Trucial chiefs in 1892, and accept a British political officer at his court in Riyadh. At the same time Mubarak again reminded Knox of the desirability of Ibn Saud's establishing himself in Hasa.[61]

The proximity and different objectives of the four overtures made in 1906 demonstrated that Ibn Saud perceived the British as instrumental in his relations with the Ottomans in both defensive and offensive terms, offering him both protection against Ottoman expeditions and aid in the occupation of Hasa. The suggestion in his final overture that he would publicly appeal for British help only after Hasa's occupation further attested to his sensitivity toward Britain's diplomatic entanglements with the Ottoman government. These four overtures convinced Cox of Ibn Saud's earnestness. Restating the arguments he had advanced on September 16, Cox endeavored to impress upon India the necessity of giving some reply, negative or positive, to the Saudis, if only for the sake of diplomatic courtesy.[62]

The government of India considered only Cox's point that, once rejected, the Saudis might approach some other power, and it did not view this argument as effective. England was supreme in the Persian Gulf. Given Ibn Saud's naval vulnerability, no matter when he delivered the coup de grace to Ottoman rule in Hasa, "it was to the British that he would be compelled to turn for protection against attacks by sea." The British would then be in a position, "if they considered it advantageous, to stretch out a hand which Ibn Saud will be compelled, in his own interest, to take." In other words, India asserted that the Saudis could, and therefore would, never pursue an anti-British policy or orientation, and therefore Cox's apprehension was unjustified. On grounds of general policy, too, it was unnecessary to accept the Saudi overture. For one thing the Porte was still deeply interested in Arabia, and it would be "a diplomatic blunder to promote the disintegration of the Ottoman Empire." For another, the growth of Saudi power, as was evident

in August 1905, had disturbing consequences for the gulf principalities. India, to be sure, believed that the Saudis would seek an
early opportunity to clear Hasa of the Ottomans. But India was
confident that the British government could defer reaching an understanding with the Saudis until this happened. The best course
of action was thus to refuse the Saudi request for protection and,
at the same time, to inform Ibn Saud that the British government
wanted to maintain friendly relations with him so long as he left
the Trucial chiefs alone.[63]

Even such a cautious policy seemed inexpedient to O'Conor, who
had closely watched the growth of Saudi power in the course of
1906. He admitted that Ibn Saud's importance had been much
enhanced by Ibn Rashid's defeat and death, but this obliged Britain
to watch with even greater care the Saudi relations with Kuwait
and the Trucial principalities. The question of Saudi independence
from the Ottomans must have occupied O'Conor, for shortly afterward he predicted that neither Ibn Saud's military prowess nor
his administrative capacity encouraged the belief that he would
be able to cope successfully with the Porte. O'Conor was consistent
in restating his views, especially in questioning Ibn Saud's ultimate
power to withstand Ottoman efforts to reassert themselves. It was
thus worthless, in O'Conor's view, to pursue a course, as was suggested by India, that implied approval of the consolidation of "the
Wahhabi power," which was bound to antagonize the Porte.[64]

The Foreign Office was swayed by O'Conor's reasoning and concluded that it would be unwise to seek an involvement of any kind
in the affairs of central Arabia. India was subsequently instructed
to inform both Qasim and Mubarak that, as Ibn Saud's proposals
"involved considerations which it was impossible for His Majesty's
Government to maintain, no reply was to be expected."[65] Because
the understanding with Great Britain, which Ibn Saud perceived
to be a prerequisite for a move against Hasa, was impossible to
reach, Saudi offensive designs in that area had to be postponed
indefinitely.

The Ottoman withdrawal from Qasim, damaging as it was to
the Porte's prestige, by no means implied an end to the Ottoman
presence in central Arabia. The completion of the Hejaz Railway,
outflanking Nejd from the west, and the shadow of the Baghdad
Railway, threatening the Saudi domains from the north, scarcely

pointed to any Ottoman intention to abandon central Arabia. Cox, aware of such developments, noted that in the absence of some diversion, "central Arabia could not escape ultimate absorption by the Ottomans."[66]

Nevertheless, by 1907 the Saudis could take pride in the fact that the whole of Nejd was clear of Ottoman forces, that the Porte had not regarded their existence and consolidation as a challenge necessitating an immediate reaction, and that consequently the Porte had not sent any expeditions into Nejd to re-establish an Ottoman foothold there. A direct effect of this state of affairs was the absence until 1913 of any further Saudi overtures to the British for defensive purposes vis-à-vis the Ottomans. This accounts for the otherwise curious fact that on February 28, 1910, in Ibn Saud's first meeting with Captain William H. I. Shakespear, who had been the political agent in Kuwait since 1909, Ibn Saud did not use the opportunity to make another approach to the British for protection against the Porte.[67]

The Tenth Overture

At the beginning of 1911, Ibn Saud renewed his overtures to the British concerning his offensive designs on Hasa. In February he sent an emissary to see Cox at Bushire, but Cox sent him away without a conclusive answer, as the envoy had brought no letter of authority.[68] Before Ibn Saud had a chance to rectify this omission, Captain Shakespear provided him with a much better opportunity to convey his message to the British government.

In March, Shakespear was on a tour of the Kuwait hinterland, where by luck or design he found Ibn Saud and his forces and camped with them. What followed was another Saudi overture identical to the one made in 1906. Ibn Saud told Shakespear that his people bitterly resented the Ottoman occupation of Hasa, but they thought an expedition against it would be fruitless if the Ottomans could bring in unlimited troops by sea. Since the British had kept the peace at sea in the Persian Gulf for a century and prevented anyone with warlike intentions from sailing on it, surely they would not allow the Ottomans to do so. By expelling the Ottomans from Hasa, which had always belonged to the house of Saud, Ibn Saud would become the ruler of part of the gulf coast.

All he asked, then, was that the British treat him as they treated all other rulers—the sheikhs of Kuwait, Qatar, Bahrain, and the Trucial Coast and the sultan of Muscat—most of whom would certainly have been overrun by the Ottomans or Persians had the British navy not been vigilant. Ibn Saud wished to reach an understanding with Great Britain that he would be treated equally with all other rulers. He emphasized that he was asking not for any British military assistance in driving the Ottomans out of Hasa but rather for an understanding that after his ejection of the Ottomans he would be protected from a naval attack alone and only from the Ottomans. Summing up his appeal, Ibn Saud asked to have such relations with the British as would make the Porte hesitate "to oppress us or interfere in our affairs"—in other words, the kind of protection Kuwait enjoyed.[69]

Shakespear protested that he had not come to discuss politics, nor had he any authority to examine political problems. Nevertheless, he explained to the Saudi ruler that Britain had always confined its interests to the gulf coast and refrained from any interference in central Arabia, that is, in Ibn Saud's affairs. Given the amicable terms that Britain enjoyed with the Porte, the British would be averse to any understanding with Ibn Saud against the Ottomans which would amount to intrigue. At Ibn Saud's request, Shakespear promised to pass on the overture to his superiors, but he warned him against entertaining any illusions as to the expected response.

In reporting his interview with Ibn Saud, Shakespear suggested that, with Ibn Saud established in Hasa, the British position would be considerably strengthened. But the higher his dispatch went, the less enthusiasm it generated. For himself, Cox would have much preferred Ibn Saud to the Ottomans as a ruler of Hasa. He asserted that Britain had "excellent reasons for maintaining cordial relations with Ibn Saud; at any rate, for not wishing to create in him a feeling of soreness and ill-will towards us." Cox went so far as to suggest that the Saudi ruler might, in return for a nominal subsidy, undertake in writing "to observe the Maritime Truce; to maintain friendly relations with the Gulf chiefs in relations with Britain; and to prohibit the import of arms by sea." But even Cox concluded that as long as diplomatic relations wth the Porte were satisfactory, or even correct, "we are no more in a position now than we were five years ago, to enter into any understanding with Ibn Saud which would envisage the expulsion of the Turks from Hasa."[70]

The India Office added that, in view of the intractable attitude of the Porte in the Persian Gulf, Britain should leave none of the weapons at her disposal unexamined, Ibn Saud being certainly one of those weapons. But it stated that on the whole the objections to "a policy of adventure" in central Arabia were no less strong then than in 1904. The Foreign Office, as had been the case in the past, reasserted "a policy of strict non-intervention in the affairs of the desert" and terminated the debate.[71]

Ibn Saud once again faced British rejection.[72] But he did not reverse his hitherto consistent position to abstain from attacking Hasa as long as he failed to reach an understanding with Britain. For the moment, it seemed as if the process by which the Saudis had restored their previous dominions had come to an end.

4

Saudi-Ottoman-British Ambiguities, 1913–1914

Ibn Saud, by occupying the Hasa coast-line, entered into the sphere of British interests. We must have relations with someone in *de-facto* control of Hasa.

Foreign Office to the Porte

It is more desirable to incur minor local inconvenience by discontinuing communications with Ibn Saud than to run the graver danger of undermining the Porte's authority in its Asiatic dominions.

Foreign Office to India Office

After I had lost faith in you, I was obliged to enter into an agreement with the Ottomans to secure immunity from their aggression.

Ibn Saud to Shakespear

IN THE SPRING OF 1913, Captain Shakespear encountered Ibn Saud in the Kuwaiti hinterland and spent four days with him. Following their talks, Shakespear expressed confidence that a Saudi occupation of Hasa was only a matter of time. Consequently, he pleaded for a reconsideration of British policy toward the Saudis, arguing that Ibn Saud was likely to lead Arabia "should any extensive combination come into being among its tribes."[1] Shakespear's prediction proved accurate, for within days Ibn Saud moved against the principal towns of Hasa, and by the end of May 1913 he was in solid control of the whole province. Ibn Saud's coherent and consistent policy of abstention from occupying Hasa was thus abruptly reversed after ten years.

The cause of this policy reversal was not Ibn Saud's economic difficulties, even though all the territory under his rule was entirely devoid of natural resources of any kind, and Hasa, the richest province in Arabia, had three ports which could yield a solid source of revenue. The severe economic difficulties that had beset Ibn Saud from 1906 to 1912 were of equal magnitude to those he encountered in 1913, yet he had refrained from conquering Hasa in that earlier period despite his expressed desire to do so. Nor was the cause of Ibn Saud's policy reversal his growing military strength following the establishment in 1912 of the Wahhabi organization, Ikhwan, which turned into the main Saudi military instrument, and the corresponding reduction in the power of the Ottoman garrisons in Hasa.² By 1906 Ibn Saud had believed that he already possessed the military capability needed to drive the Ottomans out of Hasa. Moreover, in that year Ibn Saud did not ask for British military help in the conquest itself, only for a British promise to deter a possible Ottoman sea expedition following his own occupation of Hasa. Since Ibn Saud perceived that the military strength necessary for the conquest of Hasa had existed as early as 1906, its increase could not account for his behavior in 1913.

The reason that Ibn Saud turned against Hasa and not, for instance, against the Rashidis, a target less likely to incur Ottoman wrath, had to do with a unique factor in the conquest of Hasa: the British. This factor accounted for both Ibn Saud's abstention from conquering Hasa until 1913 and the reversal of this policy in May of that year. Britain's consistent rejection of the Saudi overtures left Ibn Saud in a deadlock. Both his long-term goal, the achievement of independence, and his immediate objective, the occupation of Hasa, envisaged a prior understanding with Britain. But when the British turned down all his appeals, there seemed no way for Ibn Saud to pursue his ambitions.

Shakespear's latest rejection in 1911 provided Ibn Saud with several valuable insights into the reasons behind Britain's indifference and became the crucial element in future Saudi moves. Shakespear explained that his government would not enter into any relations with the Saudis since their territory did not lie along the coast of the Persian Gulf and was thus beyond the sphere of British interest. But Ibn Saud had sought to establish himself on the coast and could not do so only because such an act necessitated, in his perception, a prior understanding with Britain. In short, Ibn Saud saw himself as being caught in a vicious circle: he could not have relations with the British because he was not a coastal ruler, and he could not become a coastal ruler because he did not have relations with Britain. He also realized why London could not at this point treat him as equal to the other gulf sheikhs: whereas all of them were coastal rulers, he was a central Arabian one. Thus, the conquest of Jabal Shammar could not have effected any change in his position as a central Arabian ruler and hence in Britain's attitude toward the Saudis.

If Ibn Saud was ever to secure British protection and achieve independence from the Ottomans, he had to occupy Hasa, place himself within the British sphere of interest, and ipso facto "force" the British to reverse their previous policy and establish relations with him. His previous assessment that the conquest of Hasa required a prior understanding with Britain in order to frustrate an Ottoman sea attack was discarded. He now concluded that, with a Saudi conquest of Hasa as a fait accompli, the British, by virtue of their century-old policy, would be forced to prevent an Ottoman sea attack.

That this was Ibn Saud's line of thinking before he moved against Hasa is evident from the conversations he held with Shakespear shortly before Hasa's occupation. Ibn Saud for the first time did not renew his appeal for British assistance, an inexplicable omission unless he had already made up his mind to conquer Hasa. Instead, he wished to know how Britain would react if he ventured to occupy the province, a further indication of his determination to act without a prior understanding with Britain. Throughout the talks he also displayed no annoyance at the British indifference, stating that "some day you would be forced by circumstances to take up my case." Finally, when Shakespear endeavored to dissuade him from entertaining the hope that Britain would intercede on his behalf should he conquer Hasa, Ibn Saud nevertheless maintained that he would be able "to enlist British sympathy." If Ibn Saud felt that Shakespear was being less than candid in asserting that Britain would not modify her stand toward the Saudis, even if they occupied Hasa, his suspicion proved entirely justified. For when reporting his conversations to Cox, Shakespear averred that, were the Saudis to establish themselves in Hasa, "we shall be forced into relations with Ibn Saud however much we may desire to avoid him."[3]

The vicious circle that Ibn Saud saw himself following as a result of the British rejection of all his overtures was similar to the dilemma he had faced more than ten years before while still in exile. Endeavoring to reconquer Riyadh from the Rashidis, Ibn Saud had sought the prior commitment of several Nejdi tribes before launching the attack on Riyadh. Despite their sympathy with the Saudis, the tribes refused to commit themselves to Ibn Saud's cause as long as he was not successfully established in Riyadh.[4] In both instances his predicament was the same: goal A (Riyadh in 1902; Hasa in 1913) seemed obtainable only after securing a prior commitment from group B (tribes in 1902; Britain in 1913), but he could not secure the commitment from group B without first achieving goal A. In other words, he needed help to ensure success, but help was apt to materialize only after success.

The solution Ibn Saud adopted was similar as well: to take a calculated risk in attaining goal A on the assumption that the aid of group B would then follow. In 1902 he had decided to storm Riyadh, assuming that the tribes would then rally behind the Saudi banner and solidify his position, which proved to be an accurate calculation. And in 1913 he decided to occupy Hasa, assuming that the British government would come to his aid by preventing an Ottoman sea expedition, even without a prior Saudi-British understanding.

But before making the final decision to occupy Hasa, Ibn Saud had to ascertain whether Britain would not regard his conquest of Hasa as a hostile action bound to generate disorder in the Persian Gulf. His last meeting with Shakespear solved this problem, because Shakespear did not make any reference whatsoever to possible British disapproval of such a Saudi move. Shakespear's reply thus removed the last obstacle regarding the substance of Ibn Saud's decision and left open only the question of its timing.

Ibn Saud must have realized that, though his prognosis for breaking the vicious circle in 1913 was similar to that of 1902, the circumstances of each case differed in two major respects. Hasa was not Riyadh, where the adversaries to be overthrown were the Rashidis, but a stronghold of the Ottomans themselves who would most probably seek to retaliate for their defeat. In addition, the calculated risk in 1913 that Britain would prevent an Ottoman sea attack involved much graver dangers than had the risk in 1902. Whereas in 1902 the Saudis in exile had nothing to lose if their adventure proved abortive, in 1913, having re-established their state and consolidated their position in central Arabia, they had a great deal to lose if the Porte resorted to massive retaliation and Britain refused to intervene. Barely a century had passed since the Ottoman Empire had destroyed the first Saudi state, and that event was all too vivid in Ibn Saud's mind.[5] He was not so concerned with an Ottoman land expedition in view of the disastrous precedents of 1904–1906. The problem of the timing of Hasa's occupation thus focused on one crucial question: when the Ottomans would be the least likely to retaliate for their expulsion from Hasa in the form of a major sea attack.

Ibn Saud closely monitored the Ottoman difficulties in various parts of their empire. For the whole of 1912 they were engaged in a war against the Italians in North Africa following the Italian conquest of Tripoli. Simultaneously, in October 1912 the first Balkan War erupted, with the Serbs and the Bulgarians endangering the empire at its very center. So great was the perceived danger that the Porte decided to transfer many of the troops from Baghdad, Basra, and Hufuf to the capital.[6]

That Ibn Saud was very interested in and well informed about Ottoman difficulties was reported first by Captain G. E. Leachman, a British officer and traveler, who had a long conversation with the Saudi chief in Riyadh in December 1912. Ibn Saud later wrote to Shakespear that it pleased him to learn of the "heavy fighting and Ottoman losses," and he asked for "detailed information on this." When they met in the spring of 1913, Ibn Saud told Shakespear that the Ottomans' misfortunes and their present weakness provided the Saudis with an opportunity that was unlikely to recur. He calculated that the Porte would be too occupied in recuperating and reorganizing the Ottoman army after the war's conclusion to dispatch a serious expedition to Hasa and Nejd. Once the Saudi spies confirmed that the garrisons at Hufuf, Qatif, and 'Uqair had been significantly decreased, the question of the timing was resolved.[7]

On the night of May 4, 1913, Saudi forces attacked the walled city of Hufuf, and after a short battle the Ottoman garrison surrendered and was allowed to leave peacefully for Bahrain. On May 15, 'Uqair and Qatif followed suit, and by the end of the month Hasa was under Saudi control. The Ottoman authorities in Basra, stunned by Ibn Saud's coup, tried to repulse the invaders, but the

Saudis defeated the Ottoman contingent and allowed it to leave for Bahrain unmolested.[8] Instead of inflicting a serious defeat on the Ottomans, Ibn Saud preferred to minimize the provocation that his occupation of Hasa entailed for the Ottomans and avoid further humiliation.

In sum, Ibn Saud's interest in occupying Hasa went through three distinct stages from its first manifestation in 1906 until the conquest itself in 1913. In the first stage, lasting from 1906 until 1912, Britain's refusal to commit itself to frustrating an Ottoman sea attack—a commitment that Ibn Saud perceived as a sine qua non—outweighed the existing Saudi volition and capability for the conquest. The turning point occurred when it became apparent that both such a precondition could never be fulfilled and the major Saudi goal of securing independence through Britain could not be obtained without a prior conquest of Hasa. Once Ibn Saud ascertained that Britain would not view with disfavor a Saudi occupation of Hasa, the decision was made. In the third stage, the question of the timing of the attack was determined by Ottoman difficulties in the Balkan Wars. These were viewed by Ibn Saud as very likely to prevent the Ottomans from embarking on a large-scale military operation in the Persian Gulf.

Establishment of Relations with Britain

Immediately after his establishment in Hasa, Ibn Saud moved to translate his military success into a political reality by pursuing two parallel lines of action. First he sought to cover his flank by a personal approach to the Ottomans, informing them that he had been forced to take measures owing to appeals of the inhabitants against the oppression of and mismanagement by local Ottoman officials. He stressed that he had no intention of revolting against the Porte and, as proof, expressed his readiness to become a wali on behalf of the sultan and guarantee to maintain order. He stated that his recovery of Hasa was merely a restoration of the status quo which had prevailed before the Ottoman occupation in 1871, and he once again expressed his loyalty and subservience to the Porte, declaring himself "an obedient servant of the Sultan."[9]

The overture to the Ottomans was less important to the Saudi leader than his approach to the British in order to ascertain whether his calculated risk had been based on a sound assumption. Informing the British on June 13, 1913, that he had recovered his "forefathers' ancestral dominions—Hasa and its dependencies," Ibn Saud stated his desire to establish such relations with Great Britain as to deter the Porte from contemplating retaliation against the Saudis. He reiterated his promise not to injure or attack the littoral states in alliance with the British, and he demanded to be informed "if Britain is not willing to preserve former friendship so that I may look to my own interests."[10] Ibn Saud's gamble to "force" Britain into establishing relations with him by dint of his new status as a coastal ruler reached its moment of truth.

Ibn Saud's assumption that his very conquest of Hasa would force London to reconsider its whole policy proved immediately correct in at least one respect. Even before the British receipt of his letter, British officials in India and the Persian Gulf had already suggested a reassessment of British policy toward the Saudis. This was the first time that the Saudi issue had been debated not as the result of a Saudi overture but rather at the instigation of British officials themselves. The controversy that erupted within the British government as a result of the Saudi conquest of Hasa was exacerbated by a new factor, compounding British ambiguities and constraining their freedom of action vis-à-vis the Saudis. For more than two years British and Ottoman representatives had been trying to settle the three outstanding problems between the two countries: the delineation of British and Ottoman interests in the Persian Gulf; the completion of the Baghdad Railway; and the problem of Ottoman customs duties. By the time Ibn Saud drove the Ottomans from Hasa, the negotiations were approaching a successful conclusion, according to which Britain recognized Ottoman authority over "the sanjaq of Nejd," whose boundaries included Hasa.[11] Ibn Saud's recovery of Hasa thus presented the British with a difficult dilemma. On the one hand, if they were to adhere to their longstanding policy of establishing relations with coastal rulers, they had to enter into relations with Ibn Saud. On the other hand, such a move was bound to irritate the Ottomans and frustrate whatever progress had been achieved in the negotiations with the Porte.

Cox was cognizant of the dilemma Britain faced and strove to reconcile both sides on the matter. First, he identified the immediate problem: whether Britain should adhere to her policy of preventing maritime hostilities in case the Porte decided on a major sea-attack against the Saudis. Second, he suggested a policy line based on the recognition of Ibn Saud as the de-facto ruler of Hasa and the establishment of "definite and friendly relations" with him. But Cox realized that Britain could not come to terms with the Saudis behind the back of the Ottomans, and he therefore proposed to approach the Porte with a view to arriving at a mutually acceptable arrangement. Britain should persuade the Ottomans, Cox suggested, to appoint Ibn Saud as an autonomous governor of Hasa on the basis of Ibn Saud's recognition of Ottoman suzerainty. And in his capacity as a coastal ruler, Ibn Saud should be allowed to make agreements with Britain for the preservation of the maritime truce, the prohibition of the arms traffic, and the friendly treatment of the coastal rulers in treaty relations with Britain. Cox appreciated London's traditional reluctance "to be drawn into central Arabian politics," but he emphasized that "this is now a Gulf question."[12] Cox's last point demonstrated more than anything else that, had the Gulf authorities determined British policy, Ibn Saud's calculation might have well been realized in its entirety. His transformation of the Saudi issue from a central Arabian to a gulf problem was precisely what caused both Shakespear and Cox to advocate the establishment of relations between Britain and the Saudis.

The Indian government and the India Office also noted that "Ibn Saud now controls the whole hinterland of the Persian Gulf," and consequently an understanding with him would be necessary. But in view of the satisfactory course of the negotiations with the Ottomans, they agreed that it would be useless to raise the Saudi issue at this juncture and suggested waiting for further developments.[13] Thus, both also played into Ibn Saud's calculation, with the only difference that they sought to defer a decision until after the successful conclusion of the Ottoman-British treaty.

Only the Foreign Office refused to revise its traditional policy of abstention from intervening in the affairs of Nejd. "Considerations of European policy dictated our desire to consolidate the power of the Porte in its Asiatic dominions." Besides, Secretary Edward Grey was far from convinced that ultimate Saudi victory over the Ottomans was assured. From the Foreign Office's standpoint, the Saudi issue seemed insignificant when viewed against the overall context of British-Ottoman relations. The Indian authorities were consequently instructed to abstain from any intervention, direct or indirect, in Nejdi affairs, and Shakespear was personally warned to abstain from communicating with Ibn Saud.[14]

With the receipt of the Saudi letter of June 13, the issue was reopened, only to be concluded in the same manner. Consequently, Cox addressed a letter to Ibn Saud on July 9, explaining that the British government had to remain strictly neutral in the Saudi-Ottoman dispute and would not intervene in it in any way. The Foreign Office approved Cox's suggested statement that "Britain would be glad to see you reconciled to the Ottomans." But it vetoed the second part of Cox's sentence, which read ". . . and assist in promoting such reconciliation."[15] What Ibn Saud would have heartily welcomed was precisely what the Foreign Office deleted from the communication.

For a moment it seemed as if Ibn Saud's whole gamble had collapsed because of the Foreign Office's adamant opposition. Before receiving this letter, and having so far heard nothing from the British, Ibn Saud once again sought to pre-empt any Ottoman thoughts of retaliation by stressing to the Porte that the occupation of Hasa had been forced upon him by the local inhabitants and that he entertained the utmost loyalty to the sultan.[16] The receipt of Cox's letter tended to confirm Ibn Saud's impression that his gamble had proved wrong after all. The fact that this was the first time the British had ever communicated with the Saudis could have hardly consoled him, for the content of the letter dashed his expectations. Perhaps the British government was not yet fully cognizant of the repercussions of his new status as a coastal ruler, and it was necessary to demonstrate the practical implications of this reality.

In late July 1913, Ibn Saud wrote to the sheikh of Qatar demanding that he expel the Ottomans from his principality. The British were immediately concerned lest Ibn Saud force the sheikh to evict the Ottomans, failing which, he himself would take possession of Qatar. It is probable that the Saudi chief, disappointed by the British reply, sought to signal to the British that his new position on the coast enabled him seriously to threaten their interests and consequently to force a revision in their attitude. In addition, he wrote to Shakespear and Cox, warning that, if Britain did not "regard our affairs in the true circumstances, then necessity must force us to seek relief from others," and demanding a full explanation of the British attitude.[17]

To compound British apprehension, the Saudi occupation of Hasa had an immediate effect on the Trucial chiefs. Drawing a direct lesson from the past, the sheikhs of Abu Dhabi and Dubai expected a Saudi attack on their territories. The sheikh of Abu Dhabi was particularly alarmed, as he was in possession of Buraimi, which Ibn Saud regarded as a Saudi territory. To complicate matters further, a rebellion in Muscat provided Ibn Saud with an opportunity to threaten Trucial Oman as well.[18] In short, by his actions, combined with his sheer presence along the gulf, Ibn Saud endeavored to convey to the British the notion of a new state of affairs in the gulf, forcing them to establish relations with him.

This constellation of circumstances, created by Ibn Saud himself, was at the core of the shift in British policy. Cox and the Indian government reasserted their "case" with the utmost forcefulness, aimed at penetrating the brick wall of the Foreign Office. The thrust of their analysis was that "Ibn Saud entered the sphere of British influence and interest . . . and the moment has arrived for deciding whether we are to conciliate or estrange him." They pointed to the disquiet among the Trucial chiefs as an indication that the new situation had rendered obsolete the traditional policy of noninterference in Saudi affairs. In conclusion, India recommended not a treaty but an amicable exchange of views with Ibn Saud, impressing upon him Britain's hope that he refrain from "touching the Chiefs in treaty relations with Britain."[19]

In London, meanwhile, a significant change took place on July 29, 1913, when the Ottoman-British Convention was signed by representatives of both countries after three years of negotiations. Foreign Secretary Grey thus became more amenable to persuasion, and he was "convinced by the arguments of the Government of India that a case is made out for modification of views he had previously expressed."[20] Consequently, Grey approved an approach to the Ottomans, on the assumption that, once their authority over Nejd had been explicitly recognized in the convention, a British intercession regarding the Saudi issue would not arouse Ottoman suspicions.

The Foreign Office's official communication, conveyed by Alwyn Parker to the Ottoman negotiator Hakki Pasha on August 15, would have pleased Ibn Saud, had he been acquainted with its content, for the thrust of the British approach was based on the same elements underlying Ibn Saud's strategy in the occupation of Hasa.[21] Parker set the framework for the British approach by stating that Ibn Saud, by his conquest of Hasa, had entered into the sphere of British politics and commerce. Since Britain had important interests and obligations in the gulf, such as the maintenance of the maritime peace and the suppression of piracy and arms traffic, it was no longer possible for the British government to ignore Ibn Saud and pretend to treat Hasa as politically derelict. Hence, Britain was compelled to have relations and find a modus vivendi with someone in de-facto control over Hasa. Such relations, however, would not affect Britain's strictly neutral attitude in the Saudi-Ottoman dispute and its desire to see a speedy reconciliation between the parties. Furthermore, Britain was ready to offer its good offices in order to bring about such a reconciliation.

Grey's assumption regarding the Ottoman response was confirmed when Hakki Pasha appeared "more gratified than offended" by London's approach, expressing the Porte's appreciation of Britain's offer of mediation. But the Ottomans contemplated a goal diametrically opposed to that of Ibn Saud. Whereas Ibn Saud endeavored to embroil the British in his dispute with the Ottomans in order to enhance his bargaining position, the Porte sought to keep the British out of their bilateral relations with the Saudis. Hakki therefore assured Parker that his government was in contact with Ibn Saud and hoped to reach a satisfactory settlement soon.[22]

As Grey had modified his opposition and the Porte was not offended by London's approach, the Foreign Office approved India's suggestion for "an amicable exchange of views" with the Saudis. On September 11, 1913, Cox addressed a letter to Ibn Saud, expressing the desire of His Majesty's government to maintain friendly relations, provided the Saudis undertook to respect the integrity of the gulf principalities, including Qatar. Cox inquired in what directions Ibn Saud wanted the British government "to evince its friendly regard" and expressed readiness to have a meeting with Ibn Saud.[23]

The communication must have caught Ibn Saud by surprise, for its letter, as well as its spirit, was in total contrast to the first British letter of July 9. The Saudi chief was by now under strong

Ottoman pressure to mend his ways and accept Ottoman terms for a settlement. The Porte obviously sought to restore the status quo ante in Hasa and was prepared to grant Ibn Saud partial autonomy under six conditions: the former Ottoman garrisons in Hasa were to be reinstated; the qadis in Nejd were to be nominated by the sultan; all foreigners were to be excluded from Nejd; all communications from foreign powers were to be referred to the Porte; Ibn Saud was to pay an annual revenue of 3000 Turkish liras (T.L.); and no concessions were to be given to any foreigners.[24] Ibn Saud deferred his response to the Ottoman terms until after he had heard from the British, as he did not wish to commit himself to any arrangement before he had played out the British card.

Compared to the first British response, Cox's letter effected a whole new state of mind in Ibn Saud. Britain had for the first time formally and officially expressed its desire to enter into friendly relations with the Saudis. The magnitude of this change can be understood only against the background of the 1902–1913 period, when Britain had consistently refused to establish any sort of relations, to the point that Saudi letters remained unanswered. Far more important, the letter read as if the British themselves were interested in establishing contact with Ibn Saud. Cox himself was the one who raised the idea of a meeting and who inquired as to how the Saudis expected Britain to demonstrate its friendly attitude, creating the impression that the British Government was willing to support the Saudis. It is true that London had decided it could not undertake to support Ibn Saud against the Porte and could offer only its mediation; but this qualification was missing from Cox's letter, and Ibn Saud therefore had good reasons to deduce from it that Britain would support him.[25] In sum, for Ibn Saud the letter amounted to a confirmation that his gamble was justified, since its underlying assumption had proved correct. Britain, which had been indifferent to the Saudis since their reestablishment in Nejd in 1902, had been forced by the Saudi conquest of Hasa to bring about an immediate change in its policy.

Ibn Saud hurried to translate his assessment of Cox's reply into two practical lines of action. Considering his bargaining position to be improved, he first notified the Porte that he insisted on complete autonomy for Nejd and recognition of his right to Hasa and his freedom to appoint all local officials and control all domestic affairs—in short, a semi-independent status. The only issue he omitted in his reply was that of his relations with foreign powers, since he was not yet fully acquainted with the extent of British support. Next, he rushed a letter to Cox, requesting a meeting in late November when Ibn Saud would arrive in Hasa. Ibn Saud assured Cox that in the interval he would take no action "which would be likely to run counter to the wishes of the British Government," that is, commit himself to any arrangement with the Ottomans without first ascertaining the British position.[26]

Ibn Saud looked forward to the meeting, regarding it as the culmination of his eleven-year struggle to secure British protection. With the occupation of Hasa he had not only restored an integral part of his house's dominions but also forced Britain to modify its hitherto indifferent attitude toward him. But the major part of the gamble, the extent of this modification, remained as yet unresolved. Would Britain go all the way and establish its protectorate over the Saudis as it had done in Kuwait at the turn of the century? Would it confine its role to preventing the Ottomans from embarking on a naval expedition against Ibn Saud? Or would it be willing only to offer its good offices in the Saudi-Ottoman dispute without taking sides? The forthcoming meeting with British officials provided Ibn Saud with the opportunity to convey his intentions to the British government and simultaneously to learn of its position.

The British prepared themselves for the meeting in two areas. First, they had to predict the kind of problems that Ibn Saud would raise and find appropriate solutions. Second, they had to define the issues that Britain should discuss with the Saudi ruler in order to safeguard its interests along the coast.

In the first category of issues, the British included the questions of Ibn Saud's attitude toward Qatar and the Saudi-Ottoman dispute. As for Qatar, the British were apprehensive lest Ibn Saud carry out his threat and move to expel the Ottoman garrison from the principality. As a result, in the letter of September 11 to Ibn Saud, Cox chose to mention only Qatar of all the gulf sheikhdoms whose integrity Britain expected the Saudis to respect. The India Office noted that Britain could not press the Porte on that point until the Ottoman-British Convention was ratified. As a policy guideline, the Foreign Office ordered Cox to explain to Ibn Saud that the garrisons would be removed within a short time after the ratification of the convention.[27]

As for the Saudi-Ottoman dispute, the British clearly anticipated a Saudi request for support against the Porte. When this conviction came to prevail in London, the India Office ordered that Ibn Saud be informed that the British government was willing to do its best "to reconcile him with the Porte." But if he were to request British support against the Ottomans as a quid pro quo for complying with British wishes, he should be made to understand that Britain was entirely unable to support him.[28]

The second category of issues, related to safeguarding Britain's coastal interests, was up to the British authorities in the gulf to define and determine. Accordingly, Cox drafted a memorandum on December 2, 1913, containing the four major elements of British policy in the gulf: noninterference in the politics and nonencroachment on the integrity of the gulf principalities; suppression of piracy and the illicit arms traffic; maintenance of the maritime truce; and admittance of British subjects to trade freely along the shores of the gulf. The officials entrusted with interviewing Ibn Saud were to ascertain his views on these four elements and thus enable His Majesty's government to reach a modus vivendi with him. Cox also suggested obtaining an undertaking from the Porte "not to take hostile action by sea against Ibn Saud without a previous exchange of views with us."[29] This memorandum confirmed Ibn Saud's assumption that Britain would have to take up the question of an Ottoman sea action whether or not it had relations with the Saudis. The congruence of Ibn Saud's assumptions and Cox's reasoning underlined a curious, but nevertheless sensible, phenomenon. For both men, British interests in the gulf alone figured as the major, if not the only, consideration dictating British decision-making. This was natural for Ibn Saud, since the "only" Britain he knew was the one in the Persian Gulf.

On December 2, Cox ordered Major A. Trevor, the political agent at Bahrain, to proceed to Hasa in company with Captain Shakespear in order to meet Ibn Saud. Both officials arrived at Hasa in mid-December and had two long interviews with the Saudi ruler on December 15 and 16 in the coast town of 'Uqair.[30] Ibn Saud started the first meeting by giving an account of the history of Nejd, establishing the historical right of his family and describing the Ottomans as foreign usurpers. He said that what he was concerned with was his honor, the honor of his house, and the preservation of his ancestral rights, and he was asking for the support of the British government. Trevor and Shakespear inquired in what way he wanted British assistance. Ibn Saud replied that he wanted to secure his position by getting an assurance that Britain would maintain the maritime peace on his strip of the coast, Hasa, and recognize him as the de-facto ruler. The practical significance of such an assurance would be to guarantee that Britain would deter and prevent the Ottomans from dispatching a naval expedition against Ibn Saud. In a broader sense, such a guarantee would constitute the first indispensable step in the process of Saudi independence from the Ottomans.

Trevor and Shakespear responded that they could give him no such assurance. Moreover, they were convinced that the British government, in view of its friendship with the Porte, could not do so either, as the Ottomans would undoubtedly regard such a move as a hostile act. But Ibn Saud did not give up. Instead, he tried to exercise his leverage on Britain by introducing a set of inducements and penalties, the proverbial carrot and stick. The list of inducements offered by the Saudis included commitments, if provided with the British assurance, of noninterference in the politics of Qatar and the Trucial Coast, cooperation in the suppression of piracy and the illicit arms traffic and in the maintenance of the maritime truce, immediate admittance of British traders to Hasa, and a commitment to have no relations with any other power and to consult the British government in all important matters.

If the British were to turn down his request, Ibn Saud let them know that such a course would entail certain penalties for their interests. It was in this framework that he volunteered to disclose to his guests the six-point Ottoman proposal he had received in August. He claimed that the Porte would probably drop all terms in the proposal except for the two related to the exclusion of all foreign merchants and the exclusive conduct of foreign policy. He made Shakespear and Trevor understand that, in the absence of an affirmative British reply, he would be forced to conclude a settlement that would exclude all British traders from the ports of Hasa and prohibit the British from communicating with him. Ibn Saud knew that the two clauses were anathema to the British.

The reference to the second penalty came in the form of an implied threat. Ibn Saud could claim Qatar and the Trucial Coast as part of his ancestral dominions and could make his power felt there. He implied—and his guests understood the hint—that the only consideration which restrained him from overrunning Qatar and the coast after he had occupied Hasa was his desire not to alienate the sympathy of the British government.

Ibn Saud's goal was to demonstrate that his interests and objectives coincided with those of Britain and that wherever there could be a conflict of interest, he was ready to subordinate his aspirations to British wishes. At the same time, he wanted to prove to the British that the Porte's aims were clearly incompatible with Britain's policy in the gulf and that the Ottomans were not averse to working against British interests. The reality he strove to impress upon the British forced them into choosing one of two alternatives: either they provided him with the assurance, or their interests in the gulf were bound to suffer.

Ibn Saud immediately detected a change in his guests' attitude after he had alluded to the possible penalties and to the terms of the Ottoman proposal. The Porte's draft, Shakespear and Trevor explained, infringed on British interests in two respects, for Britain must be able to communicate with the de-facto ruler of Hasa, and the British could not acquiesce in a settlement excluding their subjects from any part of the coast. They stated that their government would have to take up "the question of the prejudice to their rights and interests which the existence of any clause excluding their subjects would entail." At this point Ibn Saud urged the British to take a definite stand on his request, as he had to respond to the Porte. Shakespear and Trevor, for their part, requested that he delay a definite answer until the British government had an opportunity to consider their report of the meeting.

Ibn Saud agreed immediately. He suggested that the most feasible way to postpone his reply without incurring the wrath of the Ottomans would be by informing them that the dispute could be better resolved at a meeting between himself and the wali of Basra in the spring. This would give the British government three months to consider its attitude toward Ibn Saud, who would accordingly calculate his policy vis-à-vis the Porte.

Ibn Saud assumed that even if the British government could not grant him the assurance, Britain could still play a valuable role in assisting him against the Porte. Throughout the interview he left no doubt that he preferred any Saudi-Ottoman reconciliation to be carried through under the auspices of the British. This form of British intervention would deter the Ottomans from contemplating a sea expedition and would simultaneously improve his bargaining position with the Porte.

Trevor and Shakespear's major concern was that Ibn Saud might reach an understanding with the Ottomans which would be detrimental to British interests. They therefore suggested that Britain inform him of its decision to effect a settlement between him and the Porte and thereby dissuade him from concluding such an agreement on his own. The new acting resident, J. G. Lorimer, was quick to realize that the British faced a seemingly insoluble dilemma in reconciling their dealings with Ibn Saud, the de-facto ruler of Hasa, with their recognition of Ottoman sovereignty over this province. He conceived of a solution on two levels, local and international. On the local level, questions that did not concern the Ottomans could be agreed upon between the local British authorities and the Saudi chief. Such questions included, for instance, Ibn Saud's relations with Qatar and Trucial Oman and his admittance of British subjects. On the international level, Ibn Saud had essentially requested that the British government intervene with the Ottomans on his behalf in order to secure for him the rulership of Hasa on an autonomous basis. Since his desire was irreconcilable with Ottoman policy, Ibn Saud should be informed that Britain could mediate between him and the Porte only with the consent of both parties.[31]

British Intervention in Saudi-Ottoman Dispute

Lorimer's solution was based on a major misconception that a separation between the two levels, local and international, was possible. In reality the two were intertwined, if not interdependent, for Ibn Saud was ready to reach an agreement with Britain on local problems only if it gave him some assurances in the context of his relations with the Porte. The Foreign Office rejected Lorimer's proposal for this and two other reasons. First, if Ibn Saud negotiated with the Ottomans on his own, he might be constrained to accept their six-point proposal, which would deprive Britain of any standing in Hasa. Second, if the Saudis and the Ottomans failed to reach an agreement, the Porte might be tempted to embark on a sea expedition aimed at the reconquest of Hasa, which would endanger British interests. An Ottoman military expedition was no longer merely an idle speculation once Cox, who was on leave in London, met Hakki in early March 1914 and found him convinced that the Ottomans would reconquer Hasa.[32] It was paradoxical that whereas the resident called for a cautious policy to allay Ottoman suspicions, the Foreign Office decided on a firm policy. This marked the first time that Ibn Saud's calculations and assumptions in conquering Hasa proved justified by acts of the Foreign Office and not merely of the Indian authorities.

The twofold apprehension of an Ottoman sea expedition and a Saudi-Ottoman agreement detrimental to British interests led the Foreign Office to depart from its long-standing position and intervene with the Ottomans. The British position was articulated in a detailed memorandum that Parker submitted to Hakki Pasha in London on March 9. Setting the terms of reference for the intervention—"Britain must have direct relations with the *de facto* ruler of Hasa"—the memorandum protested against the three articles in the Ottoman proposal regarding the referral of all foreign communications to the Porte, the exclusion of foreigners, and the banning of all foreign concessions. The memorandum described them as "impossible of acquiescence" and expressed the desire to see them withdrawn. It also urged the Porte to refrain from any hostile action by sea against Ibn Saud without first consulting the British and giving them an opportunity for friendly mediation. But the most outstanding feature of the memorandum was the explicit statement that British policy toward Ibn Saud was based on the four desiderata contained in Cox's memorandum of December 2, 1913, namely noninterference in the gulf principalities, suppression of piracy and arms traffic, maintenance of the maritime truce, and admittance of British traders. Although Britain did not wish to intrude itself into the Ottoman-Saudi dispute, it expected the eventual agreement between the parties "to approve Ibn Saud's undertaking to comply with the four British desiderata." Foreign Secretary Grey's readiness to pursue a firmer policy was probably motivated by the conclusion of the second Ottoman-British Convention on the very day that the memorandum was communicated to Hakki. Grey assumed that Britain's recognition in the convention of Ottoman sovereignty over the whole of Nejd and Hasa enabled him to insist on maintaining British interests in the Persian Gulf without thereby damaging British-Ottoman relations. The British intervention culminated in urging Hakki to allow Britain to mediate before undertaking military operations. Hakki was specifically told that "military actions were in fact impossible, owing to the nature of the Coast, without infringing the neutrality of Bahrain, which we . . . [could] not allow."³³

From the Saudi vantage point, the Foreign Office's communication meant that the immediate Saudi goals were about to be realized; that is, the Porte would probably abstain from dispatching a sea expedition and the Saudis would be allowed to have direct relations with Britain. Whatever consequences the British intervention might eventually bring about, it would certainly constrain Ottoman freedom of action. Moreover, from the standpoint of the long-term Saudi goal of securing independence through Britain, the intervention was a significant step forward. This was the first time that Britain officially and unequivocally claimed to have a legitimate *locus standi* in Saudi-Ottoman relations despite its recognition of Nejd and Hasa as territories under Ottoman sovereignty. The statement highlighted the change in Britain's policy of indifference to the Saudis since 1902, which had been prompted by the Saudi conquest of Hasa.³⁴

Meanwhile, the Ottomans had not failed to take notice of the first direct communication between British officials and Ibn Saud in December 1913. Consequently, they decided to apply more pressure on Ibn Saud in order to force him to accept their terms for a settlement and to dissuade the British from intervening. In mid-February 1914, the Ottoman war minister, Enver Pasha, requested Mubarak to arrange a meeting between Ibn Saud and an Ottoman envoy, 'Umar Fauzi, expressing the sultan's desire "to avoid the shedding of Muslim blood." But Ibn Saud was noncommittal. The Ottomans also embarked on military preparations to lend weight to their political maneuvers. About the beginning of January 1914, they sent arms and ammunition to Ibn Rashid, and in early March, eight hundred Ottoman troops arrived at Basra by the S.S. *Saratow*. Concomitantly, Hakki protested in London against the establishment of "direct relations between Ibn Saud and the British," reminding Britain of its formal and binding recognition of Nejd as an Ottoman province and of Ibn Saud as an Ottoman subject. Moreover, as the Ottomans intended to re-establish their garrisons in Hasa, they would deeply resent it if Ibn Saud received any encouragement from Britain.[35]

Ibn Saud was aware of the Ottoman military movements, and Shakespear, who visited Riyadh on March 9, 1914, found active preparations there for the mobilization of a large Saudi force. Ibn Saud understood that if the Ottomans decided to use the military option, he might face an attack by Ibn Rashid in Qasim, which would be followed by an Ottoman onslaught from the northeast. As spring was approaching and the Ottoman pressure on Ibn Saud was intensifying, he wrote to Trevor, reminding him that the three-month waiting period was drawing to an end. Since it was impossible for Ibn Saud to keep the Ottomans off any longer, he requested notification of the British position. To Shakespear, Ibn Saud revealed his anxiety to learn what steps, if any, the British would take in the event of Ottoman troops making for the coast. He asserted that he had no intention of committing himself to the Ottomans as long as he had any chance of arriving at an arrangement with Britain or at least obtaining British support in his negotiations with the Ottomans. But he could not wait indefinitely and continue to maintain a large force in the field. Unless he could obtain some assurances, he would be compelled to make his own arrangements in order to obtain a respite from the necessity of remaining continually on guard.[36]

By the time Ibn Saud's inquiries were transmitted to London, the British Foreign Office memorandum of March 9 had already been delivered to the Ottomans. The India Office interpreted the Foreign Office's memorandum as an intervention on Ibn Saud's behalf. Consequently, it instructed the Indian authorities to inform Ibn Saud that, as the British government was endeavoring to effect an arrangement with the Porte, "he should not take any independent action in the matter."[37]

Ibn Saud received the British communication on March 23, and his self-confidence grew considerably. At long last he had succeeded in embroiling the British in his bilateral relations with the Porte. Instead of facing the Ottomans alone with his limited resources, he was now supported by Great Britain, which was exerting its influence on future Ottoman reactions. But at this very juncture, the Ottomans renewed their pressure on Ibn Saud. At the beginning of April, Mubarak received three letters impressing upon him the urgency with which the Porte viewed the Saudi problem. The Ottoman war minister informed him of the sultan's decision "to guard zealously what was left to Islam," the wali of Basra again commented to him about the "avoidance of bloodshed," and Sayyid Talib requested him "to help energetically in this important matter."[38] The content of these letters was promptly conveyed to Ibn Saud's attention.

The Saudi chief was now in a confident state of mind, which was duly reflected in his response to the Ottoman demands. To Mubarak, Ibn Saud stated his desire to secure a status similar to that of Kuwait, namely autonomy with British protection under Ottoman suzerainty. To Talib, he wrote that though he did not waver in allegiance to Islam and obedience to the Porte, there were things that he could not do. Alluding to the British intervention with the Porte, he suggested that if the Ottomans' real intention was to arrive at an agreement, then "it was for the Porte to accomplish this with those people [the British] whose good qualities cause the countries of the world to remain in repose, whom we know and on whom we depend and do not wish to displease by actions contrary to our promises to them." Characteristically, Ibn Saud was sufficiently cautious to inform Trevor of the new Ottoman overture, demonstrating once again his sincerity in seeking coordination with Britain. He also requested a more definite reply from the British government regarding the results of the mediation effort. He was disappointed when Trevor replied that he had no further information and advised him to keep waiting.[39]

Ibn Saud's patience was exhausted several days later when Mubarak informed him of another Ottoman overture and urged him to come to Kuwait. This time it was Sayyid Talib, entrusted with the negotiations with Ibn Saud, who stated that he would arrive shortly in Kuwait at the head of an Ottoman delegation. Ibn Saud realized that he could defy the Ottomans no longer, as almost four months had elapsed since he informed them of his intention to meet their delegates. But lest they interpret his departure for Kuwait as a sign of weakness, Ibn Saud let them know that he was in a position "to do great things even as far as Iraq were it not that I do not wish to be the cause of further decline to the Ottoman Government." He emphasized that submission would be incumbent upon him only if the Porte withdrew its insistence on the restoration of Ottoman garrisons to Hasa.[40]

On April 16, Ibn Saud left Qatif for Kuwait. Before his departure, he notified Trevor that he could wait no longer for a British reply. But he requested to meet the political agent at Kuwait before his negotiations with the Ottomans started.[41]

Britain's failure to provide Ibn Saud with a definite reply was rooted in changes that had occurred in the framework of British-Ottoman relations. While the British were expecting an Ottoman answer to the Foreign Office memorandum of March 9, the Porte was seeking to delay a reply, pending the results of their efforts to effect a settlement through Mubarak. The Porte's silence further aroused British suspicions that the Ottomans were contemplating a military action against Ibn Saud. On Grey's instructions, the British ambassador, Louis Mallet, urged the Porte to avoid "any disturbances which will create widespread unrest and severely affect the security of the Coast," and he renewed the offer of mediation. In response, the minister of interior, Tal'at Bey, stated that negotiations were taking place through Mubarak and a settlement was expected soon.[42]

In view of this reply, Mallet suggested that Britain terminate its effort of mediation. Britain, he argued, could only accept an Ottoman request for mediation but could not press for one, as otherwise Britain would appear to violate the convention, which recognized Ibn Saud as an Ottoman subject. If Britain was concerned about the terms of a Saudi-Ottoman agreement, such an apprehension could be disposed of in direct Ottoman-Anglo negotiations. But Britain certainly did not have the right to prevent the Porte from consolidating Ottoman authority in Ottoman territory.[43]

As a result of Mallet's communication, the Foreign Office reverted to its old position of noninterference, ironically depicted by Arthur Hirtzel of the India Office as "pretending that Ibn Saud does not exist." The Foreign Office's intervention originated from concern about both an Ottoman military action and an Ottoman-Saudi agreement inimical to British interests. Mallet's telegram dispelled both problems, the first by making it apparent that the Ottomans were relying on negotiations rather than on military means, the second by persuading Grey that Britain had no *locus standi* in the Ottoman-Saudi dispute despite the fact that vital British interests were at stake. In addition, as negotiations were conducted through Mubarak, a staunch friend of Britain, there was little concern that their results could hurt British interests. Arguing that "there is no justification for an intimation being conveyed to an Ottoman subject that he should not negotiate with his own Government," the Foreign Office instructed India to inform Ibn Saud that he was free to negotiate with the Ottomans on his own.[44]

Ibn Saud arrived at Malah, ten miles south of Kuwait, on April 26, 1914, and two days later the political agent at Kuwait, Lt. Colonel W. Grey, came to convey to him the British decision. Ibn Saud was disappointed and at first inclined to think that the British government had allowed him to entertain hopes which could not be realized. But Grey managed to dispel this notion, explaining that it was the Ottomans who had declined the offer of mediation and that the British government could not force upon them assistance which they did not desire.

The conversation that ensued was crucial to Ibn Saud's subsequent behavior in his negotiations with the Ottomans. In view of Grey's message, Ibn Saud realized that entering into negotiations with the Ottomans had become inevitable. But if they insisted on restationing their garrisons, the question of whether he should accept it or break off the negotiations depended on the possible British reaction to the breakoff of the negotiations. Ibn Saud, therefore, addressed two questions to Grey: should the negotiations break off, would the British then give him the assurance that the Ottomans would not be allowed to take hostile action by sea, and would there be any chance of securing the mediation of Britain? Although reluctant to give Ibn Saud any assurance, Grey predicted that the Porte would most probably ask for British mediation, which would then be offered.

Ibn Saud concluded that, as the door was still open for British intervention, the Ottomans would not hasten to take military actions against him. If the Porte were to insist on the reinstatement of Ottoman garrisons, he could adhere to his opposition even to the point of breaking off the negotiations, without running the risk of Ottoman retaliation. To induce Britain further to intervene, he warned that "the Ottomans would undoubtedly compel me to prohibit the presence of all foreigners in Hasa." Reporting on the meeting, Grey concluded that Ibn Saud would use "every possible means to draw us into the negotiations, e.g., by accepting, under the plea of compulsion, such conditions which he knows we will be loathe to recognize."[45]

The Ottoman deputation arrived at Kuwait on April 29. It was headed by Sayyid Talib and consisted of Baha al-Din, chief of staff at Baghdad, 'Umar Fauzi, chief of staff at Basra, and Sami Pasha, mutessarif of Hasa. Accompanying the delegation were the brothers 'Abd al-Wahhab and 'Abd al-Latif Mandil, land proprietors and Ibn Saud's agents at Basra.

The negotiations started at Subaihiyya on May 2, 1914, with the Ottomans demanding that their garrisons be reinstated in Qatif and 'Uqair, that all forts in Hasa be surrendered to them, that all arms be handed over to their troops, and that Ibn Saud have no connection with any foreign powers. In return for Saudi acceptance of these conditions, the Ottomans agreed to recognize Ibn Saud's local autonomy, to allow him to collect all local taxes, and to give him verbal permission to retake Qatar and Trucial Oman when he chose. The Ottoman conditions were essentially similar to those they had demanded all along, since they were based on the two principles of restoration of the status quo ante in Hasa and surrender of Saudi foreign relations. The only striking difference lay in the Ottoman promise to let the Saudis retake the coastal principalities. Ibn Saud probably raised the subject with the purpose of alienating the Porte from the British, who could not acquiesce in such a provision and thus would be influenced to intervene. Ibn Saud's terms, which were also similar to those he had agreed upon in August 1913, were that he should retain Hasa under Ottoman suzerainty, that he should pay the Porte T.L. 3000 per annum as tribute, and that he shoud be at the disposal of the Porte in the event that armed assistance was required.[46]

There was agreement on most of these issues, the only unbridgeable gap being the question of the reinstatement of the Ottoman garrisons. The debate reached its peak when 'Umar Fauzi warned Ibn Saud that if he did not accept the garrisons, he would be compelled to do so. The Saudi chief arose and, half-drawing his sword, ordered Fauzi to leave the assembly. The negotiations nearly ended in a fight before being suspended altogether. The Ottoman deputation returned hastily to Basra on the night of May 5, and Ibn Saud hurried back to Riyadh.

The Ottoman position was probably based on the miscalculation that Ibn Saud would modify his stand and relinquish Hasa once he understood that British mediation was excluded. This was the underlying reason for Hakki's continual requests in London that Britain dispel the Saudis' illusions that the British might come to their support. The Ottomans were caught off balance by the strong posture Ibn Saud displayed, which was incomprehensible from their point of view. Not surprisingly, therefore, they tended to attribute Ibn Saud's intransigence to some secret British encouragement, the more so when they learned of Grey's meeting with the Saudi chief on the eve of the negotiations. Accordingly, Hakki protested in London that Ibn Saud could be so intransigent only if he had a reason to believe that Britain would intervene. But if Britain were to convey to Ibn Saud the impression that the British would not view with disfavor an Ottoman sea expedition, he would easily come to terms.[47]

Thus, in the aftermath of the failure of the negotiations, both parties had diametrically opposed expectations about the British. While the Saudis waited for the British to intervene now that negotiations had reached a deadlock, the Ottomans grew more adamant in their opposition to British mediation. The Foreign Office was completely swayed by the "Ottoman" case. Secretary Grey did not wish "to lend color" to the Porte's suspicions that Britain supported "Ibn Saud's policy of making himself independent." Grey now tended to discount all indications that the eventual Saudi-Ottoman settlement would be inimical to British interests, and he disregarded the Foreign Office's very arguments in the March 9 memorandum. Not only was Britain not going to offer her mediation, but also "no communications with Ibn Saud should be held except in cases where they cannot be avoided."[48] In short, Britain's policy toward Ibn Saud reverted once more to the position that had prevailed prior to the Saudi occupation of Hasa.

The shift in British policy was caused by the developments in Europe, where the deteriorating situation would in a matter of weeks lead to the outbreak of World War I. Striving to pre-empt a potential German-Ottoman alliance, the Foreign Office was determined to abstain from any action that might arouse Ottoman susceptibilities. Viewed against this background of the European theater, the Saudi issue and even British interests in the gulf were perceived as marginal.

Conclusion of Saudi-Ottoman Treaty

Britain's failure to intervene once more left the Ottomans and the Saudis with the necessity to settle their differences on their own. Ibn Saud had had now his army mobilized for almost three months, and he badly needed a respite. He assumed that the Ottomans had drawn the proper lesson from his strong posture during the negotiations and consequently would be more forthcoming. But simultaneously he gathered from the consistent Ottoman determination to reinstate their troops that for the Porte the issue had become a symbol of Ottoman authority over that part of the peninsula. And he calculated that in the final analysis the Porte would be content with the restoration of only a symbolic garrison. He decided, therefore, to accept a small Ottoman force deprived of any military significance, which would both satisfy the Porte and not conflict with Saudi interests.

The Ottomans, for their part, reciprocated in kind and displayed a more accommodating state of mind. As Ibn Saud was ready to recognize their sovereignty over Nejd and Hasa, and as agreement had been reached on most of the issues, they could not let the one issue of the garrisons block a settlement. The Ottoman Empire was in no way ready to undertake large-scale military operations in eastern Arabia, the more so after Britain had so clearly demonstrated its opposition to any Ottoman naval operation in the Persian Gulf. With the exclusion of the military option, the only alternative was a settlement, if Ibn Saud could be made to accept a face-saving formula regarding the garrison.

With both parties disposed to an accommodation over the issue of the Hasa garrisons, a bargaining situation evolved. Ibn Saud's agent in Basra, 'Abd al-Latif Mandil, and the Ottoman authorities there easily reached an agreement, which was approved by the Porte and came to be known as the Ottoman-Saudi Treaty of May 1914 (see Appendix A). The sultan issued an imperial firman, or decree, on July 8, which officially and publicly nominated Ibn Saud as the wali of Nejd, thereby elevating the Saudi territories to a wilayet, the highest administrative unit in the Ottoman state. The war minister then congratulated Ibn Saud for strengthening "the great Ottoman Government." A month later, the Ottoman minister of interior conferred upon Ibn Saud "the august dignity of supreme ministership" in recognition of his "sincere loyalty and great attachment to the Ottoman throne."[49]

The treaty was signed by Ibn Saud himself and by the wali of Basra, Sulaiman Shafiq Ibn 'Ali Kamali, and was dated "4th Rajab 1332—15th May 1914." The identity of the signatories and the date of the treaty raise several questions as to when and where the treaty was actually signed. That the treaty was not signed at the end of the negotiations at Subaihiyya is evident from two factors. First, the Ottoman deputation and Ibn Saud left Subaihiyya on May 4, the deputation returning to Basra and Ibn Saud to Riyadh, so that the treaty, dated May 15, could not have been signed there. Second, the wali of Basra, who signed the treaty on behalf of the Porte, was not present at all in the Subaihiyya negotiations. Moreover, the treaty could not have been signed by the wali and Ibn Saud on the same day, May 15, because the wali was then in Basra and Ibn Saud in Riyadh.

In fact, two different dates appear at the top of the document, because the Muslim date 4th Rajab 1332 did not correspond to May 15, 1914, but rather to May 29, 1914. This apparent "mistake" provides the answer to the whole dilemma. The wali signed the treaty on May 15, and then 'Abd al-Latif Mandil, Ibn Saud's agent, had to deliver it to Ibn Saud in Riyadh for his signature. Mandil later confided to the British agent in Bahrain that he had been sent to Ibn Saud with a royal firman and a draft treaty.[50] Ibn Saud signed the treaty and dated it 4 Rajab, which was May 29. Thus, the two dates on the treaty represent the actual dates on which the signatories affixed their signatures on the treaty: May 15 *and* 4 Rajab (May 29).

In the treaty, Ibn Saud recognized Ottoman sovereignty over Nejd and himself as an Ottoman subject. He promised to hoist the Ottoman flag on all government buildings and undertook to support the Porte in case it had "to fight with a foreign Power" or to restore order in other wilayets.[51] In foreign affairs, Ibn Saud explicitly surrendered his external sovereignty. He undertook "not to interfere with or correspond about foreign affairs and international treaties" and promised not to grant concessions to foreigners. The compromise regarding the garrisons provided for the stationing of "Ottoman soldiers and gendarmerie," whose number would be determined by Ibn Saud. In exchange, the Porte appointed Ibn Saud the wali of Nejd, and the wilayet was conferred upon the Saudi family on a hereditary basis.

There was no reference in the treaty to Qatar and Trucial Oman, against which the Porte allegedly gave Ibn Saud a carte blanche, and it is impossible to ascertain whether there was any verbal agreement to this effect. At any rate, Ibn Saud's future attitude toward the gulf principalities could hardly be affected by an Ottoman promise. As his past and future behavior indicated, his perception of Britain's predominant status in the gulf dictated his policies vis-à-vis the sheikhdoms. Britain's presence determined his conduct in two respects. First, despite the conclusion of the treaty with the Ottomans, he still needed Britain to achieve his ultimate aim of independence from the Porte, and he could therefore not afford to alienate the British by moving against the principalities. Second, he realized that Britain was committed to the independence of the sheikhdoms and could crush him if he were to act against its interests.

Ibn Saud's agreement with the Porte functioned in three contexts: Ottoman, British, and domestic Saudi. In the context of Ottoman-Saudi relations, the treaty signified substantial gains for Ibn Saud. He managed to avoid a military encounter with Ottoman might by embroiling the British in the dispute and by proceeding cautiously between an early, uncompromising bargaining position and a timely realization of the inevitability of compromise. He not only incorporated Hasa into the Saudi entity but also secured Ottoman recognition of the new reality just several months after the Porte had expressed its determination to restore its direct authority over Hasa. He managed to prevent the reinstatement of the Ottoman garrisons in Hasa, thus removing what might have become a constant threat and irritant to his freedom of action. Compared to the terms of the initial six-point Ottoman proposal, the treaty constituted a substantial improvement as far as Saudi interests were concerned. Finally, the treaty reflected the new status Ibn

Saud secured for the Saudi entity. In the previous Ottoman-Saudi agreement of February 1905, the Porte had recognized the territories under Saudi control as constituting merely a qadha and the Saudi ruler as merely a qa'im-maqam. Now the Saudi territories were elevated by two ranks to the top rank, a wilayet.

In the context of British-Saudi relations, the May 1913–May 1914 period was pivotal for Ibn Saud. His occupation of Hasa propelled the Saudi issue to the forefront of British attention. After displaying an indifferent attitude toward Ibn Saud for eleven years, Great Britain had to modify its policy and enter into relations with the Saudis. This period witnessed both the first official communications between the parties and the first official meetings between Ibn Saud and British officers. Although the ultimate Saudi goal of securing official protection from Britain along the lines of the Kuwaiti model remained still in limbo, the Saudis succeeded in achieving their immediate goal of drawing Britain into the framework of their bilateral relations with the Porte and using British power as a counterweight to Ottoman pressure. Britain's intervention in March and April 1914, both by offering mediation and by protesting against Ottoman policies, significantly constrained the Ottoman freedom of action against the Saudis and consequently improved Ibn Saud's bargaining position. Local British authorities were conscious of their contribution, indicating that, by "causing the Porte to believe that he was applying for British protection, Ibn Saud extracted better terms than he would otherwise have obtained."[52] The final reversal in Britain's position and her withdrawal from active intervention could not change this reality, for by then the Ottomans had already become aware of both British-Saudi contacts and Britain's opposition to any Ottoman operation in the Persian Gulf.

The domestic Saudi context is the most difficult to fathom, owing to the paucity of available information. According to Mubarak, who was well-informed of the situation in Nejd, a strong anti-Ottoman atmosphere prevailed in Riyadh. In an interview with Grey, Mubarak volunteered to predict that Ibn Saud would find it impossible to reach any agreement with the Porte, even if he wished to do so, because of the prevailing mood.[53] The opposition to any Saudi agreement with the Ottomans, so strongly displayed in 1905, must have been of no less a magnitude in 1914. With the increase in

Saudi strength since 1905 and the extension of Saudi rule over most of Nejd, there was presumably a concomitant increase in the hostility toward the Porte. But such opposition did not deter Ibn Saud or prevent him from concluding a treaty with the Ottomans when he viewed it as inevitable or essential to Saudi interests. It is probable that he had to conceal the existence of the treaty from the ulama in Riyadh, which accounts for the fact that the Saudi archives contain no reference to the treaty and all biographies of Ibn Saud ignore the issue.

Following the conclusion of the treaty there was a sudden absence of Saudi correspondence with the British. For nearly two months the British authorities were left in the dark regarding the fate of the Saudi-Ottoman negotiations, and it was not owing to Ibn Saud's efforts that the situation was finally clarified. The first to learn of the conclusion of the negotiations were the four political agents at Basra, Kuwait, Bahrain, and Muscat, who gathered from scattered information that a treaty had been concluded. The British did not learn about the full scope of the treaty until January 1915, after they had captured Basra and found the treaty in the Ottoman archives there.[54] Given the intensive correspondence that Ibn Saud had conducted with the British prior to the conclusion of the treaty, his abrupt silence was striking.

The reason had to do with the double role that Ibn Saud envisaged for Britain. In the short run, he sought to draw the British into his dispute with the Ottomans in order to solidify his occupation of Hasa, prevent an Ottoman sea attack, and improve his bargaining position. With the conclusion of the treaty, both objectives were secured, and there was no immediate role that Britain could play. In the long run, Ibn Saud strove to induce the British to establish a protectorate over the Saudi entity similar to the one they had established in Kuwait. But his two interviews with British officials—with Shakespear and Trevor in December 1913 and Grey in April 1914—led him to conclude that this was unobtainable in the foreseeable future. He learned from Grey that Britain had just concluded an agreement with the Ottomans and would certainly not jeopardize its entente with the Porte for the Saudi cause. He realized that considerations beyond his control dictated the British attitude toward him and that there was no chance Britain would grant him protection against the Porte.[55] With his immediate goals secured and with Britain incapable of playing the long-term role he had designed for it, Ibn Saud had no reason to pursue his correspondence with British authorities and thereby violate the treaty he had just concluded with the Porte.

Ibn Saud could be satisfied with his achievements so far. Just twelve years after he had made a modest reappearance in Riyadh, he had succeeded in restoring the two traditional centers of the Saudi state, Nejd and Hasa. His long-term goal of securing independence from the Ottomans through Britain could not be achieved for the time being, because for Great Britain the relations with the Porte by far outweighed the Saudi issue. Viewed from London, Ibn Saud's significance was too marginal to allow a disruption in Ottoman-British relations. It became apparent to him that a change in Saudi-British relations, and hence a possible realization of Saudi goals, might emerge only from a radical change in the bilateral relations between Britain and the Porte. When Ibn Saud concluded the treaty with the Ottomans in May 1914, he could not possibly have known that such a radical change would occur just three months later.

5

Independence and British Protection, 1914–1915

The British Government invite your cooperation in liberating Basra from the Ottomans. In return we promise to enter into treaty relations with you.

Knox to Ibn Saud

I am a person who desires to remain quiet and in repose so that my state may not become impaired. As for the war, I hope God will give the victory to those from whom advantage comes to us.

Ibn Saud to Knox and Mubarak

The desirability of concluding a treaty with Ibn Saud flows not only from the exigencies of the War but also from his postwar status as master of a long strip of the Coast.

India Office to Foreign Office

THE OUTBREAK OF World War I in the autumn of 1914 was to change the nature of the Saudi-Ottoman-British triangle drastically. It was also to constitute a turning point in the history of the Saudi state, bringing about in just fourteen months the realization of a long-desired Saudi goal.

As the Ottoman Empire slid into alliance with Germany, the British sought to ensure the cooperation of Persian Gulf rulers should a war against the Ottomans become inevitable. This raised in particular the question of Ibn Saud, the only real uncertainty in the situation, which had been generally settled by 1914 through the Persian Gulf treaty system. Having rejected all his overtures since 1902, the British found themselves in an awkward relationship with Ibn Saud, who could be an asset to either side in a war. As an ally, Ibn Saud could conceivably attack from central Arabia west toward the Red Sea, north into Syria across the Ottoman line of advance into Egypt, or northeast into Mesopotamia. As an enemy, he could threaten the British position in the Persian Gulf and advance against the western flank of the Indian Expeditionary Force to be sent into Mesopotamia. Nevertheless, most British officials did not foresee any reason for concern in this respect. The acting resident in the gulf, Knox, predicted that the Arab chiefs would rise against the Porte even without British encouragement. And Gertrude Bell, a well-known traveler before she joined the Arab Bureau in 1915, reasoned that as Ibn Saud had been most anxious to secure some definite British recognition, he would be easy to recruit as an ally.[1]

The Porte, to be sure, faced precisely the same problem, securing the support of the Arab chiefs, and Ibn Saud's importance must have been highly appreciated. As early as July 1914, three months before war was declared between Great Britain and the Ottoman Empire, the Ottoman war minister, Enver Pasha, assigned to Ibn Saud a role for the contingency of war. Ibn Saud would have to end his quarrel with Ibn Rashid and move northward to an area between Kuwait and Zubair in order to protect Basra against a possible British advance. Arms, ammunition, and officers would be sent to him in preparation for an offensive against the British and those in Treaty relations with them. As a sign of goodwill, Enver's communication was accompanied with a gift of T.L. 10,000 for Ibn Saud.[2]

As in the past, Ibn Saud was quick to notify the British of the Ottoman approach, expecting to learn their reaction before he responded.[3] Aware of the outbreak of the War in Europe, he hoped the British would reconsider their attitude toward him, as their vital interests might now be at stake. Ibn Saud's calculation proved justified, for the Saudi communication, received by the resident on September 27, promptly alarmed the British government. The previous British confidence in Ibn Saud's behavior was now replaced by a concern that he might be persuaded to side with the Porte. Furthermore, reports reaching British Intelligence in Cairo indicated that Ibn Saud had "definitely identified himself with the Turks whom he had promised to assist by the dispatch of a considerable force."

To forestall Ibn Saud's subversion, the India Office proposed to send an emissary to convince him to side with Britain in the event of war. The choice of Captain Shakespear as the emissary was unanimously endorsed by all British officials concerned with Arabian policies, by virtue of his being the most competent British political officer on Saudi affairs. Shakespear and Ibn Saud had met no less than five times previously and spent altogether nineteen days in discussions, cultivating a strong personal friendship and enjoying a high regard for each other. Shakespear was also an ideal envoy because of his fluency in Arabic, military background, profound knowledge of the tribes, and political flair for dealing with the chiefs of Arabia and the Gulf. Even Mallet in Constantinople, previously averse to British contacts with the Saudis, supported the scheme of using Ibn Saud against the Ottomans.[4]

In early October, Knox informed Ibn Saud that Shakespear was being dispatched to him with a message from the British government. The political agent at Bahrain was instructed to make the Saudi ruler understand that the situation was "urgent." The British also employed Mubarak, who wrote to Ibn Saud that Germany was working to alienate the Ottomans from Britain and that it was hoped that he would use his influence to maintain peace in Arabia.[5]

Ibn Saud must have wondered when he found himself in the unprecedented position of being wooed by both powers. But most significant for him was the fact that it was the British who were soliciting his help, whereas in all previous occasions, it had been he who had sought their support. He understood that if the British government had deemed it necessary to dispatch Shakespear all the way from England, his assistance was greatly needed. While determined to take full advantage of his newly created position, he decided to remain noncommittal until the British position was completely clarified.

Accordingly, on October 24, 1914, Ibn Saud replied to Knox's letter by pointing to the "love and friendship" between the British and the Saudis, but he made no reference to his position, stating merely that he was expecting Shakespear. In another letter, welcoming Shakespear, Ibn Saud's caution and desire to remain noncommittal were all the more apparent. Apprehensive lest the Ottomans find out about his imminent meeting with Shakespear, he advised Shakespear to stay at Bahrain and correspond from there. If a personal meeting was inevitable, he asked Shakespear to come only on the condition that he disguise himself as an Arab so that "no one should know of your coming," as "we must first know the reality and be on the look out." Proceeding on the same lines, he accepted gifts of money and some armaments that the Ottomans had sent to him, but he deferred a response to their approach until after the British offers became known.[6]

In short, at this stage Ibn Saud was sitting on the fence. He was unwilling to commit himself to the British before their position was clearly stated, lest he alienate the Ottomans without having first obtained solid British support. And he was similarly reluctant to side with the Ottomans, being permanently hostile to them and hoping that the coming events might produce at long last the long-sought British protection.

British Offer of Protection

The last day of October 1914 witnessed the turning point when Great Britain and the Ottoman Empire found themselves at war. On that day the British issued a proclamation to all Persian Gulf rulers, "who have sought freedom from the Ottoman oppressor," to preserve order and reject the "talk of *Jihad*." A second proclamation was issued the next day, guaranteeing the holy towns of Arabia and the holy places in Iraq from any attack by British forces. The official declaration of war between Britain and the Ottoman Empire then came on November 5.[7]

On November 3, Knox informed Ibn Saud of the invitation of His Majesty's government to him to cooperate with Mubarak and Khaz'al, the sheikh of Muhammara, in the liberation of Basra from the Ottomans. Alternatively, Ibn Saud was asked to prevent any Ottoman reinforcements from reaching Basra until the British arrived to seize the place and to protect British subjects and their goods from plunder. In return, the British promised to protect Ibn Saud from an Ottoman attack by sea, recognize his independence in all Nejd, Hasa, and Qatif and conclude a treaty with him. Attached to the letter were the texts of the two proclamations to the gulf rulers as evidence of British sincerity. Simultaneously Ibn Saud received Shakespear's letter insisting on a personal meeting and claiming that, as he was an official representative of the British government, he could not come in disguise.[8]

Once acquainted with the declaration of war, Ibn Saud wished for a total Ottoman defeat. The Porte's victory could not but spell the end of all Saudi hopes of independence. But British victory was by no means guaranteed, and a vengeful Ottoman return was a horrifying prospect. Even given a British victory, one could not exclude the possibility of an Ottoman-British agreement following the war that would provide for the restoration of the Ottomans to certain parts of Arabia. If a total alienation of the Porte was therefore undesirable, Ibn Saud could not comply with Britain's request that he participate in liberating Basra from the Ottomans.

Another thing, however, became clear to Ibn Saud: as the British and the Ottomans were already at war and the probability of obtaining independence loomed large, there was no reason for him to commit himself to the Ottoman plan conveyed by Enver. The Saudi chief, to be sure, did not couch his response to the Porte in anti-Ottoman terms. Instead, he cited local inhibitions as preventing him from participating in the Ottoman scheme: he had to stay and defend his domain and could not come north until Ibn Rashid had actually moved against Egypt.[9]

As a response to Knox's letter of assurances was also necessary, Ibn Saud was confronted with an immediate dilemma. On the one hand, the British offered him all he had been asking for since 1902: independence and protection. But on the other hand, he could not and did not want to comply with their request that he participate actively in liberating Basra. In short, Ibn Saud sought to obtain the British assurances without having to deliver his part of the bargain as stipulated by the British.

Accordingly, on November 28, 1914, Ibn Saud responded to both Knox and Shakespear, assuring them that "I am one of the great helpers of the British" and that "my hopes are strong in God and then in the Glorious Government." Offers of practical assistance, however, were conspicuously absent, and Ibn Saud described himself as "a person who desired to remain quiet and in repose so that my state may not become impaired." As for the assurances, he was eager to discuss them with Shakespear and was leaving toward Kuwait for the purpose of negotiations. For Ibn Saud, the achievement of full independence was secondary in importance to retaining his present possessions. If he perceived that attaining independence entailed a serious risk of "impairing" the possession of his territories, then the risk was not worth taking. Ibn Saud's cautious conduct contrasted with that of Mubarak, who received a similar letter of assurances from Knox and mobilized his forces promptly.[10]

Meanwhile Shakespear arrived at the gulf on November 7. Cox, who reassumed the post of the gulf resident, instructed Shakespear to remain as permanent emissary to Ibn Saud and endeavor to bring him northward to cooperate with the British forces in Mesopotamia. The assistance that Cox intended to obtain from Ibn Saud was by no means confined to the occupation of Basra. As soon as the town was occupied on November 22, Cox informed the viceroy that he had sent Shakespear to bring Ibn Saud north "to help suppress hostile activities by the tribes between Basra and Baghdad."[11] The original British aim was to secure Ibn Saud's active alliance against the Ottomans in Mesopotamia.

In the meantime, the Ottomans renewed their pressure on Ibn Saud to participate in their scheme. In early December they dispatched four ulama to Nejd to preach the obligation of jihad incumbent upon any devoted Muslim once his ruler faced the Christian infidel. From Basra they sent Sayyid Talib to Ibn Saud in order to achieve a reconciliation between the Saudis and the Rashidis and enlist Ibn Saud in a jihad against the British. Shakespear was apprehensive that Ibn Saud might be persuaded to comply with the Ottomans' demands, but the Saudi leader had already decided to abstain from participating in the Ottoman plan. Once the four Ottoman emissaries arrived, Ibn Saud placed them in an honorable confinement lest their preaching become too effective. To offset any possible anti-British sentiments among his people, Ibn Saud had the British Proclamation on the Holy Places read in one of his public assemblies, comparing the British government, which, though of another faith, was prepared to bind itself by such a proclamation, to the Ottomans who, though of the same faith, had continually oppressed their subjects.[12]

At the same time, Ibn Saud's decision to refrain from active support of the British in Mesopotamia was reinforced, paradoxically, by Cox himself, who reasoned that "your affairs will now prosper because your territory will become free of Ottoman annoyance and interference from which you have suffered hitherto."[13] If Ibn Saud was to get rid of the Ottomans anyway, without active struggle against them, he did not see why he should undertake an active military role with all the risks it entailed. But he did want the treaty and the protection the British offered him in exchange for his support. When Shakespear arrived on December 31, 1914, the problem of how to attain these goals without paying the price had to be resolved.

Rejection of Active Military Role

Ibn Saud and Shakespear met at Khufaisa and conducted the negotiations during the first three days of 1915.[14] Ibn Saud felt obliged to explain his failure to comply with Knox's request that he assist in the onslaught on Basra. It was not that he did not trust the British any more or had abandoned his desire to come under British protection. But Knox's letter had placed him in a delicate position: he had been asked to wage war against his sovereign by a power which, six months earlier, had left him to negotiate on his own. At the same time, the assurances he had been offered were informal, did not constitute a binding instrument, and did not even specify whether they were limited merely to the war or remained valid for the postwar period. The risk of alienating the Ottomans permanently and irrevocably was too great to be outweighed by vague promises. Nor could he now commit himself any further until he possessed a definite signed treaty with Great Britain.

In order to expedite the conclusion of such a treaty, Ibn Saud submitted to Shakespear six main proposals: Ibn Saud would be recognized as the independent ruler of Nejd, Hasa, and Qatif, with a dynastic guarantee; in boundary disputes with chiefs under British protection, decisions would follow ancestral rights; the *Shari'a* would apply to all Muslims in his territories, whether Saudi subjects or not; Great Britain would defend the Saudi territories from external aggression by land or sea; Great Britain would not harbor refugees from his territory; and the British government would treat Saudi subjects in its territories with the same consideration as its own. In return, Ibn Saud was prepared to undertake four guarantees of his own: to have no dealings with any other power and to give no concessions except after consulting with the British government; to protect trade within his territories; to protect British subjects and protégés in his ports; and to prohibit the arms traffic, provided he could obtain his own needs through the British government.

Ibn Saud's suggestions, prima facie, were striking in the sense that they did not contain any reference to the British *raison d'être* for the talks, namely the role he was to play in the British war effort against the Ottomans. This was chiefly the result of his refusal to fight the Ottomans before their expulsion from Arabia became irreversible and his reluctance to play a military role far from his territories, leaving them vulnerable to a Rashidi attack. His proposals thus revealed that the explanations he had given in November for failing to comply with Knox's request were excuses. For if the only reason he could not support Britain in Mesopotamia was that Knox's letter was not a binding instrument and did not ensure British protection beyond the war period, then once British assurances were embodied within a binding treaty not limited to the war period, Ibn Saud's military assistance should have been unquestionable. Nevertheless, his proposals, while envisaging a comprehensive treaty containing all the British assurances, lacked any reference to the military services he was asked to render. Ibn Saud clearly sought the British assurances for which he had longed since 1902 without having to reciprocate by a binding military role.

The British could not be expected to conclude a treaty on the lines he suggested if it would not secure the goal that had prompted their very approach to him. The Saudi leader therefore sought leverage to induce the British to conclude a treaty without committing himself to fight the Ottomans in exchange. The leverage he employed focused on the damage he was capable of causing the British, should he opt to side with the Ottomans, rather than on the assistance he was prepared to contribute to the British effort. Using moderate language, he threatened that if the treaty was not concluded soon, "I fear force of circumstances may drive me to give some overt demonstration of my intention to side with the Porte." The presence of the four Ottoman emissaries was promptly brought to Shakespear's notice in order to lend weight to the warning.

The contribution that Ibn Saud offered the British was thus essentially of a negative and indirect character. It consisted of three elements: he would not implement his part in the Ottoman plan and would not take any actions that could prejudice British interests; he would prevent Ibn Rashid from advancing toward Egypt; and by not joining an Ottoman-Rashidi alliance, he would secure the British in Mesopotamia from attack on their western flank. By his sole decision, Ibn Saud could therefore cause the miscarriage of the whole of the original Ottoman plan. As a further sign of goodwill toward Britain, he dismissed the four Ottoman emissaries with a message to the effect that, as Ibn Rashid was actually engaged in hostilities with him, no cooperation was possible. He also informed the Ottomans that he could not align himself with their forces lest the British attack his seaboard on the Persian Gulf. The Ottomans did not treat Ibn Saud's argument as a pretext. One of their chief commanders expressed understanding of Ibn Saud's inaction "as he was too near the English who could do him enormous harm."[15]

Transformation of British Perspective

That Shakespear understood Ibn Saud's position is evident from his conclusion that Ibn Saud had no intention of abandoning his freedom to make his own terms with the Ottomans, from whom he was confident he could secure a very good "second best," until he held a signed treaty with Britain. Shakespear's report constituted the first step in the process whereby Britain's expectations from the Saudis, in exchange for British obligations, underwent a thorough transformation. Listing the advantages likely to accrue from a Saudi-British treaty—control of the Arab littoral of the Persian Gulf, control of the arms traffic, impetus to British trade, and exclusion of foreign powers from central Arabia—Shakespear made no reference to Saudi assistance to the British war effort. Aware that Ibn Saud had not addressed himself to any of the original British requests for military support, Shakespear sought to convince his superiors that a binding understanding was nevertheless necessary: "The cooperation Ibn Saud has furnished by his own attitude and his influence with other Arab chiefs has been of no less value than the active support asked for by our letter of assurances of 3 November 1914, and deserved generous response from His Majesty's Government."[16]

That Cox understood the nature of Ibn Saud's position is evident from his immediate reaction: "we could not expect any help from Ibn Saud in the region of the Euphrates." In addition, Cox was alarmed by the leverage Ibn Saud had employed, his undisguised threat to give some overt demonstration "of my intention to side with the Ottomans," which Cox did not treat as a bluff. Ibn Saud's threat was now matched by Cox's admonition. Reminding Ibn Saud that the Ottomans had been worn at all points and were in a weak position, Cox advised him not to commit himself to any action which "could prejudice your position in the eyes of His Majesty's Government." As for the treaty, Cox assured him that it was possible to reach an agreement on the lines Ibn Saud proposed, even though it would take time to draw up.

Transmitting Ibn Saud's proposals to India, Cox added that Ibn Saud should undertake five additional points: to receive a British political agent at Hasa or Riyadh; to abstain from waging war by sea without British consent and to cooperate in the suppression of piracy; to protect pilgrim traffic passing through Saudi territory; to agree to extraterritoriality for British non-Muslim subjects; and to levy custom dues at reasonable rates, allow British merchants' vessels to visit Hasa ports, and locate post and telegraph offices at one of Hasa's ports. Concerning Ibn Saud's desire to extend British protection to any external aggression by land, Cox commented that, as the only potential power in question was the Ottoman Empire, the British government incurred little risk by giving the desired undertaking, subject to the reservation that "aggression be unprovoked."[17]

Outstanding in Cox's draft was the absence of any allusion to Ibn Saud's participation in the British war effort. This omission illuminated not only the success of Ibn Saud's tactics but also the transformation of Cox's conception of Saudi support from an active military role in Mesopotamia to a friendly neutrality or, at best, indirect and passive assistance. Proposing Ibn Saud's terms as well as his five additional points as the basis for a treaty, Cox asked authorization for the draft to be negotiated by Shakespear.

The government of India, which expected an agreement with the Saudis on the lines of Knox's letter of assurances of November 3, was surprised by the detailed comprehensiveness of Cox's draft. Ibn Saud's terms specifically raised many touchy problems, such as the boundaries of his state, the dynastic guarantee he sought, and last but not least, his demand for jurisdiction over Muslim-British subjects. The resolution of these problems would take a long time, and meanwhile, Ibn Saud might make good his threat.

Accordingly, India informed Cox that, as a detailed treaty on the lines suggested by Ibn Saud was fraught with difficulties, it preferred to conclude an immediate preliminary treaty, containing four broad principles. Britain would recognize Ibn Saud as the independent ruler of Nejd, Hasa, and Qatif and guarantee hereditary succession, subject to the reservation that the ruler was accepted by the tribesmen and approved by the British government. In the event of unprovoked aggression by any foreign power, the British were prepared to aid Ibn Saud to such an extent and in such a manner as the situation required. In return, Ibn Saud would agree to have no dealings with or grant concessions to any power. And finally, Ibn Saud and Great Britain would agree to conclude soon a detailed treaty in regard to other matters jointly concerning them.[18] Significantly, the Indian government did not even raise the question of Ibn Saud's active military support, in exchange for which the original British assurances were to be granted, for by now all Indian authorities had become convinced that such Saudi support was unlikely to materialize.

The framework of the Saudi-British deal, which India had sought since October 1914, had thus undergone a veritable metamorphosis. Whereas the three initial British assurances were to be matched by active and direct Saudi assistance, India was now ready to grant the same assurances, in the framework of a treaty, in exchange for Saudi neutrality only and, at best, indirect assistance coupled with British domination over Saudi foreign policy.

At this moment, London was completely unaware of the transformation. Having learned of Ibn Saud's forthcoming battle with Ibn Rashid, the India Office inquired how that battle would affect "Saudi cooperation with us in Mesopotamia in return for which our assurances had been given." The Indian authorities then had to acquaint the India Office with the new parameters, indicating that, as the November assurances were contingent upon the Saudi cooperation in Basra, a condition not fulfilled, the assurances were no longer valid without the conclusion of a further treaty.[19]

The India Office, obliged to explain the proposed Saudi-British deal to the Foreign Office, submitted a masterful essay in statesmanship.[20] It offered a new conceptual framework for the recently transformed British position and created thereby the basis for future Saudi-British relations. It was true, the India Office argued, that Ibn Saud had not actively supported the British effort in Mesopotamia. But then he was engaged in hostilities with Ibn Rashid, who had been supplied with Ottoman money, arms, and officers. Indirectly and negatively, therefore, he might be said to have assisted the British so far as to justify favorable consideration for his claim. But an even more important factor heightened the desirability of a treaty with Ibn Saud. This was not the exigencies of the war but rather the general situation that would be created in the Persian Gulf if Ottoman rule finally disintegrated because of the war. In the interest of peace, it would be essential for Britain, as the power that controlled the Persian Gulf, to have a working arrangement with Ibn Saud, who would be left the master not only of central Arabia but also of a long strip of the gulf coast. The common denominator in these two sets of considerations was that both Ibn Saud's demands and the price Britain was prepared to pay for his friendship had to be measured not so much by the services which the Saudi ruler was expected to render but by the potential power for mischief which he did and would possess.

By adding the new consideration of Ibn Saud's postwar importance in the gulf context, the India Office introduced a new dimension, unrelated to the war, which was anchored in Ibn Saud's status as a gulf ruler. Implicit in the India Office's argument was the claim that British interests required that the Saudi entity, by virtue of its conversion into a gulf principality, be absorbed into the network of treaties which bound all other gulf territories to Great Britain. Indicative of this underlying assumption and of the importance attached to the gulf context was the India Office's proposal to add a clause to the four already suggested by the Indian government, binding Ibn Saud to abstain from interference with the affairs of Kuwait, Bahrain, Qatar, and the Trucial Coast. Thus, all five proposed clauses bore a close relationship to the gulf network of treaties and none whatsoever to the British war effort.

The Foreign Office raised no objections. On the contrary, Oliphant, an assistant secretary, noted that he "earnestly" supported the "immediate conclusion of a preliminary treaty," and Nicolson, the under-secretary, suggested that the British not be "too cautious" about the terms of the treaty. Accordingly, the Foreign Office not only concurred in the proposed draft but also asserted that Secretary Grey "shares the views expressed in the India Office's letter." On February 6, 1915, the government of India authorized Cox to enter into negotiations with Ibn Saud through Shakespear.[21]

The debate within the British government seemed somewhat academic, for on February 6 Shakespear had already been dead for two weeks, something that Cox did not know until February 16. After learning of Shakespear's arrival at the Saudi camp and apprehensive of a forthcoming British-Saudi alliance, the Ottomans had been determined to abort such a dangerous contingency. Thus, they supplied Ibn Rashid with money, arms, and ammunition and urged him to attack the Saudis at once. Ibn Saud, alerted to the Rashidis' preparations, was confident of his ability to defeat them. Even Shakespear predicted that "Ibn Saud's victory appears to be certain." The battle erupted at Jarab on January 24, with Shakespear present at the scene on the Saudi side. Accounts of the proceedings of the battle, in which Shakespear was a conspicuous figure dressed in British uniform and sun helmet, differ as to whether or not he was a combatant. The details of the battle notwithstanding, there is no doubt as to its result: the fight ended inconclusively, both sides suffering heavy casualties, including Captain Shakespear's death. Ibn Saud tried for some time to conceal his failure, informing Cox that the Rashidis "were slaughtered and defeated," but independent reports reaching Kuwait refuted his claim.[22]

Measured by the expectations he entertained, the battle was a serious setback for Ibn Saud. But the battle, coupled with Shakespear's death, did not influence the whole conduct of the war in the Middle East. Nor did this prompt the British to shift the focus of their Middle East strategy from Ibn Saud to Sharif Husain of the Hashemite family, who had been the guardian of the holy places in the Hejaz on behalf of the Ottomans from 1908 until aligning himself with Britain during the war. From the standpoint of British policy, Sharif Husain was religiously, politically, strategically, and militarily much more important than Ibn Saud. Hence, according to Gary Troeller, "Shakespear's untimely death would not have altered the factors which led Britain to concentrate her support on Husain."[23] Furthermore, from the standpoint of Saudi policy, Shakespear's death was even less significant. Ibn Saud never under any circumstances intended to assume an active military role in the British war effort, similar to the one assumed by the Sharifian family, by leading the Arabs in a fight against the Ottomans. This was the hopeful role assigned to him by Britain which he consistently rejected, as shown by his negotiations with Shakespear. Ibn Saud's firm position was formed on January 4, before the fateful battle of Jarab, while Shakespear was still alive, confident in Saudi power, and while Ibn Saud expected an easy victory. It could not, therefore, have been affected by the results of the January 24 battle.

Ibn Saud's position expressed in the negotiations contained profound and fundamental differences with that of Sharif Husain regarding their roles in the war. Throughout the negotiations, for example, Ibn Saud made it abundantly clear that he would not take part in active fighting against the Ottomans, even in exchange for a treaty, British protection, and recognition. Thus, he consistently refused to declare war against the Porte, despite the British urging. Husain, in contradistinction, did not have any reservations about declaring war and fighting the Ottomans. Ibn Saud was thoroughly reluctant as well to commit himself to large-scale military operations beyond the confines of his territories in Nejd, the reason being that "my state may become impaired." The whole thrust of Husain's commitment was based on a large-scale military role outside his territories in the Hejaz. Moreover, Ibn Saud had never expressed any desire to assume an all-Arab role beyond the Saudi context in Arabia proper. None of the points in his draft transcended the Saudi limits of Nejd, Hasa, and Qatif. The difference in this respect was striking, as Husain's demands envisioned a pan-Arab scheme, illuminated by both his pretentious title, "King of all Arabs," and the independent Arab state he sought to create. All British authorities accepted Ibn Saud's refusal to assume an active anti-Ottoman military role, and they conducted the entire negotiations prior to the Jarab battle on this basis. In the Sharifian case, however, the British negotiated from the position that any promises to Husain were to be granted only in return for an active "Arab Revolt" against the Ottomans.

The parameters of the proposed agreements were fundamentally different in many respects. In the Saudi case, there was to be no reference whatsoever to a Saudi contribution to the British war effort, the tacit understanding being that the Saudis would remain

neutral or, at best, provide indirect assistance. The British commitments to recognition of Saudi independence and protection of
the Saudis thus did not depend on any services the Saudis were
to render. In the Sharifian case, however, the British commitments
were directly related to and conditional upon the services Husain
was to provide the British effort.

Finally, the course of events following the Jarab encounter made
clear that the process of negotiations for the conclusion of the treaty
was affected neither by Ibn Saud's setback nor by Shakespear's
death. Ibn Saud immediately requested the resumption of negotiations without changing any of his previous stands. All the British
authorities involved emphasized the necessity to conclude the
agreement on the precise lines suggested before the battle. And the
draft treaty Cox dispatched to Ibn Saud on February 28 was precisely the same one he had been about to send to Shakespear before
his death became known.

The question comes down to the reasons behind Ibn Saud's pas-
sivity during the war. As far as Ibn Saud was concerned, he had
never been willing to commit himself to an active anti-Ottoman
role, and he had held this position consistently since the very first
British approach. His position did not originate from either the
Jarab battle or Shakespear's death. As for the British, until mid-
January they had indeed expected an active Saudi contribution to
their war effort. Once, however, Ibn Saud's reluctance became
known, all concerned authorities abandoned such expectations.
This shift occurred before the results of the Jarab encounter and
Shakespear's death became known in mid-February. In short, the
battle and Shakespear's death affected neither British-Saudi relations nor the terms of the proposed treaty and certainly not Ibn
Saud's contribution to the British war effort. A line of continuity
runs from early January, when Ibn Saud's and Shakespear's views
were presented in the negotiations, to February 28, when the negotiations were resumed, undisrupted by the January 24 battle
and Shakespear's death.

Ibn Saud lost no time after his setback at Jarab in making contact with Cox. Eager to resume the treaty negotiations, he suggested that either another British officer, "familiar with Arabic,"
be sent to him or negotiations be conducted with Cox through
correspondence. Cox, no less determined to pursue the negotia-

tions, sent Ibn Saud a draft treaty and urged him to sign it without delay (see Appendix B). The draft consisted of the four clauses suggested by the government of India, the one added by the India Office, and two added by Cox himself, committing Ibn Saud not to grant concessions to any power and to keep open the roads to the holy places. Cox assured the Saudi chief that as soon as the treaty was concluded, an officer would be dispatched to him to discuss the details of a second treaty. Attached to the draft treaty was a letter from the viceroy to Ibn Saud, expressing friendship to the Saudis, pointing to their common interests, and requesting him to sign the draft.[24]

As Cox was in Mesopotamia and Ibn Saud in Nejd, correspondence was maintained through the Saudi agent in Basra, 'Abd al-Latif Mandil. Hence, not until mid-April 1915 did Ibn Saud become acquainted for the first time with the preliminary treaty sought by the British, which was significantly different from the comprehensive one in which he was interested. But he accepted the new framework, while introducing a considerable number of modifications in the British text. These reflected Ibn Saud's desire to limit the extent of British control over Saudi affairs in scope and time, in order "to re-assure the governing family of Ibn Saud." Thus, he objected to the provision subjecting the selection of future Saudi rulers to the approval of the British government. Similarly, he deleted the word "unprovoked" from the provision defining the kind of aggression which entitled him to British protection. And, instead of allowing the British to determine the extent and manner of their aid, he stipulated that such aid would be "in all circumstances and in all places." In the same vein, he objected to the formula obliging him to follow "unreservedly" the advice of the British government and instead inserted the words "where his interests require it." Ibn Saud signed his draft (see Appendix B) and attached it to a letter to the viceroy, expressing friendship and goodwill toward the British government.[25]

Cox intended to belittle the significance of Ibn Saud's modifications. He was confident in his ability to convince the Saudi ruler in a personal meeting to yield on points unacceptable to the British and to reach a compromise on other points. On August 16, the Foreign Office concurred in the terms of the proposed text; one of its officials described as "satisfactory" Ibn Saud's readiness to accept the treaty "with only a few modifications." Cox was subsequently authorized to arrange a meeting with Ibn Saud to conclude the treaty. Addressing Ibn Saud personally, the viceroy expressed the hope that before long a treaty would be concluded, "which will formally seal the sincere friendship that exists between you and His Majesty's Government."[26]

In the meantime, Ibn Saud was preoccupied with more crucial developments within his own domain. After the encounter at Jarab, he faced what had occurred so often before in his moments of weakness: a tribal revolt, this time by the 'Ajman tribe in Hasa. He was fortunate to secure an understanding with Ibn Rashid on June 10, and for the moment he managed to avoid the necessity of fighting on two fronts. But in mid-July, in one of the severest encounters with the 'Ajman, Ibn Saud was seriously wounded, and his brother Sa'd was killed. Asking Cox for urgent assistance, Ibn Saud indicated that, as anxious as he was to meet Cox to conclude the treaty, he could not come to the coast for a while. Cox inquired as to the kind of assistance Ibn Saud was seeking, and as a temporary measure, he sent him 300 rifles, ammunition, and 10,000 rupees.[27]

By early September, Ibn Saud could divulge to Cox the nature of his present difficulties. An Ottoman officer had approached him, requesting an interview to deliver a letter and a present from the Ottoman war minister.[28] When the Saudi chief replied evasively, the Ottomans decided to take a more forceful stand against him. They pressed Ibn Rashid to break his recent agreement with the Saudis and encouraged the rebellious 'Ajman to pursue their revolt, supplying both with large amounts of arms and money. Ibn Saud now faced troubles on two fronts and asked Cox to furnish him with 3000 rifles, ammunition, and a loan of 50,000 rupees.

Cox viewed the new circumstances from two perspectives. On the one hand, if Ibn Saud were to be allied with the British, it was in their own interest that he should be the strongest element in central Arabia. Accordingly, Cox suggested a loan of 20,000 pounds, 1000 rifles, and 200,000 rounds of ammunition. On the other hand, Ibn Saud's troubles were useful in the sense that they might make him more tractable for the purpose of the treaty. Cox therefore suggested that, when informed of the British assistance, Ibn Saud should be asked to sign the revised treaty. The Indian government, the India Office, and the Foreign Office all agreed to Cox's proposals, except that only 374 rifles, available for immediate dispatch, were approved by the War Office. But as Cox was about to implement his plan, new circumstances again forced a change in the scheme. The Saudi forces in Qasim managed to repulse Ibn Rashid, and those in Hasa routed the 'Ajman. Ibn Saud, emerging from his domestic difficulties, asserted that a meeting was necessary in order to discuss "many matters in regard to which the interests of both parties are involved."[29]

It was now Britain's turn to delay the proposed meeting. Advancing in Mesopotamia with the Expeditionary Force as its chief political officer, Cox witnessed its defeat in Ctesiphon on November 25, 1915, retreated to Kut, and arrived back in Basra in early December. By then, two major developments compounded the defeat at Ctesiphon and endangered the British position both in the Persian Gulf region and in central Arabia. The Ottomans doubled their strenuous efforts to create an anti-British diversion in Arabia and decided to purchase some 40,000 camels for an attack on Egypt. At the same time Mubarak of Kuwait, a staunch ally of Britain, died, and his successor, Jabir, was reported to be under the influence of pro-Ottoman circles in Kuwait.[30] Against such a background, an alliance with Ibn Saud seemed all the more important and urgent. Cox left Mesopotamia and on December 26 crossed to Darin on the island of Tarut, where he and Ibn Saud met for the first time.

Given the ten-month period that had elapsed since Cox dispatched the draft for Ibn Saud's signature on February 28 until their meeting on December 26, the lengthy delay might suggest that following the Saudi defeat at Jarab and the death of Shakespear, the government of India had given up on Ibn Saud, whose active support could have been of use only to attack the Ottomans in Mesopotamia.[31] Active Saudi support in Mesopotamia, however, had been ruled out as early as mid-January, before the Jarab affair. Moreover, India continued to pursue the treaty negotiations as enthusiastically as it had done before the Jarab encounter. The delay must be attributed instead to objective reasons unrelated to both sides' desire to conclude a treaty. In the initial phase, lasting from February 28 to mid-August, the delay was caused by both Cox's presence in Iraq and the fact that the correspondence was conducted through the interior. This caused a lapse of four months between Cox's dispatch of the draft on February 28 and his acceptance of Ibn Saud's counterdraft on June 24. Another seven weeks passed while the draft was sent by sea from Basra to India and then to London, from June 26 to August 10. In the second phase, lasting till mid-October, Ibn Saud was engaged by the 'Ajman rebellion. In the final stage, Cox could not travel to Hasa until mid-December owing to the campaign in Mesopotamia.

Prior to negotiating the various clauses of the treaty, Cox expressed to Ibn Saud his apprehension lest Ibn Rashid advance toward Kuwait, and Cox urged the Saudi chief to win the Rashidis over to the British side. Ibn Saud replied that Ibn Rashid would not dare advance too far for fear that the Saudis would cut in against Hail in his rear. Ibn Saud would offer to be reconciled with them on condition that they came over to the British side or, failing that, agreed to remain neutral.[32]

Conclusion of Saudi-British Treaty

The negotiations between Cox and Ibn Saud focused mainly on the wording of Articles I, II, and IV, which had been the stumbling block all along. Ibn Saud was adamant against a provision in Article I subjecting the selection of future Saudi rulers to the approval of the British government. Cox tried to convince him that in the absence of such a clause, the British might find themselves committed to support an incompetent son, unpalatable to the tribes or unfriendly to the British. Ibn Saud retorted that in practice this was impossible, as the ruler had to enjoy the confidence of his tribes. The compromise stipulated that the ruler "shall not be antagonistic to the British government in any respect."

In Article II Ibn Saud insisted on the omission of the term "unprovoked," claiming that the word "aggression" (ta'adi) in itself implied the absence of justification. He was apprehensive lest the wording enable the British to refrain from assisting him, if at any time it would be inconvenient for them to do so. Similarly, he rejected the provision that left the extent and manner of British aid to the sole discretion of the British government. After all, the protection issue had been a cornerstone of his policy since 1902, and he wanted the clause now to be as unequivocal as possible.

Cox compromised on both points. He replaced "unprovoked" by "without reference to the British Government . . . giving them an opportunity of composing the matter." And he qualified Britain's sole discretion by adding "as the British Government . . . may consider most effective for protecting his [Ibn Saud's] interests and countries."

Ibn Saud rejected the provision in Article IV committing himself to follow "unreservedly" the advice of the British government, the more so as the Arabic translation seemed to render such an undertaking a general one. But then Cox opposed the Saudi phrasing, "where his [Ibn Saud's] interests require it." Finally they settled for a new formula, whereby Ibn Saud was to follow British advice "unreservedly, provided that it be not damaging to his own interests."

On December 26, 1915, Cox and Ibn Saud affixed their signatures on the treaty, which was duly ratified by the viceroy on July 18, 1916 (see Appendix C). Ibn Saud thus realized his two long-desired goals: independence from the Ottomans and British protection. The treaty constituted the first legal document attesting to the new international status of the Saudi state.[33] The major tactical achievement of Ibn Saud lay in his securing the treaty without having to commit himself to an irrevocable rupture with the Ottomans by declaring war and joining in active fighting against them, as the British would have liked him to do. He calculated that, even if the Ottomans did manage to return to Arabia following the war, he would still be able to mend relations with them by claiming that the treaty had been imposed on him by Britain, blaming Ibn Rashid for his failure to respond to Ottoman requests, and citing his refusal to participate in the British campaign and declare war against the Porte as signs of his friendly feelings. In contrast, if he had fought the Ottomans directly, totally alienating them, a possible Ottoman return would inevitably have been vengeful, similar to the one that had occurred a century before. He would have faced a grave dilemma had the British insisted that he participate in fighting the Ottomans in return for the treaty. But fortunately for him, the British did not, and he thus succeeded in transforming his role in the bargain from that of an active anti-Ottoman actor to that of a neutral, albeit friendly, Arab chief, sympathetic to the British. Furthermore, it was Ibn Saud himself who introduced the very notion of a treaty, increasing the level of British assurances from that of a temporary, nonbinding letter to a permanent formal agreement, while at the same time decreasing his commitment from that of active support to friendly neutrality.

Ibn Saud's diplomatic success was all the more remarkable when compared with Sharif Husain's conduct and demands in his negotiations with Britain. Whereas the Saudi leader insisted on a formal treaty, the sharif was content with a deal whose parameters were assurances embodied within nonbinding letters, in exchange for which he was prepared to offer an active military role—in other words, the very elements rejected by Ibn Saud. The British were aware of the basic difference. A Foreign Office memorandum explicitly noted that "our commitments to Husain are not embodied in any agreement or treaty signed, or even acknowledged, by both parties; in this, they differ from those given to Bin Saud." Another memorandum concluded that "the [Saudi] treaty, though never intended to be exhaustive, is on sounder lines than our treaty with the Idrisi [the ruler of Asir who signed a treaty with Britain on April 30, 1915] or our more informal arrangements with Husain." The sharif, in enthusiastic anticipation of his future status as king of an expanded territory, also neglected to assure that in any case his territorial base, the Hejaz, would be independent and protected. Ibn Saud, as much as he entertained the idea of further expansion, sought first and foremost to secure the independence of "Nejd, Hasa, Qatif, Jubail and the towns and ports belonging to them." Although Husain's immediate rewards were incomparably greater, in the long run these rewards could not safeguard his throne or guarantee the existence of the Hejaz as an independent state. In comparison to the sharif, therefore, Ibn Saud had more diplomatic skill.[34]

As for the British, their position had undergone a fundamental metamorphosis. Their initial approach to Ibn Saud, reversing a twelve-year policy, was wholly within the context of the war and aimed at securing Saudi participation in the Basra campaign and then northward in the region between Basra and Baghdad. Once the ice was broken, the process acquired a dynamic and momentum of its own. Thus, even when it became apparent that the expected Saudi role had to be ruled out, and furthermore when Ibn Saud demanded a treaty and not merely assurances, the British did not withdraw from the deal but accepted the new framework introduced by Ibn Saud. They did so because a Saudi-British treaty was imperative primarily in another context, the Persian Gulf network of treaties. And from January 21, 1915, it was this framework which acquired precedence over the war context. From the British point of view, a treaty with Ibn Saud had become a necessity in May 1913, when he assumed control over a part of the Persian Gulf coast. But priority had to be given for fifteen months to a higher set of considerations which emanated from British-Ottoman relations and focused on the sacred principle of "preserving the integrity of the Ottoman Empire." Once the outbreak of war removed the Ottoman obstacle, the road was open for the establishment of formal British-Saudi relations, culminating in the treaty.

As a whole, the treaty was patterned after the treaties concluded earlier with other Persian Gulf chiefs. British recognition and protection were reciprocated by pledges of nonalienation of territory and surrender of foreign relations. The major value of the treaty, as far as the British were concerned, lay in its negative aspects: pre-empting a possible Ottoman-Saudi alliance, preventing Saudi interference in the affairs of the gulf principalities, and excluding other powers from influence in the region. Another achievement was its success in avoiding a comprehensive treaty along the lines suggested by Ibn Saud, which would have involved determination of the boundaries of the Saudi territories, something that Britain wished to avoid.[35] In view of Ibn Saud's expected pretensions along the gulf coast, evident from his reference to "ancestral rights" as the criterion determining territorial disputes, this was no small achievement.

All British authorities were united in their support of the concluded treaty. Cox, the Foreign Office, the viceroy—all defined the final text as "satisfactory." In Cairo, that "Sharifian bastion," Dr. Hogarth wrote to the viceroy that the treaty was all to the good provided no pledge had been made to support Ibn Saud against Husain.[36] And such a pledge had never been made.

The treaty reflected the convergence of the Saudi interest in independence from the Porte and British protection with the British interest in absorbing the Saudis into their gulf treaty system and securing their friendly neutrality during the war. It was not a wartime instrument on the level of the British arrangement with the sharif or the treaty with the idrisi of Asir, though the initial impetus for the negotiations envisaged this type of agreements. The sharif committed himself to declare war and to launch the "Arab Revolt" against the Porte in exchange for which British commitments were granted: "If the Emir of Mecca is willing to assist Britain in the war against Turkey, England will guarantee . . ." etc. Similarly, the idrisi undertook "to attack and endeavor to drive the Turks from their stations" in a treaty whose "main objects are to war against the Turks," and as a quid pro quo, Britain undertook to safeguard and protect him. The Saudi leader, in contradistinction, did not undertake any such military role, and the Saudi-British treaty was devoid of any reference to the war. Indeed, the Foreign Office described the Saudi-British treaty as "containing all the elements of a true trucial treaty" and did not refer to it as a wartime instrument.[37]

Ibn Saud realized his two goals in 1915 in part because of a shift in British policy, external to any particular Saudi successes in this year. The outbreak of the World War caused a radical change in British-Ottoman relations, initiating the British overture to Ibn Saud. Had the Ottomans not aligned themselves with Germany against Britain, the British would not have been forced to invade Mesopotamia; hence they would not have approached the Saudis with the intention of securing their support in the campaign; and consequently they would not have concluded a treaty with them. In other words, had the previous pattern of Ottoman-British relations persisted after 1914, Ibn Saud would not have had the opportunity to attain his goals. Mubarak's success in 1899 was greater than Ibn Saud's in 1915. Whereas Ibn Saud managed to secure British protection only after British-Ottoman relations had undergone a radical change, Mubarak had succeeded in mobilizing British protection while the conciliatory framework of Ottoman-British relations was intact. But the rupture in British-Ottoman relations in the autumn of 1914 did not fully explain the conclusion of the treaty. The rift made possible a British overture to Ibn Saud, but it did not necessitate the conclusion of the treaty, especially after Ibn Saud failed to comply with the British request that he participate in the Basra campaign.

Thus, the roots of the treaty were not the outbreak of the war and Knox's first approach to Ibn Saud but rather Ibn Saud's own action, which obliged Britain to conclude a treaty with him. His occupation of Hasa forced the British government not only to establish relations with him but also to institutionalize such relations formally, with all the obligations that entailed. This necessity could not be, and was not, affected by his refusal to fight the Ottomans, because it emanated from the British interests in the Persian Gulf and transcended the war effort in time and scope. Had Ibn Saud not occupied Hasa, thus remaining merely a central Arabian ruler, the Persian Gulf dimension, which compelled the British to conclude the treaty with him, would have been nonexistent. Under such circumstances, his failure to participate actively in the Mesopotamia campaign would have spelled the end of the British readiness to enter into treaty relations with him. It is highly questionable whether the British would have been ready to pay in the form of a treaty for the mere neutrality of a central Arabian entity. But with the Saudi state controlling a significant part of the coast, Ibn Saud did not have to commit himself to a military role in Mesopotamia in order to secure the treaty. What started as a British effort to mobilize the Saudis in their war effort ended in a treaty, establishing a framework for Saudi-British relations and thereby rectifying, from a British point of view, an anomaly that had existed since May 1913.[38]

6

Between the Hammer and the Anvil, 1916–1918

As for your letter requesting assurances, such a letter could emanate only from a man bereft of his reason or of an absent mind.

Sharif Husain to Ibn Saud

We do not intend our own interests but those of the British Government. If you decide to . . . then that is my opinion too, as your opinion is the highest and superior.

Ibn Saud to Cox

As for your inciting us to fight the Turks, we have not done so . . . because we must consider our advantage and our harm.

Ibn Saud to Sharif Husain

WORLD WAR I CONFRONTED Ibn Saud with severe dilemmas which at times seemed insurmountable. He was forced to navigate his state, which had just recently acquired its independence, in and through four major spheres of activity that significantly curbed his freedom of action. These spheres were interdependent in the sense that Ibn Saud's achievements in any one of them had immediate adverse impact on the other three.

First, Ibn Saud was plagued by the revolts of the 'Ajman and al-Murra tribes in the east and south. These two tribes, which had caused him considerable trouble since the second half of 1915, threatened his flank and prevented him from operating against Ibn Rashid in the north. This in turn upset the British, who were expecting Ibn Saud to harass Ibn Rashid and confine him to Hail, thus preventing him from assisting the Ottomans in Mesopotamia. Consequently, the British were less inclined to support Ibn Saud militarily and financially, which in turn compounded his difficulties in suppressing the domestic revolts. In addition, the tribal revolts were exacerbated by the refuge Kuwait had granted the 'Ajman tribe in 1916, which complicated the already strained relations between Ibn Saud and the Kuwaiti successors of Mubarak.[1]

Second, the Ottomans had yet to be totally defeated by the British, and Ibn Saud could not rule out their possible return to Arabia. This raised serious problems concerning the attitude he was to adopt toward the Porte and the extent of his cooperation with Great Britain. On the one hand, his active and direct support of the British might earn him the Porte's antagonism after the war, if the Ottomans made good their return. Such a contingency was by no means a remote one, especially in the aftermath of the disastrous British defeat of Kut al-Amara in April 1916.[2] On the other hand, he had great confidence in ultimate British success, which converged with his own aspirations in seeing the Ottomans permanently expelled from Arabia. It was through the British that he had achieved his long-desired independence, and to alienate them at this stage would run contrary to his own interests and to the obligations he had undertaken in the treaty. The dilemma was thus how to appear to support the British without antagonizing the Porte.

Third, the proclamation of the Arab Revolt by Sharif Husain on June 5, 1916, and, more specifically, the British request that he cooperate with Husain in fighting the Ottomans further complicated Ibn Saud's problems. He had grievances against Husain as a result of Sharifi-Saudi encounters going back to 1910, when a dispute had broken out between the two over the allegiance of the 'Utaiba tribe, whose strategic location along the Nejdi-Hejazi border exacerbated the conflict. Later, when Ibn Saud's brother, Sa'd, was captured by the Sharifian forces, the Saudi leader was forced by Husain to acknowledge Ottoman sovereignty and agree to pay £1000 as a yearly tribute for the area of Qasim, in exchange for which Sa'd was released. The incident created considerable bitterness in Ibn Saud and governed Saudi-Sharifi relations for years to come. Beyond the personal insult, the episode taught Ibn Saud that Husain constituted a major obstacle for the implementation of Saudi goals and that their respective interests were diametrically opposed. The most recent encounter between the two had occurred in November 1915, when Husain attempted to exploit Ibn

Saud's problems with the 'Ajman tribe in order to advance his position in Qasim.[3] Now that the British had requested him to cooperate with Husain, Ibn Saud was reluctant to have any dealings with the Sharifians. Husain's designs beyond the Hejaz, as manifested by his assumption of the pretentious title "King of all Arabs," could only strengthen Ibn Saud's perception of the sharif as an enemy with whom no cooperation was conceivable. In addition, assisting Husain meant fighting the Ottomans directly, which Ibn Saud sought all along to avoid. Finally, in view of the tribal revolts and the lack of funds and arms, the Saudis were in no position to assist the sharif even if they wanted to. But at the same time, a refusal to assist Husain completely meant defying the British, a situation Ibn Saud had always successfully avoided. The crucial question was how to refrain from cooperating with the sharif without appearing to defy the British.

Fourth, there was widespread disenchantment in Nejd with the pro-British policies Ibn Saud pursued.[4] The Nejdis had several complaints against the British. The asylum granted to the 'Ajman by Kuwait, a British protectorate, did not prevent the tribe from attacking Saudi tribes, while the British compelled Ibn Saud to refrain from retaliating. The blockade that the British sought to enforce on goods reaching the Ottomans in Mesopotamia and Medina also entailed serious losses for the Nejdi merchants. The main source of Saudi income, the camel trade with Syria, was interrupted by the war and the blockade, virtually exhausting Saudi revenues. Finally, Husain's machinations and pretensions for lordship over all Arabs alarmed the apprehensive Nejdis. That Britain was perceived as encouraging such pretensions raised serious doubts as to the prudence of Ibn Saud's policy of friendly relations with Britain. Ibn Saud thus had to placate his disenchanted people without effecting any change in his pro-British stance.

Above all, Ibn Saud was too weak militarily and financially to offer any significant contribution to the British offensive. He was confronted with enemies from three directions—the 'Ajman in the east, Ibn Rashid in the north, and the sharif in the west—and he could not employ all his forces in any one direction without exposing the other two flanks. Ibn Saud's vulnerability enhanced the British perception of him as inferior to Sharif Husain and confirmed their determination to concentrate their war efforts on the

Sharifians rather than the Saudis. This decline in stature vis-à-vis the sharif was to haunt Ibn Saud throughout the war period and nurture his fears that British-Sharifian schemes had designated to the Saudi state a status of vassalage under the overlordship of Husain, "King of all Arabs." In short,the very Saudi independence, just recently acquired, was once more at stake.

Under these circumstances, Ibn Saud had only one instrument to employ against the British, the recently concluded Anglo-Saudi Treaty. If he were to honor all his obligations in the treaty, the British would have no pretext to renege on their commitments, chief among which were the recognition of Saudi independence and its protection against foreign powers. The overriding consideration in Saudi policy henceforth focused on the desire not to alienate the British in a way that would enable them to renounce their obligations in the treaty. In view of the multitude and complexity of the problems confronting Ibn Saud, it was indicative of his statesmanship and military leadership that he emerged from World War I with his territory intact and his political status undiminished.

Saudi-Sharifi Enmity

The year 1916 started with Ibn Saud's journey to the south to suppress the revolt of the al-Murra. His departure afforded Ibn Rashid the opportunity to advance northward in Iraq to assist the Ottomans. The British, obviously disappointed that Ibn Saud failed to confine Ibn Rashid to Hail, did not conceal this from the Saudi leader. But by mid-1916 there was a more urgent field requiring Saudi help, the Arab Revolt in western Arabia. Informing Ibn Saud of the sharif's declaration of war against the Ottomans, Cox requested him to unite with the Sharifian forces in their common struggle against the Porte.[5]

Ibn Saud was eager to avoid any British disillusionment with him. By June he had successfully emerged from the tribal revolts and was in a position to dispatch a large force to operate near Hail. The impact was immediate: Ibn Rashid received urgent instructions from the Ottomans to return to Hail. But as the resources at Ibn Saud's disposal were insufficient, he informed Cox that he could not launch a general war against Ibn Rashid in the absence of a considerable amount of arms and ammunition.

Fighting Ibn Rashid was one thing; assisting the sharif was quite another. It entailed cooperation with an avowed adversary, active and direct fighting against the Ottomans, and exposal of Riyadh to a Rashidi onslaught. But in his reply to Cox, Ibn Saud wished to ignore the last two considerations, which might have exposed both his reluctance to fight the Ottomans and his military weakness, so he emphasized only the first. Above all, he assured the British that their wartime goals were identical with his and that he had been pleased with the sharif's revolt. But the official communiqué that Cox had sent to him referred to "the Arabs" as a compendious whole, which implied the loss of Saudi independence. Reminding Cox of the old feud between him and the sharif, Ibn Saud stated that the Saudis would never tolerate any Sharifian lordship. He sought to ascertain whether Britain recognized the sharif's supremacy, which might have superseded British recognition of Saudi independence. He reasoned that, although Cox could appreciate his fears, it was probable that "the representative of the British Government who is actually conducting negotiations with the Sharif is not acquainted with the position." It is remarkable that Ibn Saud, a Bedouin chief, had a sense of the Cairo-Baghdad rivalry over the direction of British policy in the Middle East.[6]

In August, Ibn Saud received a letter from the sharif informing him of Mecca's occupation and requesting Saudi assistance. In response, Ibn Saud reminded the sharif of "past misunderstandings" and made the Saudi cooperation contingent upon a Sharifian promise of noninterference: "If you are desirous of our services and cooperation, then we desire you to give us a promise so that our mind may be at rest in regards to your attitude . . . especially regarding the question of interference with our tribes and subjects."[7]

In communicating the exchange to Cox, Ibn Saud strove primarily to establish a solid framework for his future relations with the sharif. He emphasized that he entertained the proposal of cooperation with Husain only because Britain desired it. He therefore had to know whether in the British government's view his relations with the sharif were a matter concerning only the two chiefs or a subject also involving British interests. In the former case, he would devise his plans on the basis of Husain's reply and would take the necessary steps to protect his own interests. In the latter case, however, he would subordinate his own preferences to those of the British government.

In the same vein Ibn Saud wrote to Cox regarding his relations with Ibn Rashid, inquiring whether the issue was a matter concerning the two chiefs *inter se* or a subject affecting British interests. In the former case, he would embark on an all-out attack on Hail only "at a suitable opportunity," explicitly noting that "the present political juncture appears unfavorable." This was an allusion to his reluctance to expose his territories to two potential adversaries, the sharif and the 'Ajman. In the latter case, however, he would conform to British wishes, provided he was supplied with the necessary arms.[8]

Meanwhile, the Porte deposed Sharif Husain and nominated 'Ali Haidar as the new emir of Mecca. On August 14, 'Ali Haidar informed Ibn Saud of his nomination, warned him of Husain's machinations, and requested Saudi support. Ibn Saud's handling of the letter illustrates his method of extricating himself from a delicate situation. To Haidar, Ibn Saud wrote that "the family of Husain have produced nothing but injury and discord by their rebellion. He desires independence and for this will indulge in any kind of intrigue and incitement. His position is now weak and we can easily defeat him if supplies of ammunition are made available." Thus Ibn Saud managed to portray a friendly attitude toward the Ottomans without committing himself to any specific action on their behalf. But at the same time he took advantage of the issue in order to promote his standing in the eyes of the British. He dispatched to Cox a copy of Haidar's letter as a sign of cooperation, informing Cox that he had explained to Haidar "the resentment of all Arabs towards the Turks by reason of their actions" and concealing all other parts of his reply which were not favorable to the British, to say the least.[9]

Cox accepted Ibn Saud's explanations respecting both the Sharifi and Rashidi issues. He suggested to India that the Saudi leader be assured that no understandings with Husain would prejudice British adherence to the Anglo-Saudi Treaty. Hence, Ibn Saud could unite with the sharif without any misgivings. Simultaneously, Cox advised, it was essential to assure an appropriate reply on Husain's part to Ibn Saud's letter, which would not contain the term "Arab

Kingdom." Acquainting the sharif with the terms of the Saudi treaty could remove any illusions he might have entertained as to the firmness of the British undertakings toward Ibn Saud. Cox agreed that Ibn Saud could not be expected to attack Hail without British assistance and left it for his government to decide whether to offer Ibn Saud such assistance.[10]

Despite initial doubts, the Foreign Office finally instructed Cairo to acquaint the sharif with the Saudi-British Treaty and assure him that the British government was using its influence to persuade Ibn Saud to give the sharif all possible assistance. The Saudi ruler was to be informed that Britain had no reason to suppose the sharif had any designs on his territories and that the British government would use its good offices on his behalf as long as he respected the treaty. But reference to the treaty was to be confined to Article I concerning British recognition of Saudi independence, as Article II, relating to British protection of the Saudis, was not binding on the British against other Arabs, only against foreign powers. Once possessing these assurances, Ibn Saud should be encouraged in every way to support the Sharifian rebellion.

As for Saudi military contribution, India thought it was undesirable to press Ibn Saud to take any specific action: "If he does so spontaneously, well and good; but otherwise we should be content with the immense asset we have secured in the passive friendship of Nejd." This was an obvious allusion to the parameters of the British-Saudi Treaty, whereby British obligations were not given in exchange for a Saudi military role. The India Office, however, seemed to forget the terms of the treaty, contending that "we did not make a treaty with Ibn Saud in order that he might do nothing." The office finally settled for a limited Saudi role, "assisting us indirectly by holding Ibn Rashid in check and preventing him from attacking the Sharif or Basra."[11]

By October 18, 1916, Cox was in a position to give Ibn Saud definite assurances on both the Rashidi and Sharifi issues. Britain wished him to support the sharif in some way, as by attacking Ibn Rashid or by winning Ibn Rashid to the British side. But it was left to Ibn Saud's discretion to determine without prejudice to his own interests. Cox assured him that the British government had not reneged on recognizing him as an independent ruler and the sharif had to acknowledge this status.[12]

Ibn Saud could be pleased with Cox's letter on several accounts. First, Britain had reiterated its adherence to the treaty and to Saudi independence. Second, the sharif's designs against the Saudis were neither initiated nor encouraged by the British. Third, Britain did not force on Ibn Saud any military role on either front; hence he managed to fulfill his goal of avoiding large-scale operations outside Nejd without antagonizing the British.

Several days later not only Ibn Saud's confidence was shattered but, primarily, the whole British effort to allay Saudi fears. Although London instructed McMahon to ensure that Husain responded appropriately, Husain's reply had already been dispatched more than two weeks earlier. Returning Ibn Saud's letter so that "you may reflect on what you wrote to us," the sharif stated that such a letter could emanate "only from a man bereft of his reason or of an absent mind."[13]

Ibn Saud's apprehensions were now compounded, as Husain's letter tended to confirm his anxiety over Sharifian designs in Nejd. Worst of all, in Ibn Saud's perception, Husain could not entertain such designs without the support or at least tacit connivance of Britain. Nothing could dispel such an impression except for a personal meeting with Cox. In an urgent letter Ibn Saud sought to impress Cox with the extent of his cooperation with Britain, noting that he had recently detained Ibn Far'un, an Ottoman envoy, and seized his seven hundred camels, and that he had also reinforced the blockade against trade and communication with the Ottomans. Finally, he renewed his request for a meeting with Cox. Cox detected Ibn Saud's anxiety that there had been a secret British-Sharifian understanding detrimental to Saudi interests."[14] He therefore agreed to meet Ibn Saud, and the two met, for the second time, at 'Uqair on November 11, 1916.

Ibn Saud's principal objective at the interview was to demonstrate that he was doing his utmost to support the British cause despite serious domestic and external constraints. He informed Cox that there was a growing opposition in Nejd to his pro-British policy. Because of the blockade he had enforced on trade between Nejd and Syria at the British request, his people had lost one of their main sources of revenue. His subjects also could not conceive of an alliance with a power that was perceived as encouraging their enemy, the sharif. In this context Ibn Saud showed Cox the sharif's letter, proving that it was Husain who was responsible for the lack of Saudi-Sharifi cooperation, and Cox had to admit that the letter was "extremely discourteous and arrogant." Ibn Saud was deeply bitter against the sharif, noting that under normal circumstances Husain's contemptuous attitude could only have been obliterated by blood. But then these were not normal circumstances, as his bilateral relations with the sharif were of great importance and concern to British wartime interests. As a result, Ibn Saud was ready to swallow his grievances against Husain for the sake of the British cause. He offered to send one of his sons with a symbolic force of fifty men to join the Sharifian army's maneuvers "as a token of identification with the Sharif's cause." He would do so, however, only if the sharif sent a friendly request to this effect.[15]

Ibn Saud thus assured that in any contingency he could not be accused by the British of failing to cooperate with the sharif; at the same time, he compromised none of his principles. If the sharif did not make the friendly request, then it would be Husain's fault that cooperation could not materialize. If the sharif did request Saudi support, then the fifty-man force would participate only in maneuvers and would not fight the Ottomans. On the Rashidi issue, however, Ibn Saud assured Cox that Saudi military operations were feasible only if Britain could provide him with the necessary material assistance. In order that his apprehensions be dispelled, Ibn Saud also had to be officially reassured that Britain did not support whatever ambitions the sharif might contemplate in Nejd. Such an assurance was all the more urgent as only a week earlier the sharif had proclaimed himself "King of all Arabs," implying sovereignty over all Arabs, including the Saudis.[16] Cox attempted to mollify Ibn Saud, informing him that Britain had insisted that the sharif "made formal admission that he claimed no jurisdiction over the independent Arab rulers," but this did not satisfy the Saudi ruler.

Inviting Ibn Saud to attend a durbar of Arab chiefs in Kuwait, Cox suggested to the Indian government that Ibn Saud be awarded the Knight Commander of the Most Eminent Order of the Indian Empire (K.C.I.E.) and that he be taken to visit British headquarters in Basra. The Indian authorities approved Cox's proposals, and the

India Office ordered them to give Ibn Saud the British government's fullest assurances.[17]

British Assurances to Ibn Saud

On November 18, 1916, Ibn Saud arrived at Kuwait and two days later attended the great durbar where several hundred Arab dignitaries were present. Cox informed him that His Majesty's government had decided to invest him with the K.C.I.E. "as a token of their confidence in Your Excellency . . . and your cooperation with ourselves . . . In their dealings with the Sharif, His Majesty's Government have been careful to reserve all your rights, and the Sharif has expressly stated that he had no intention of interferring with Ibn Saud."[18]

Receiving such a sweeping assurance, Ibn Saud sought to reciprocate with a strong and unusually overt manifestation of his pro-British feelings, compensating for the little active contribution he could offer. Striking the durbar's keynote speech, which was "as spontaneous as unexpected," Ibn Saud pointed out that, "whereas the Ottoman Government had sought to dismember and weaken the Arabs, Britain's policy aimed at uniting and strengthening us. By committing iniquities against other Muslims, the Ottomans had placed themselves outside the pale of Islam. The Sharif's action should be praised and all true Arabs should cooperate with him in forwarding the Arab cause." In direct response to the British communication, Ibn Saud addressed a letter to Cox, expressing gratitude for the British assurances. "As for the Sharif's promise not to interfere in my affairs, I am tranquil thanks to the presence of Great Britain. The state of affairs between me and the Sharif will be according to your wish, viz. that I should agree with him."[19]

From Kuwait Ibn Saud was taken to Basra, where he had the first opportunity to acquaint himself with modern arms. As Gertrude Bell, who accompanied Ibn Saud as Oriental Secretary to Cox, described: "We took him in trains and motors, showed him airplanes, high explosives, anti-aircraft guns, hospitals, base depots—everything. He was full of wonder but never agape." Ibn Saud at this time had the first chance in his life to meet a European woman. Cox observed, "The phenomenon of one of the gentler sex occupying an official position with the British Force was one quite outside his Bedouin comprehension." His British hosts were impressed not only by his statesmanship but also the way he reacted to modern technology, like "a man who was eager to learn rather than bewildered." Ibn Saud in turn drew his own lesson; he was convinced by what he had seen that "the British had come to stay" and that "victory will be the ally of the British."[20]

After being assured that the British had no complaints against him, Ibn Saud felt secure enough to submit his request for material assistance. He admitted to having been engulfed by domestic difficulties which significantly limited his ability to offer the British substantial support. But he had done his utmost in the way of moral cooperation by his visits to Kuwait and Basra and by his statements in support of the British and the sharif. Ibn Saud asked for three thousand rifles, some machine guns with the necessary ammunition, and such monthly subsidy as the British determined.

Ibn Saud sought to link the assistance to British interests in two ways. First, he dwelt at length on the growing opposition at home to his pro-British policies. Given the loss of income caused by the interruption of the camel trade with Syria and the inability of Ibn Saud to subsidize his tribes, the Nejdis were increasingly anxious that they not be put "in the opposition camp to the Ottomans." Though they were still loyal to Ibn Saud, he expressed concern as to their future attitude in view of his inability to placate them. The real extent of unrest in Nejd and whether it reached such dangerous proportions cannot be ascertained, although it is reasonable to assume that Ibn Saud endeavored to exploit such real, or imagined, domestic difficulties in order to extract from Britain a price for the friendship of such a vast territory as Nejd. Second, Ibn Saud noted that the assistance could be used against Ibn Rashid, thus indirectly promoting the British war effort in Mesopotamia. In this context, Ibn Saud proposed to maintain four thousand armed men in Qasim, if provided with a subsidy, so as to threaten Ibn Rashid's flank and harass and attack him as opportunity offered.[21]

The current Saudi request for assistance was fundamentally different from all previous ones in that it envisaged British aid on a permanent basis. Ibn Saud sought to create some overt and practical manifestation of the close relations with Britain and to establish a permanent and solid channel of British support. In addition, he wished to equate himself with the sharif, who had been receiving a large monthly subsidy of £200,000 since his proclamation of the Arab Revolt. A permanent subsidy from Britain would tie Ibn Saud to the British in a way that would obstruct the sharif's hostile designs on Nejd. Conveying his friendship directly to the viceroy, Ibn Saud informed him that Jabir, who succeeded Mubarak in November 1915, Khaz'al, and he had decided to unite with the British government "in the exalted interests" of its war effort.[22]

Cox proposed a favorable response to Ibn Saud's request for arms and advised his superiors to agree to a £5,000 monthly subsidy. Ibn Saud's military contribution, Cox admitted, did not amount to much, but his moral cooperation was "very considerable." At any rate, compared to the sharif's subsidy, Cox argued, the proposed amount was "moderate," which was an understatement. India and London accepted Cox's recommendations unreservedly, and on January 1, 1917, the Treasury sanctioned the subsidy "as a temporary arrangement for not more than six months."[23]

Ibn Saud could be content that his greatest concern that Britain had reverted from her undertakings in the treaty and had made conflicting promises to the sharif was clearly dispelled by an official and formal communication. He was also pleased with the monthly subsidy and the modest military assistance, which indicated also that the British did not perceive anything in his conduct as either damaging their interests or violating his own undertakings in the treaty. As for the subsidy and the military assistance, they did not bind him to an all-out offensive against Hail, which might have endangered Riyadh. The durbar also produced a temporary settlement, for the duration of the war, of the Kuwaiti-Saudi dispute over the 'Ajman. Last but not least important, it was the sharif, and not Ibn Saud, who was blamed for the lack of Saudi-Sharifian cooperation.

That the British government held Husain responsible for the Sharifi-Saudi rift was evident by the strenuous measures that the Foreign Office took to convey to Husain its displeasure with the way he had treated Ibn Saud. In early October 1916, the British agent in Jidda, C. E. Wilson, had handed over to Husain a copy of the British-Saudi Treaty and reminded him of his commitment to respect "treaties made by His Majesty's Government with Arab Chiefs." The Foreign Office also advised the sharif that the British government was prepared to recognize him only as "Ruler of the Hejaz," not as "King of all Arabs," and insisted on a formal admission that he claimed no jurisdiction over independent Arab rulers. Once acquainted with the sharif's insulting letters to Ibn Saud and to the rulers of Kuwait and Muhammara, the Foreign Office ordered that a message of complaint be conveyed personally to Husain, expressing regret that three Arab rulers "have reason to feel aggrieved at the reception of their advances" by the sharif. The message concluded with a reprimand, warning Husain that British efforts to mobilize all Arabs for his cause would be of no avail if he himself repelled "those whom His Majesty's Government had attracted to his support."[24]

The Foreign Office was once again late in forwarding its protest, as two weeks earlier Husain had managed to commit another act bound to deepen Saudi apprehensions. On November 15, he sent a letter to Riyadh, informing Ibn Saud of his recent coronation in Mecca, and he signed it "King of Arabian Countries." Ibn Saud hurried to dispatch the letter to Cox, noting that it confirmed his suspicions regarding the sharif's designs over Nejd. Cox responded that "the title which the Sharif uses or does not use has no meaning in reference to yourself, and you can completely rely on our assurances and our treaty."[25] It was one thing to be aware of Husain's hostile schemes; it was quite another to fear that the British acquiesced in such schemes. Once Ibn Saud was officially assured of Britian's opposition to the sharif's ambitions, the nature and danger of these ambitions became much less important and urgent.

Ibn Saud endeavored to comply with all British requests so that the onus for the lack of Saudi-Sharifi cooperation would fall on Husain's shoulders. In this respect, his efforts were highly successful. By the end of 1916 the Foreign Office had defined his attitude as "very satisfactory," while at the same time it criticized the sharif for "repelling" the Saudi ruler "whom the British Government had attracted to his support."[26]

Flirtation with the Ottomans

Ibn Saud's growing overt cooperation with Britain brought him into confrontation with the Ottomans. One of his main goals since the beginning of the war had been to avoid alienating the Ottomans to the point of an irreparable breach, and he still adhered to this principle. It partly accounted for his refusal to declare war against the Ottomans and his abstention from fighting them, two acts the sharif was not hesitant to undertake. Indeed, in response to Husain's request that the Saudis declare jihad and "fight the Turks," Ibn Saud replied that he could not do so "because we must consider our advantage and harm." But two recent actions of Ibn Saud caused some alienation among the Ottomans: his detention if Ibn Far'un and the seven hundred camels, and his public statements at the durbar in Kuwait in support of the British. In early 1917, an Ottoman mission was sent from Medina, the only remaining Ottoman stronghold in Arabia, to Riyadh to protest Ibn Saud's recent actions, and the Ottoman commander, Fakhri, wrote several letters to Ibn Saud, demanding assistance in supplies and camel corps.[27]

The full scope of Ibn Saud's reaction to these demands is unknown, mainly because the Saudi archives are inaccessible. Philby, a year later while on a mission to Nejd, saw Fakhri's letters and claimed that their contents "made it clear that Ibn Saud never even replied." Even Hogarth from the Arab Bureau argued, after seeing "evidence derived from a secret source," that Ibn Saud in all likelihood did not respond. But Philby later admitted that Ibn Saud was "in friendly though guarded correspondence with Fakhri," divulging neither the context in which the letters were exchanged nor their contents. In addition, there was a general feeling of mistrust over Ibn Saud's good faith among various authorities in the British government. Some of them suspected that "Ibn Saud may all the while be intriguing with the Turks." R. E. A. Hamilton, the political agent in Kuwait, indicated while in Riyadh that "it is rumored and universally believed that Ibn Saud has received subsidies from the Turks." Alois Musil, a Czech historian and geographer who was in Arabia during the war and had good contacts on the Ottoman side, also reported that in the early summer of 1916 Ibn Saud established direct communication with the Turkish forces at Medina and supplied them with camels. Furthermore, claimed Musil, in September 1916 Ibn Saud sent a delegation to Damascus to discuss various questions with the Ottoman authorities.[28]

An Ottoman source is even more revealing. In his memoirs the commander of the Ottoman Armies in Palestine, Sinai, and Syria, Jemal Pasha, compared the sharif's treacherous and "double-faced role" during the war with Ibn Saud's positive attitude. He revealed that Ibn Saud "made himself very useful to us by sending camels to the army from the far depth of Nejd." It is thus safe to assume that Ibn Saud sought to balance his anti-Ottoman behavior and statements by alleviating the condition of the besieged Ottoman garrisons in Medina. If he calculated that this would render his image in Ottoman eyes more positive, he was correct, as was shown by Jemal's conclusion that "Ibn Saud could not give us any direct assistance as he was too near the English who could do him enormous harm."[29]

Besides his desire to avoid alienating the Ottomans, Ibn Saud's support for the entrenched defenders of Medina was rooted in another set of considerations. His attitude toward the Ottoman enclave in general and his interest in enabling it to survive in particular were a microcosm of the complexity of the Saudi position during the wartime period. On the one hand, Ibn Saud had yearned all along for the total expulsion of the Ottomans from Arabia and should therefore have been satisfied with the defeat of their last stronghold in Medina. On the other hand, a Sharifian victory in Medina would have considerably strengthened Husain vis-à-vis Ibn Saud and, in view of the sharif's ambitions, might have diverted his energies toward Nejd. Of the two considerations, the second carried more weight, for a Sharifian victory entailed potential serious danger to Nejd, whereas the sole Ottoman enclave in Medina posed no immediate threat. In order, then, to pre-empt a Sharifian victory and enable Medina to withstand Sharifian assaults, it was important that supplies to the town were not cut and that the trade route via Qasim remained open. But such a course would have conflicted with Ibn Saud's promises to Britain to enforce the blockade on all supplies to the enemy through his territories. The problem thus centered on the crucial question of how to let Medina survive without antagonizing the British.

The question was mitigated to a large extent by the fact that Ibn Saud did not have to supply Medina with the necessary provisions to help it withstand the siege. All he had to do was to refrain from a strict enforcement of the blockade in the Qasim region, allowing supplies to pass from Kuwait and Iraq to Medina. The merchants in Qasim, attracted by the high prices the Ottomans offered for the smuggled goods, could be trusted to take care of the supplies; all that was needed was Ibn Saud's tacit connivance. Jemal's memoirs therefore report that "Ibn Saud permitted the export of merchandise from his country to Syria." At times when the British expressed their disappointment at the contravention of the blockade, Ibn Saud excused himself by citing his inability to exert an effective control on the Qasimis, who were left with no source of income because of the cessation of the camel trade with Syria.[30] It is not a coincidence that the question of the blockade was to haunt the British throughout 1917 and until the end of the war, constituting a constant divisive issue in Saudi-British relations. It led the sharif to accuse Ibn Saud of collusion with the Ottomans, a contention that was not unfounded.

Another major source of friction between Ibn Saud and Britain was the British attempt to win over disaffected sections of Jabal Shammar that were inclined to desert Ibn Rashid and perhaps effect a coup in Hail. Although some British authorities doubted the real strength of the defector, al-Subhan, others agreed with Cox that every opportunity to eliminate Hail as a pro-Ottoman stronghold must be exhausted. The India Office argued also that Ibn Rashid's defeat would remove one of Ibn Saud's major problems and enable him to move against the Ottomans in Medina. Cox, who knew better, expected Ibn Saud to be offended by the British attempt to install in Hail a pro-British emir, thus depriving the Saudis of the possibility of restoring Jabal Shammar to their dominions. Ibn Saud chose to conceal his disappointment and instead sought to belittle al-Subhan's importance, depicting him as having "about ten followers" and questioning his sincerity. Domestically, the issue caused Ibn Saud considerable difficulties. It afforded his followers another cause to voice their disapproval of his support of the British, who were not averse to aiding their Rashidi enemy.[31] But Ibn Saud understood that the question was one of military considerations and that the British attempt was not motivated by any anti-Saudi calculations.

Meanwhile, Ibn Saud moved to implement his part of the bargain agreed upon at the durbar, and at the end of January 1917, he left Riyadh for Qasim. From there he continuously harassed Ibn Rashid, preventing him from assisting the Ottomans in both Iraq and Medina. It was obvious, however, that Ibn Saud was not en-thusiastic about occupying Hail, lacking the necessary arms and being militarily too weak to wage an all-out attack. Philby, who visited Riyadh at the end of 1917, found that all the guns the British had supplied Ibn Saud against Hail "were in cold storage." Fur-thermore, if he were to eliminate the Rashidi, the British would then justifiably demand that he move against Medina, which he sought to avoid. Reluctant as he was to eliminate Hail, this was precisely what the British intended him to do in the coming months.[32]

On March 11, 1917, the British finally conquered Baghdad. En-couraged by their success, they sought to accelerate Ottoman de-feats on other fronts, too, foremost in Medina and Hail. Cairo demanded a concerted attack on Hail, with Nuri Sha'lan, the sheikh of the Ruwala section of the large 'Anaza tribe, whose influence was paramount from Jabal Druze to north of Jabal Shammar, moving from the north and the Saudi forces from the south in order to prevent "a diversion by Ibn Rashid in the direction of Medina." On May 10, Mark Sykes and Colonels C. E. Wilson and Leachman, Political Agent of the Desert, all agreed that "it is most desirable for Ibn Saud to take Hail" and suggested that Leachman proceed to Ibn Saud to discuss the implementation of the plan. Cox followed suit and suggested to Ibn Saud "to take advantage of the reduced state of Ibn Rashid" and capture Hail before this was done by the northern tribes.[33]

But at this juncture, a fundamental change occurred in Hail. Weakened by growing desertions and by Ottoman defeats in Mes-opotamia, Ibn Rashid made peace overtures to Ibn Saud. The Saudi chief was not interested in peace with Ibn Rashid, because the Rashidis were the hereditary enemies of the house of Saud and because peace with Ibn Rashid would have obliged him to do pre-cisely what he wished to avoid: fight the Ottomans and support the sharif. But to reject the Rashidi overtures would have run counter to the obvious British interest in winning over Hail and eliminating it as an Ottoman stronghold. The question was thus how to render a Rashidi-Saudi peace impossible without alienating the British.

Ibn Saud's solution was to inform Cox that he was ready to make peace with Ibn Rashid only because it was "in the British interest to bring him over to us," but the extreme peace terms he proposed to Ibn Rashid rendered an agreement a remote possibility. By Ibn Saud's conditions, Ibn Rashid would have had to sever relations with the Ottomans, befriend the British, and align himself with the sharif. The third condition was illustrative of the two goals Ibn Saud sought to attain. It both demonstrated his support of Britain and made it impossible for Ibn Rashid to accept the Saudi terms. Ibn Saud was in all likelihood not surprised when several days later Ibn Rashid rejected his terms as "unacceptable to the interests of our religion and our world."

Relaying the exchange to Cox, Ibn Saud endeavored once again to impress the British with the extent to which he was prepared to subordinate his preferences to British interests. "I did not intend peace with Ibn Rashid for any personal motive but only for the interests of the British Government and the Sharif . . . we do not intend our own interests but we safeguard the interests of our friend and the pleasure of their friends like the Sharif." As for Cox's suggestion that he take Hail, Ibn Saud merely stated that he intended to do so "sooner or later." But his explanations did not conceal his reluctance to eliminate Ibn Rashid.[34]

Cox detected not only Ibn Saud's lack of enthusiasm but also the interconnection, from the Saudi standpoint, of the Rashidi, Ottoman, and Sharifi questions. He realized that Saudi anxieties over their western front had a direct negative impact on their ability to operate in the north, and consequently he sought to receive a full picture of Ibn Saud's concerns and considerations. Concurrently, the British strove to ensure the cooperation of the sharif in their efforts to dispel Saudi apprehensions. As a result, they proposed to send Ronald Storrs, the Oriental secretary in Cairo, to Ibn Saud and a second officer, Colonel Leachman, to the sharif. Storrs was to ascertain the Saudi capabilities for attacking Hail, to discuss ways of enforcing the blockade, and to allay Ibn Saud's anxieties concerning Husain. It was expected that Storrs, in his capacity as an official of the Arab Bureau in charge of Sharifian affairs, would be an ideal official to convince Ibn Saud that his fears were unfounded. Storrs left Kuwait on June 9, 1917, but suffered a severe sunstroke three days later and was forced to return.[35]

A previous British attempt on the other side of the peninsula to effect a reconciliation between Husain and Ibn Saud had failed as well. In a meeting at Jidda, Faisal, Husain's son, suggested to Sykes that Britain induce Ibn Saud and the Idrisi to recognize Husain's position as "Leader of the Arab Movement," without any infringement on their independence and rights. Sykes endorsed the proposal, but Cox rejected it, stating that such a request would only make Ibn Saud "suspicious of my *bona fides*" and might cause him to "go the other way."[36] It was remarkable that Ibn Saud's apprehensions constituted such a primary consideration in Cox's thinking.

Meanwhile, the question of the blockade continued to be a constant source of aggravation for the British. Smuggled goods found their way not only to Hail but also to Medina, which could otherwise not have withstood the Sharifian siege. There were two areas where the blockade could possibly have been contravened, Kuwait and Qasim. Both the Saudi and Kuwaiti rulers therefore exchanged accusations, blaming each other for the failure to ensure an efficient enforcement of the blockade. Hamilton argued that Qasim was the main source of supplies reaching both Hail and Medina, but he refrained from blaming Ibn Saud for the situation. Instead, he claimed that Ibn Saud's insecure position in Qasim, given its people's resentment of his policies, prevented an effective blockade.[37] Significantly, Hamilton did not even raise the possibility that Ibn Saud might have been interested in letting supplies pass to Medina for reasons related to his relations with the sharif.

It was hardly a coincidence that at the very time Hamilton complained of violations of the blockade in Qasim, Ibn Saud sought to circumvent a possible British attempt to hold him responsible for the violations. In a letter of June 3, he endeavored to convince Cox that the fault lay in Kuwait and Iraq, "places that are under the British Government." He specifically referred to two caravans that had left Kuwait in early May whose place of destination was enemy territory.[38]

Such accusations could not solve the problem, which culminated at the end of September with the arrival at Kuwait of an enemy caravan of three thousand camels, coming through Qasim with a passport signed by Ibn Saud's son, Turki. The irony of the situation was illustrated by the fact that Turki was in command of the Saudi forces in Qasim entrusted with enforcing the blockade. The debacle was completed by the clearance of the caravan with the sanction or connivance of Salim, the Kuwaiti ruler, in spite of specific British orders to detain it.[39] It was obvious that a radical, comprehensive solution to the problem was long overdue.

Failure of Saudi-Sharifi Reconciliation

Meanwhile, the Saudi-Sharifi rivalry intensified. Husain was as adamant as always in his hostility to the Saudis, who considered him "as convicted a *kafir* (infidel) as the Turks" and who disputed his claims to the 'Utaiba and Mutair tribes. Husain tried unceasingly to convince the British that the Saudi ruler was only ostensibly supporting their cause, while in reality being in league with the Ottomans. To substantiate his charges, the sharif cited Ibn Saud's failure to fulfill his promises and conquer Hail.[40] But when the discussion shifted to the possibility of arming the Saudis to enable them to overrun Hail, the sharif rejected the idea vehemently, for fear that the arms might be directed against him and out of a desire to retain Hail's independence until he himself would be in a position to take it over.

On the Saudi side, there was a new source for outrage at Husain. Since part of the sharif's handsome subsidy was lavished on certain tribes, the Saudi ruler could not compete and found it difficult to keep his own chiefs content. He was constantly aware of the extreme disproportion between his subsidy and that of the sharif, and he complained to the British indirectly on the paucity of his allowance. In late September he sent a verbal message to Cox, protesting that his tribes, specifically Harb and 'Utaiba, had been attracted by higher pay offered by the sharif. Citing Husain's encroachment on the Nejdi tribes as proof of the sharif's hostile ambitions, the Saudi ruler emphasized that he had refrained from counteraction only because of his friendship toward the British. And he was extremely anxious for the visit of the special officer that Cox had promised to send in June.[41]

Information regarding Ibn Saud's domestic difficulties also reached Cox from Dr. Harrison, an American doctor working in Bahrain, who had visited Riyadh in August. Ibn Saud told him that he was greatly hampered and preoccupied by the difficult task of "making his tribes pull together," and he thought the British did not fully realize this. The tribes resented the severe restrictions placed upon their trade at a time when the Hejazi tribes were so lavishly subsidized by the sharif. As a result, "public feeling in Nejd" was not really pro-British and only owing to Ibn Saud was there no overt talk against them."[42]

Ibn Saud was not held responsible for the rift with Husain. Even the sharif's own patron, the Cairo Arab Bureau, confirmed Ibn Saud's allegations that Husain was "assiduously buying over such Saudi tribesmen from their allegiance as he can." On the whole, Cairo admitted that "we have failed to induce the Sharif to cultivate friendly relations with Ibn Saud."[43]

Cox, for his part, detected the threat implied in Ibn Saud's message, that in the absence of British friendship there would be nothing to inhibit him from attacking Husain. The last thing the British needed in the midst of the war was an inflamation of the rivalry between two of their protégés. The problems that had prompted the idea of a mission to Ibn Saud in June not only remained unresolved but also grew more pressing. As the hot-weather season reached its end, Cox revived the project of the mission, consisting of political officers from Baghdad and Cairo, with the Cairo officers enjoying the confidence of Husain.

The Nejd Mission was to clear the air between the sharif and Ibn Saud and examine the military problems involved in a concerted Saudi attack on Hail. It was also hoped that both Husain and Ibn Saud would exchange envoys so that each of them could become acquainted with the other's point of view. According to the plan, Philby, now in the Iraq Political Department, and Lieutenant Colonel Cunliffe-Owen were to represent Baghdad, while Storrs was to be sent from Cairo. The India and Foreign Offices supported the idea wholeheartedly. So did Cairo, hoping that the mission would "enhance Ibn Saud's prestige and reassure him of our confidence and determination to safeguard his interests," while serving as "a useful object lesson to the Sharif."[44]

While the mission from Iraq was proceeding to Nejd in November 1917, serious problems emerged with the Sharifian part of the project, hampering the mission in embryo. From the very beginning Husain had viewed the idea with growing suspicion and was doubtful of its political motives. Being in "an uncompromising state of mind," he suggested that the mission desist from seeking a permanent settlement of the political questions separating Ibn

Saud and himself. Wingate criticized "the folly of Husains' policy of suspicion," but he hoped that time would cause the sharif to reverse it and seek reconciliation "with his nearest powerful neighbor."

Worse was yet to come when the sharif reversed his previous agreement to grant Storrs a pass through his territories. Husain now claimed that he could not guarantee safe passage from the Hejaz to Nejd, owing to the risks from the tribesmen. London and Cairo were both infuriated by the sharif's latest decision, and a Foreign Office aide noted that it was "very difficult to grasp the mentality of an Arab of the desert." More troubles were in store when on November 26 Husain also rejected the second component of the Hejazi part of the mission and refused to send a representative to Riyadh to attend the talks with Ibn Saud. Wilson concluded from his meetings with Husain on November 24–25, 1917, that, as the sharif aspired to be the paramount power in Arabia, he wished to avoid anything that might convey an impression of equality between himself and Ibn Saud. The dispatch of a deputy to Riyadh was apparently perceived by Husain as creating just this impression.[45] The British interest in enhancing Ibn Saud's prestige was precisely what prompted Husain to deprecate the mission and to view it as a constraint on his future claims vis-à-vis the Saudis. Husain's adamant stand was based on the realization that never after the war would he enjoy the strong position he possessed now, either tribally or financially. And he was intent on doing the utmost to weaken Ibn Saud by achieving for himself during the war a prominent position, one that Ibn Saud could never challenge.

The idea of a Hejazi Mission to Ibn Saud, consisting of a Cairo official and a Sharifian delegate, was abandoned because of the sharif's obstinacy. None of the British authorities blamed Ibn Saud for the perpetuation and deepening of the Saudi-Sharifi rivalry. Moreover, Cairo concluded that the sharif had failed to exploit Arabian animosity toward the Ottomans and to secure common action by the peninsula chiefs, which "augurs ill for the success of his more ambitious schemes."[46]

Meanwhile, the mission from Iraq arrived at Riyadh and had its first meeting with Ibn Saud on December 1. A wide range of subjects were discussed, such as Saudi-Kuwaiti relations and the 'Ajman problem, the contravention of the blockade, Saudi-Sharifi relations, and a possible attack on Hail.[47] The common denominator in Ibn Saud's position on each of these subjects was his unconcealed desire to acquit himself from any damage that the British interests might have incurred and to shift the onus onto others. Thus, he blamed both Britain and Kuwait for failing to comply with the agreement regarding the 'Ajman. Similarly, he declined to accept any responsibility for the failure of the blockade, pointing to Kuwait as the source of leakage. As for Ibn Rashid, Ibn Saud reverted to his long-standing argument that, if provided with considerable British assistance, he would mobilize fifteen thousand men for an attack on Hail.

The one issue on which Ibn Saud's effort to clear himself of all suspicions was redundant was his relations with the sharif, for none of the British authorities blamed him for the failure to effect a reconciliation. Nevertheless, Ibn Saud displayed once again consuming jealousy of the sharif, whose continuing use of the title "King of Arab Countries" could hardly dispel Saudi fears. Philby also detected that at the "back of Ibn Saud's mind" the suspicion regarding some secret Sharifi-British understanding still prevailed. The Saudi chief could not grasp that the sharif could act with such impunity against the will of the British government.

As usual, Ibn Saud asked for assurances, specifically referring to equality of treatment both politically and financially with the sharif. But in a departure from the past, the Saudi ruler introduced a new element by requesting more definite assurances of postwar delimitations of territory and tribal spheres. Ibn Saud's request was based on his perception, similar to Husain's, that his position and importance during the war were superior to the status he would enjoy in the postwar period. Hence, this was the optimum time to extract the most solid assurances from Britain in order to counter future Sharifi designs. One thing Ibn Saud sought to make abundantly clear was that he would never accept a position of vassalage to the sharif. Furthermore, he aspired to a status in Nejd not inferior to that of Husain in the Hejaz. Throughout the discussions, Ibn Saud evinced no offensive aspirations vis-à-vis the Hejaz but rather strove to impress his guests with a clear defensive orientation stemming from anxiety over the sharif's ambitions. This led the India Office once more to instruct that Ibn Saud be assured that the British government did not recognize the title

"King of Arab Countries," the only title authorized for Husain being "King of the Hejaz."[48]

Following his talks with Ibn Saud, Philby, without asking his superiors, decided to carry on the mission to the Hejaz privately, assuming that Cox would not have authorized it otherwise.[49] Though outraged by Philby's unauthorized journey, Husain finally met with him and Hogarth, who had replaced Storrs. The last stage of the mission was to remove any vestige of hope that a Saudi-Sharifi reconciliation could ever be secured and to unite all British authorities in holding Husain responsible for the rift. Husain and his son 'Abdallah, who took an active part in the discussions, were in a highly uncompromising state of mind. They expressed irritation each time Ibn Saud's name came up, and 'Abdallah went so far as to call him "son of a dog" and declare him "true to treacherous stock from which he sprung." Husain at first refused to discuss the Saudi subject, arguing that Ibn Saud was powerless and of small importance. But inasmuch as Hogarth, let alone Philby, had come all the way to Jidda for this purpose, Husain finally had no other choice but to discuss the Saudi issue and amplify his position.

The sharif focused on three main goals when articulating his attitude. First, he sought to convince the British of the Saudi disloyalty toward Britain, citing Ibn Saud's failure to conquer Hail, his correspondence with the Ottomans in Medina, and his incitement of his people to attack tribesmen friendly to the sharif. When Philby tried to refute the allegations, Husain refused even to listen, leading Hogarth to conclude that the sharif "absolutely declined to be persuaded from first to last." Second, Husain strove to dissuade the British from providing Ibn Saud with military assistance to attack Hail, arguing that the Saudis would employ the arms also against the Hejaz, that the independence of Hail was desirable as a buffer region preventing the spread of Wahhabi tenets northward, and that the conquest of Hail was of no military importance. But the sharif's real motive was clear: Husain wanted Hail for himself and therefore deprecated any British act bound to place it in Saudi hands. Third, Husain endeavored to receive some British confirmation of his self-proclaimed status as the pre-eminent ruler of all Arabs, reversing the British position, which recognized him only as the king of the Hejaz and denied him an all-Arab status. He agreed not to provoke a conflict with Ibn Saud for the duration of the war, and the British could infer therefrom that, following the war, the sharif might move eastward to make good his claims.

The British reaction to the sharif's positions was totally negative. Wingate himself in a comprehensive policy formulation admitted that Britain and the sharif had contradictory conceptions of the British undertakings prior to the "Arab Revolt" and consequently of the sharif's position vis-à-vis other Arab chiefs. It was high time for Husain to be informed that Britain did not support his claim to a pre-eminent status nor did it approve his attitude toward Ibn Saud. Hogarth was accordingly instructed to convey four points to Husain in response to his charges against Ibn Saud. First, Britain did not believe Ibn Saud to be guilty of treachery of any of the counts mentioned by Husain, and it intended to respect its treaty with the Saudis. Second, Britain expected Husain to respect the Saudi rights, both territorial and tribal. Third, British support should not be looked for by Husain in either any hostile action against Ibn Saud or any claim to suzerainty over Nejd. Fourth, should the British think fit to arm Ibn Saud and encourage him to attack Hail, they would not consider it incompatible with their undertakings to the sharif.[50]

Thus Cairo, the sharif's own patron, clearly blamed him for the failure to effect a Saudi-Sharifi reconciliation. Wingate himself admitted that he had no reason to doubt Ibn Saud's "good intentions" and explicitly stated that he shared Cox's "appreciation of Saudi-Sharifi relations." None of the British authorities ever leveled any charges against Ibn Saud for the rift. The sharif was well aware of this reality, as he had bitterly complained time and again that the British accused him for everything which passed between himself and Ibn Saud.[51] In view of Ibn Saud's constant aim to avoid any act that might give rise to British displeasure, this was no mean achievement.

As the first objective of the Nejd Mission, promoting better relations between Ibn Saud and the sharif, had failed, the British turned to the second goal, examining a Saudi military role against Hail. By the beginning of 1918, however, with the British occupation of Palestine in late 1917 and the rapid advance of the British offensive, the Ottoman strongholds in Arabia, Hail and Medina, lost much of their significance. There was general agreement that the capture of Hail was not "an object of sufficient importance to

warrant paying Ibn Saud a blank check for its accomplishment"
and that Ibn Rashid was in no position "to do us much harm."
Under these new realities, the question of Ibn Rashid was no longer
determined by British wartime considerations but instead by postwar Arabian politics in general and by the need to maintain a
balance of power between the sharif and Ibn Saud in particular.
India was convinced that retaining Ibn Rashid's independence would
greatly assist in maintaining such a balance. The net result was
that there was no need to provide Ibn Saud with assistance for the
elimination of Hail. The new situation was reflected in a change
of British priorities vis-à-vis Ibn Saud and Husain: whereas hitherto all efforts had been aimed at securing cooperation between
them, from the beginning of 1918 all efforts focused on preventing
an overt Saudi-Sharifi collision. Thus, Cox had to reject Ibn Saud's
request for postwar assurances that his position in Nejd would not
be inferior to that of the sharif in the Hejaz. Cox commented that
it was impossible to give Ibn Saud any fresh status or assurances
at that point, as such an act would excite the sharif's suspicions.
All Britain could do was to assure Ibn Saud that the treaty stood
firm, that his independent status as guaranteed by Britain was
safeguarded, and that he had to rest content with that for the
moment.[52]

For Britain, the decision not to provide Ibn Saud with considerable military assistance was rooted in the promising course of
the war. From Ibn Saud's standpoint, however, Britain's aban-
donment of the Hail offensive was an outcome of the discussions
that the mission had held with Husain. Ibn Saud interpreted the
decision as a clear manifestation of British deference to the sharif's
importance and as a British attempt to conciliate Husain at his
expense. Ibn Saud felt that his interests had been subordinated to
those of Husain and that the Sharifian factor was henceforth to
determine the nature of his relations with Britain in general and
of British support for his state in particular.[53]

Under this new configuration, the Saudis almost lost sight of
what might otherwise have been a cause for jubilation: the final
removal of the Ottoman threat. This major development had lost
much of its impact in 1915 when the Saudis were assured of British
protection, and the gradual process by which the Ottomans were
pushed back tended to minimize the significance of their disap-

pearance. In addition, the expulsion of the Ottomans from Arabia was more a political change than a transformation of physical reality, as they had not displayed their presence in Saudi dominions since 1913. But the major reason for the lack of Saudi exhilaration over the disappearance of the Ottomans was the perception that the threat formerly posed by the Porte had not really disappeared, since the sharif could prove an even more implacable enemy.

For Ibn Saud, the 1916–1918 period differed substantially from the years 1902–1915 in the sense that the Saudi entity did not initiate any processes but was instead an object of policies determined by the belligerent powers, Great Britain and the Ottoman Empire. Given the complex network of problems, external and domestic, facing the Saudi state, Ibn Saud's conduct throughout the period was characterized primarily by its defensive approach. The major Saudi effort was aimed at retaining the achievements secured in 1902–1915 rather than striving for new objects of expansion. Ibn Saud's policy in this period suggests that he comprehended the existing state of affairs which relegated him to the role of a passive actor. He operated within this framework and did not engage himself in policies that exceeded his resources and capabilities.

Ibn Saud managed to secure four major goals, all of which reflected his defensive orientation and hence were of a negative character. First, he fulfilled his wish not to fight the Ottomans, and thus he avoided an irreversible rift with the Porte. Second, he managed to avoid cooperation with the sharif, which he rejected because it would have involved fighting the Ottomans, would have left Riyadh vulnerable, and would have implied an admission of inferiority vis-à-vis the sharif. Third, he successfully avoided large-scale military operations beyond the confines of Nejd which might have endangered his flanks. Fourth, and most important in Ibn Saud's perception, he was able to secure the first three goals without alienating Great Britain, thereby giving her no pretext to renege on her obligations toward the Saudis. These accomplishments were all the more remarkable in that Britain wished him to do precisely the things he managed to avoid: fight the Ottomans, cooperate with the sharif, and support the British in Iraq. In view of the anti-British atmosphere prevailing in Nejd, his last accomplishment, remaining Britain's friend and being regarded as such by all British authorities, was the most impressive of all.

The shift in British policy toward Ibn Saud in 1918, from one prompted by wartime considerations to one based on the exigencies of the postwar period, heralded a fundamental transformation in Saudi policy and marked a turning point in the history of the third Saudi state. Both shifts were rooted in the increasing British military successes which spelled the end of World War I. For the British, these successes rendered the elimination of Hail unnecessary. For the Saudis, they brought about a total change in the identity of their primary enemy: the Ottoman sultan was replaced by Sharif, now King, Husain.

The 1916–1918 period thus constituted a double process whereby the gradual erosion of the Ottoman threat to the Saudis was accompanied by the gradual emergence of the Sharifian menace. The process reached its climax in mid-1919 when, along with the final withdrawal of the Ottomans from Arabia (Medina was the last enclave), the first overt confrontation took place between Ibn Saud and Husain over sovereignty over the Khurma area.[54] For Ibn Saud there was a common denominator in the Ottoman and Sharifian enemies, for both placed the very independence of the Saudi state in danger. Moreover, in two respects the Sharifian enemy constituted a more serious danger than the Ottomans. First, contrary to the remote Ottoman sultan, for whom Nejd was a peripheral province, the sharif was an Arabian potentate bordering on the Saudi territories. Second, whereas the Ottomans did not enjoy Britain's friendship, the sharif was Britain's ally and was perceived as acting with at least the tacit approval of the British government. That Ibn Saud failed to secure from Great Britain any postwar assurances concerning his relations with Husain tended to exacerbate the Sharifian threat. For the Saudi ruler, whose foreign policy since 1902 had been based on mobilizing Britain as a counterpoise to his principal enemy, there could have been no more ominous prospect than a potential British alliance with his major adversary.

As early as the second half of 1917, Ibn Saud had started to doubt whether his preferences for a British victory and an Ottoman defeat in the war were not ill considered. Visitors to Nejd reported that he was busy calculating the disadvantages that would accrue to him should the war result in the victory of the Allies or the Central Powers. The conviction that came to dominate his mind was that, if the British won the war and the Ottomans were driven out of Arabia, the Saudis would find the sharif "firmly established as an influential and powerful monarch able to count on the support of Great Britain," whereas Ibn Saud would remain "a mere Bedouin chief—as he was before the war, but with the Shammar and the northern tribes lost, and the Sharif claiming overlordship over the border tribes." If, on the contrary, the Central Powers won, "Ibn Saud will have the satisfaction of seeing Husain go down, while relying on his own political acumen to drive some sort of bargain with the Turks." At this juncture it occurred even to the British that "this is perhaps the reason that Ibn Saud has not attempted seriously to take Hail."[55]

The final elimination of the Ottoman threat in 1918 had significance not only in the short-term context of the third Saudi state but also in the wider context of Saudi history. As the traditional enemy of the house of Saud for two centuries, who had brought about the destruction of the first Saudi state precisely a century before, the Ottomans were now permanently removed from the Saudi scene. But the Sharifian problem proved no less menacing than the Ottoman one. It was to haunt Ibn Saud as the major foreign policy problem for the next decade and was to determine the final Saudi boundaries by the late 1920s. In a wider context, the vestiges of the Sharifian threat were to figure prominently in Saudi foreign policy for the next forty years, until they were superseded by a more profound and dangerous threat, radical pan-Arab Nasserism. The year 1918 thus constituted a watershed in Saudi history. The Saudi-Ottoman-British triangle that had prevailed since 1902 was replaced by the Saudi-Sharifi-British framework of relations, which was to shape the final territorial size of the third Saudi state.

7

Patterns of Saudi Foreign Policy

I am aware that in the past we had frequently to take measures against the Wahhabis for interference with the Trucial chiefs and Bahrain, but in this connection now I am convinced that Ibn Saud would be only too glad to furnish us with any undertaking we desired for the maintenance of the *status-quo* in the future.

Captain W. H. I. Shakespear

Hamdan bin Zayid, Sheikh of Abu Dhabi, is under the protection of my friend the British Government, and on account of my friendly relations with her, I cannot attack him.

Ibn Saud to Cox

FOR THE FIRST THREE DECADES of the twentieth century, Ibn Saud and his people were unqualifiably referred to as "Wahhabis" by the outside world. Later the terms "Saudis" and "Wahhabis" were used interchangeably, until "Saudis" acquired precedence and "Wahhabis" disappeared. The timing of this transformation—undoubtedly prompted by the new name the state acquired in 1932, "Saudi Arabia"—testified more to the shifting perception by foreign powers of the Saudi state than to any change in the nature of Saudi policies. In essence, the change of terms attested to a thirty-year-old reality that had just received external recognition.

For the world at large, the re-establishment of the Saudi entity in 1902 had meant primarily the revival of eighteenth- and nineteenth-century Wahhabism, which entailed first and foremost an unchecked, religiously motivated drive for expansion. Concerned with this external aspect of Wahhabism, foreigners involved with Arabian affairs conceived of the emerging third Saudi state only in terms of continuity and expected it to follow in the footsteps of its predecessors. But in the field of foreign policy the twentieth-century Saudi state, from its very inception, constituted a break with the traditional pattern of Wahhabi conduct and thus a turning point in Saudi history. In the period between 1902 and 1918, three main changes from past Wahhabi experience were adopted in Saudi foreign policy: a new strategy toward the mobilization of one power against the other, a new pattern of behavior toward the Ottoman Empire, and a new attitude toward Britain and her protégés along the Persian Gulf coast.

Ibn Saud, who shared with his ancestors the goal of independence from the Ottomans, sought to achieve it by political means, through mobilizing Great Britain as a counterpoise to Ottoman power. None of his predecessors had ever adopted such a strategy, though it could have changed the course of Saudi history at such critical stages as the 1814–1818 and 1838–1840 Egyptian occupations and the Ottoman conquest of Hasa in 1871. Saud's invoking of British support in 1871 was motivated by the Ottoman occupation of Hasa, *ex post factum,* and did not amount to a strategy. Moreover, Saudi alienation of the British during the two preceding decades had practically ruled out a positive British response.

In employing Britain against the Porte, Ibn Saud was an astute student of his mentor Mubarak. Driven to ask for British protection of the kind accorded to Kuwait against the Ottomans, Ibn Saud cited the position of Mubarak as representing what he desired. The Saudi leader favored the policy for a number of reasons. Ibn Saud realized that Britain was the paramount power in the gulf region and that the Ottomans had always retreated in the face of British determination and resolve. He assumed that "any understanding with Britain, however nebulous it might be," would make the Ottomans hesitate to attack and oppress him or interfere in Saudi affairs in Nejd. Such relations would not only relieve him of the Ottoman menace but also enable him to repudiate the allegiance to the sultan, which he had repeatedly been forced to offer. Ibn Saud was willing to make public any definite understanding he could reach with Britain, confident that the mere existence of such relations with Britain would relieve him of Ottoman pressures. Furthermore, he detected a fundamental difference between British and Ottoman interests in both the gulf and central Arabia. Whereas the Ottomans actively interfered in the small entities in both areas, seeking to assert control and influence over their affairs and curbing their independence, the British chose not to interfere in the entities any more than was necessary to prevent any other power from challenging their hegemony in the gulf. Thus, the Saudis need have no concern that Britain might replace the Porte as the power curbing Saudi independence. Ibn Saud himself recognized this, admitting that "Cox had raised me from nothing to the position I am holding today."[1] Last but not least, Ibn Saud adopted this strategy although it involved the employment of a Christian power, Great Britain, against a Muslim power, the Ottoman Empire. That Mubarak, whose life-style reflected his estrangement from Islam, could pursue such a policy was understandable. But that Ibn Saud, a profoundly devout Wahhabi Muslim, adopted such a course was remarkable. Nevertheless, the Saudi leader had no reservations regarding this aspect of his strategy. In fact, on several occasions he compared the Ottomans, "who sought to oppress and divide their subjects," unfavorably with the British who, "though of another faith," endeavored to support the Arabs.

Ibn Saud sought to legitimize this strategy on two grounds. First, he argued on religious grounds that Ottoman defeats and losses in the Balkan War and in North Africa were the judgment of Allah on a people who, while calling themselves Muslims, had for many years "neglected their religion, oppressed their subjects, embezzled religious endowments, broken every ordinance of the Qur'an and subverted the Caliphate." The present sultan was regarded as holding his throne only as "the puppet of a clique of politicians" and hence could not be considered the lawful head of the Islamic community. The Ottomans' misfortunes were taken as conclusive proof that Allah had abandoned them, and it was therefore incumbent upon good Muslims, namely Wahhabis, to rid themselves of all contact with them. Second, Ibn Saud argued on practical grounds that what "the Saudis saw under Turkish government" contrasted with the "justice, truth, equity, material prosperity and religious freedom which the Muslims under the British flag" enjoyed. Even on religious grounds, Ibn Saud favored the British. Looking with "abhorrence" on the "loose religious principles of the Turks," Ibn Saud explained to Shakespear that in his eyes "the infidel was preferable to the Turks, since the latter broke the rule he professed to follow, while the former acted in accordance with his own law." Despite the profound hatred and enmity of previous Saudi rulers toward the Ottomans, an alliance with infidels against Muslims and a comparison between Muslims and Christians favorable to the Christians would have been inconceivable to them.[2]

The second major change in Saudi foreign policy involved the new pattern of behavior toward the Ottoman government. Having failed to obtain British protection between 1902 and 1914, Ibn Saud was determined to avoid any confrontation with the full power of the Ottomans. His position was based on his own assessment of the disparity in strength between his forces and those of the Ottomans. Whereas he felt able to hold his own against Ibn Rashid or other rulers, and even against combinations of them, he was aware that the addition of Ottoman troops to assist his enemies would probably be his undoing. He knew that the Porte kept a close watch on the growth of Saudi power in Nejd and viewed it with disfavor. Consequently, he regarded it as extremely important to prevent any Ottoman interpretation of Saudi expansion in Nejd as aimed against the Porte. To that end, Ibn Saud maintained official, diplomatic correspondence with the Porte, offering submission and surrender, in order to "smooth over difficulties and placate the Ottomans." He also consistently recognized Ottoman authority after each major defeat of Ibn Rashid. Hence, Ibn Saud concluded two agreements with the Porte whereby he assumed Ottoman titles: qa'im-maqam in 1905 and wali in 1914.

Ibn Saud's overriding consideration in recognizing Ottoman authority was the consolidation of his state and the prevention of a Saudi-Ottoman showdown, which had led in the past to disastrous results. Foremost in his mind were "unhappy recollections of how the Ottomans ordered their Viceroy in Egypt to invade Nejd and destroy the Saudi state" in 1811, and how "the Turks came to reconquer Hasa in 1871." Ibn Saud was determined "to give the Turks no opportunity for a further advance into Najd."[3] As a result, he consistently refused to commit himself to an active military role against the Ottomans during World War I, despite the urging of the British and in marked contrast to the sharif. It was not that Ibn Saud "sought support for his continued rule in Najd from either Britain or the Ottoman Porte." Rather, the central component in Ibn Saud's strategy was to place both powers on different levels, adopting a distinct attitude toward each.

Similarly, Ibn Saud's negotiations with the Ottomans and the treaty he concluded with them did not indicate that he was pro-

Ottoman. He was profoundly imbued with anti-Ottoman sentiments on dynastic, religious, and political grounds. His correspondence with the Porte and his submission to Ottoman authority
could only be attributed to Britain's reluctance to establish relations with him. In Ibn Saud's own words, "If the British had brought
the al-Saud under their wing, none of these shows of submission
and other expedients would have been necessary." Thus, whenever
he was ordered to render a service to the Porte or publicly demonstrate his allegiance, he refused to abide by such instructions as
long as he had hopes that the British government might reconsider
his "old request to come under their protection." Ibn Saud's recognition of Ottoman sovereignty was no more than lip service, a
fig leaf for the continuation of Saudi consolidation. Ibn Saud contemplated the idea only as a last resort and only after his overtures
to the British had been rejected. Because his hatred of the Ottomans "to the last degree to the end of this world" was as implacable
as that of his ancestors, he did not mean what he had signed. That
despite his animosity toward the Ottomans he recognized their
sovereignty and concluded a treaty with them tends all the more
to confirm the assumption that, in dealing with foreign affairs, Ibn
Saud was a pragmatic leader, driven by pragmatic considerations
and not by religious fanaticism.[4]

The final change in Saudi foreign policy found expression in a
new pattern of conduct toward the British in the gulf. Ibn Saud
not only perceived Britain's predominant position in the region
but also demonstrated his awareness of its vital interests along the
Arab littoral of the gulf. His desire to avoid alienation from and
confrontation with Britain stemmed from two considerations. Alienation of the British would have rendered it impossible to obtain
British protection against the Ottomans, which was the basis of
his strategy. And a confrontation between Saudi aspirations and
British interests along the coast might, in view of the balance of
forces, portend disastrous consequences for the newly established
Saudi state. Because of Britain's determination to maintain the
integrity of the gulf principalities, Ibn Saud had to modify the
traditional Saudi drive for domination over these entities so as to
avoid a confrontation with Britain. It was not that the Saudis
lacked the drive for expansion in the direction of the gulf. Ibn
Saud's people in fact complained to him that "we are prevented

by your friends [Britain] from touching our rightful heritage—Bahrain, Oman, Qatar and other places." It was rather that Ibn Saud started from an early stage to regard the British as an "insuperable and permanent obstacle to the realization of Saudi dreams along the Gulf, and was prepared to accept such reality." Indeed, Ibn Saud explicitly admitted that, as the sheikh of Abu Dhabi was under the protection of "my friend the British and on account of my friendly relations with Britain, I cannot attack him." A Saudi-British encounter along the lines of the 1840s and 1850s, culminating in the British bombardment of Saudi ports in 1865, became inconceivable as a result of Ibn Saud's new attitude. Thus, it is no mere coincidence that all the gulf principalities, which in the eighteenth and nineteenth centuries were subjected to constant Saudi pressure and occupation, have retained their independence until the present day. There could be no better appraisal of the new Saudi attitude toward Britain than the testimony by Cox: "Ibn Saud has been extraordinarily correct and statesmanlike in all he has done. We have never been able to put him wrong."[5]

These three changes did not constitute isolated and marginal aspects of Ibn Saud's policies in the first two decades of the century. Viewed against the background of the two former Saudi states and in the light of subsequent Saudi policies, they amounted to nothing less than a thorough transformation of the central component of the external manifestation of Wahhabism, unchecked expansion. In the Wahhabi doctrine, the ruler's main function was to uphold the law *(shari'a)* and expand the community until it embraced all men. In order to expand the community and deepen its bases, jihad or, literally, a crusading effort was invoked, which had to be exerted by every member of the community to the fullest extent possible. This concept included the idea of "holy war," especially if waged against polytheists *(mushriqun)* and even Muslims, such as the Shi'ites, who deviated from the right path of Islam.[6] Expansion was thus an ongoing, unceasing obligation of individual Muslims as well as of the Islamic community as a whole. Furthermore, expansion was a process which, by definition, could not come to an end unless and until all those who had deviated from Islam were brought back into the fold of the righteous community. Hence, Wahhabi expansion was conducted on the basis of a religious ideal, which should not take into consideration practical realities which stood in its way. Rather, it was incumbent on the Wahhabis, on behalf of this idea, to change these practical realities and not succumb to them.

In contrast to his predecessors, Ibn Saud approached the issue of expansion from a perspective totally different from the Wahhabi ideal, assessing the existing political realities. He understood that he did not operate in a vacuum where he could enjoy complete freedom of action. His training in Kuwait had made him realize that Saudi actions affected other powers which might be provoked to react in case he encroached on what they perceived as their vital interests. And as he was aware of the existing balance of power between himself and the other powers, he saw that their superiority enabled them not only to check his expansion but also to crush the Saudi state altogether. Ibn Saud deduced from past Saudi history that as long as his ancestors extended their rule within the interior of Arabia, they had only the peninsula chiefs to reckon with. Once they appeared at the fringes of the peninsula, however, they encountered the superior forces of other powers—Egyptians, Ottomans, or British—whose pressure they could not withstand. Ibn Saud concluded that he had to distinguish between areas where he had complete freedom of action, such as Nejd, and areas where he was bound to encounter the resistance of foreign powers, such as the gulf coast. This distinction was to prevail in Saudi foreign policy and to outlive Ibn Saud. It accounted for the Saudi occupation of the whole of the interior of the peninsula and for its nonoccupation of the gulf principalities, Iraq, Transjordan, and Yemen, even after the Yemeni army was defeated by the Saudis in 1934.

Ibn Saud's new policies were prompted in part by the trauma that the Saudis had suffered from the destruction of their two former states. Yet this was not their sole basis, for otherwise the Saudis would have derived the appropriate lessons following the destruction of their first state in 1818 rather than a century later. The more important factor was that Ibn Saud's conduct was not confined to the framework of relations with the Ottomans, who had brought about the trauma, but constituted a general pattern of behavior in foreign affairs, encompassing all aspects and all periods. In capsule form, the transformation of Saudi policy derived from one major realization, that the process of Saudi expansion was not unlimited. Ibn Saud's awareness of existing political realities made him appreciate the external constraints placed upon his policies in the form of powers inimical to Saudi expansion. The nineteenth century's trauma had proved that, if provoked, these powers could not only check the expansion but also destroy Saudi independence altogether.

It was not that Ibn Saud lacked the drive for expansion. This was in fact one of his most significant motivations. But the nature of his drive differed. Its raison d'être had undergone a metamorphosis. Whereas under previous rulers the drive had been anchored in Wahhabi-religious ideals, under Ibn Saud it became motivated by political, pragmatic aspirations, which were modified, controlled, and subjected to scrutiny by existing political realities. As a result, Ibn Saud's expansionism could be, and was, brought to an end, whereas no end could have been envisaged to former Wahhabi expansionism. The desire to extend Saudi rule over the Buraimi area differed from traditional Wahhabi expansionism because it was motivated by political, not religious, considerations. Thus, the issue was not the incorporation of the whole of Oman and other gulf principalities, as was the case in the nineteenth century, but rather the extension of Saudi rule over a small, limited part of neighboring territory.

Cox appreciated Ibn Saud's statesmanship and restraint in foreign affairs, but he fallaciously attributed them to the subsidy the Saudi ruler started to receive from Britain in 1917, which caused him to feel obliged "not to annoy the British Government." Once the subsidy came to an end, Cox claimed, Ibn Saud would try to annex Oman, feeling free to pursue his own policy without the constraint imposed by the British allowance. In Cox's assessment, the British subsidy, a temporary expedient, was the cause of Ibn Saud's temporary restraint. Cox failed to detect that for fifteen years prior to the period of subsidies Ibn Saud's activities had shown a pattern of restraint imposed by the presence of Great Britain. Similarly, Ibn Saud's conduct deferred not only to the positions and interests of Britain but to those of other powers as well. This general restraint, based on an "understanding of the realities of existence" and not on the British subsidy, accounted for Ibn Saud's being "extraordinarily correct and statesmanlike in all he had done."[7]

The change in Saudi foreign policy in the twentieth century was not a result of World War I, which brought into existence the modern Middle East system with the new concepts of the "nation-state" and "boundaries." This is shown by a number of factors. Ibn Saud's acceptance of the independent existence of the gulf principalities went back to 1905 and could have nothing to do with the new, post–World War I realities. The Saudi conquest of the Hejaz, a kingdom in close relations with Britain, also took place several years after the post–World War I settlement and in defiance of it. Moreover, Ibn Saud's policies toward the Ottoman Porte and Britain in the 1902–1918 period, before application of the new concept of the nation-state, had already displayed a new pattern of political activity motivated and guided by considerations of realpolitik. Finally, Ibn Saud's stand on the issue of expansion was not a response to the post–World War I concept of boundaries but emanated rather from his perception of Saudi freedom of action in each arena—Nejd, Hejaz, the gulf, Iraq, Yemen—and his policies had been based on this principle long before the notion of boundaries was introduced into the Arabian Peninsula. These factors suggest that, unlike the Arab states in the Fertile Crescent, modern Saudi Arabia is essentially the product of the pre–World War I period, and its early development, let alone its foreign policy, is to be understood within the context of its own evolution and not the general post–World War I modern state system. The twentieth century had not "created a unique historical context" in the sense that "Saudi expansion into Muslim areas unsympathetic to the Wahhabi doctrine, in particular the Hejaz, produced outcries in the Muslim world," for this had also been precisely the situation in the early nineteenth century, after the Saudis conquered the Hejaz in 1803–1804. Indeed, foreign European intervention was not a unique factor in the twentieth century which "checked Saudi physical growth."[8] Such intervention had been prevalent throughout the nineteenth century in the form of the British presence in the Persian Gulf, which prevented the extension of Saudi rule into the gulf sheikhdoms. The unique factor in the twentieth century was therefore a change not from without but primarily from within, rooted in Ibn Saud's distinct background, education, and legacy, which resulted in a new pattern of Saudi foreign policy.

It is true, as Bayly Winder pointed out, that "the West's military weapons twice stopped the onrushing Wahhabis as they attempted to spill out of their desert into the Fertile Crescent and beyond. On the first occasion, in 1818, it was the Egyptians; on the second, exactly a hundred years later, it was actual Westerners, the British."[9] Yet there was a basic difference between the two cases. In the nineteenth century, the Wahhabis were indeed stopped by others under circumstances of a brutal confrontation, and their state was destroyed. In the twentieth century, in contradistinction, it was Ibn Saud himself who stopped before the West had to contain him. Preempting such a confrontation with the West, Ibn Saud prevented a possible destruction of the Saudi state and ensured its survival. This difference marked the turning point in Ibn Saud's foreign policy in the twentieth century.

Ibn Saud, the Statesman and Man

Ibn Saud was a desert ruler, albeit of genius, who had no personal political experience of the world outside the confines of Arabia. Yet for some reason he was able to grasp the complexities of international politics before, on the eve of, and during World War I. He mastered the art of diplomatic negotiations with all the linguistic nuances and subtleties that it entailed. He even comprehended the difference between "where his interests require it," a wording that he offered and the British rejected, and "it be not damaging to his interests," on which he finally compromised. The key to understanding this phenomenon lies in the period of Ibn Saud's exile in Kuwait, which not only had a profound impact on his cultural background and his political and religious worldview but also served as a political and diplomatic apprenticeship. The Kuwaiti experience exposed Ibn Saud, while in his formative years, to a world unknown to his ancestors, acquainted him with international politics and diplomacy, made him aware of the paramount power of Britain in the gulf, showed him how similar his goals and Kuwait's were, and finally taught him the strategy he was to pursue in order to achieve independence from the Ottomans and British protection.

The new Saudi foreign policy was essentially conceived and pursued by only one man, Ibn Saud, with the usually tacit but sometimes active participation of his father, 'Abd Al-Rahman. On more than one occasion Ibn Saud told Shakespear that only his father, not even his brothers, knew about his policy toward Britain. His emissaries to the British resident and agents always left Riyadh secretly, their purpose and destination unknown to his brothers and entourage.[10] Although the Kuwaiti experience explains the motivation behind Ibn Saud's new foreign policy, it cannot account for his ability to pursue such a policy. The domestic foundations of Ibn Saud's policy rested solely on his personality, but there were checks and constraints on his power and freedom of action that he was also able to circumvent.

The roots of that ability lay partly in a new configuration of forces within the Saudi community in the twentieth century, particularly in a new relationship between the Saudi dynasty and the upholders of the Wahhabi ideology. Ibn Saud had to have been placed in a position different from that of the former Saudi rulers vis-à-vis the Wahhabi ulama in order to be able to act as freely as he did on the basis of purely pragmatic considerations. In the aftermath of the death of the founder of Wahhabism, Ibn 'Abd al-Wahhab, and the destruction of the first two Saudi states, the Wahhabi movement lost much of its dynamism. This was reflected in a distinct weakening of the power of the traditional representatives of the Wahhabi establishment, the ulama, and in a decline in the stature of the family of the sheikh, 'Abd al-Wahhab. Not only were the Wahhabi leaders much weaker than in previous periods, but they were also reluctant to challenge Ibn Saud politically, lest they trigger disunity, which might have brought about the disintegration of the Saudi state for the third time.

Moreover, the Saudi polity at the beginning of the twentieth century was still modeled after the traditional Islamic concept of relations between the ruler and his subjects. Politics and diplomacy were the prerogative of the ruler, and it was incumbent upon the people to comply with his orders. Thus, not only could Ibn Saud maintain diplomatic correspondence with both Britain and the Porte, but he could also conceal it from his people. There were several other objective factors that helped Ibn Saud overcome opposition, such as the desert conditions, the lack of modern means of transportation and communication, the huge distances, and the absence of information. The net result of all these factors was that the checks and constraints on Ibn Saud's power were of small significance and he enjoyed a high degree of freedom of action. When Ibn Saud's charisma and natural sense of leadership are added to this equation, they explain why his power base in Nejd was so broad and why the various constraints did not really hinder him from conducting his own foreign policy.

Indeed, throughout the period Ibn Saud managed to overcome opposition to his flexible foreign policy. In 1905, the ulama called for a defiant attitude toward the Ottomans and criticized Ibn Saud; but he arrived at an agreement with the sultan and recognized his sovereignty. In 1914, Ibn Saud concluded a treaty with the Porte despite the widespread anti-Ottoman sentiments prevalent in Nejd, probably by concealing the very existence of the treaty from his people. And during World War I, he managed to remain pro-British despite growing opposition to and disenchantment with his policies. The only exception in this regard was the Ikhwan, who were ready to challenge Ibn Saud. However, until 1926 they did not constitute a real constraint on his power because territorial expansion, their major concern, was still in full swing. After 1926, when Ibn Saud brought expansion to an end, the Ikhwan did attempt to check his freedom of action and impose on him their own Wahhabi preferences, but Ibn Saud managed to crush their uprising in 1929 and defeat them.

The change in Ibn Saud's conduct of foreign policy, as compared to his predecessors', had its parallel in the personal conduct of Ibn Saud and his brothers. Their close contacts with foreigners, mainly Christians, in Kuwait relieved them of the xenophobia with which the term "Wahhabi" had become associated and made them tolerant of phenomena occurring outside the scope of the Saudi domain. Captain Shakespear became aware of this attitude when he met Ibn Saud for the first time in Kuwait in February 1910. Expecting to encounter the traditional stereotype of a Wahhabi, Shakespear was struck by the fact that "despite their Wahhabi reputation, Ibn Saud's family was much interested in the ways of foreigners and the outer world. They dined with me, appreciated a Western table and menu, and even submitted to the camera," actions that could hardly be conceived of and related to former Saudi-Wahhabi rulers. All struck Shakespear as "particularly intelligent," and Ibn Saud was "a broad-minded man who could probably be trusted further than most Arabs." Shakespear was surprised to discover that Ibn Saud did not evince any xenophobic sentiments or display "a trace of the fanatical spirit which might have been expected from the ruling Wahhabi family." When Shakespear discussed with Ibn Saud "matters of doctrine, custom and religion, which are held to be anathema by the Wahhabi sect," he was always answered with "calm and intelligent reasoning without a trace of fanatical heat." In subsequent meetings, Shakespear had long and intimate discussions with Ibn Saud, in which "all my questions regarding the country, its customs and resources were answered in the frankest manner." Shakespear was allowed to "wander and move among the tents in the Saudi camp and freely converse with the people without arousing that suspicion which generally attaches to a foreigner amongst Arabs of the desert." He was also allowed to attend Ibn Saud's majlis and join in the discussions. The reception that Ibn Saud accorded Shakespear was always friendly and hospitable, with the Saudi ruler displaying pleasure and satisfaction "to renew our old acquaintance." By the second meeting Shakespear was already addressed as "brother," and he noted that "if I had been one in fact, I could not have been treated more as one of the family."[11] Shakespear's impressions contrast with those gathered half a century earlier by the British resident, Pelly, who found the atmosphere in Riyadh less than welcoming, "the stern Wahhabis deeply resenting the presence in their midst of the representative of an infidel Power."

Ibn Saud's unique conduct was manifested on other occasions. In 1916, while visiting Basra, Ibn Saud did what would have been inconceivable for his predecessors: he asked to attend a Sunday service of his British hosts. In the absence of a chaplain, the service was conducted by a rear admiral. According to A. T. Wilson, "in the end Ibn Saud expressed his appreciation of the reverence shown by the congregation as well as of the fact that an Admiral himself conducted the Services." On the same visit, Ibn Saud had another opportunity to demonstrate his familiarity with the outside world upon being introduced for the first time in his life to a European woman. According to Cox, "Ibn Saud met Miss Gertrude Bell with complete frankness and sangfroid as if he had been associated with European ladies all his life." A further example of Ibn Saud's tolerance of foreign customs and religious aspects occurred in 1916 when he needed an urgent operation on his throat. Having invited

Dr. Harrison from Bahrain to operate on him, Ibn Saud asked him first to say his prayer "in your Christian way as I am told is your custom."[12] A Wahhabi would have been hard put to contemplate the recitation of a Christian prayer for his own health.

On several other occasions Ibn Saud demonstrated that he lacked the religious frenzy characteristic of his predecessors and of his contemporary Nejdians. When British officials, such as Cox and Dickson, visited him on the coast, he offered them "superb Egyptian cigarettes," "big black cigars," and "sealed bottles with the name Johnny Walker upon them." Once when riding in the desert with a small group of followers, Ibn Saud suddenly looked around and said: "As there are no Ikhwan with us, he who has a good voice will now start singing." When the singing started, "Ibn Saud was most pleased." None of the former Saudi rulers had ever offered tobacco and alcohol to their guests or allowed and enjoyed singing. Ibn Saud's conduct, indeed, drew the wrath of the Ikhwan, who reproached him for his lack of religious fervor and, particularly, for dealing with the British.[13] Ibn Saud thus represented, as Shakespear remarked, a new type of Saudi-Wahhabi ruler, distinct from his predecessors in background, character, and personal conduct.

Characteristics of Saudi Foreign Policy

The policies that Ibn Saud pursued during the period 1902–1918 revealed some of the principal motifs that would come to dominate Saudi foreign policy throughout the twentieth century, outliving Ibn Saud himself. The Saudi leader demonstrated extreme caution in dealing with Britain and the Porte, and later with other powers, feeling reluctant to take any risks that might embroil him in a confrontation with superior forces. Thus, although he expressed willingness and possessed the capability for occupying Hasa as early as 1906, he consistently abstained from the conquest because his major prerequisites had not been fulfilled. Likewise, despite his desire to restore the former Saudi dominions on the gulf coast, he retreated from the coastal principalities once he became aware of the British determination to protect their independence. Ibn Saud similarly refrained from occupying the Hejaz until 1924, even though in 1919 he had already possessed the willingness and capability to do so after annihilating the 5000-troop Sharifian army at Khurma.[14] This restraint resulted from his assessment that Britain would not acquiesce in a Saudi attack on the Hejaz and that a Saudi attempt might provoke a major Saudi-British confrontation.

Despite such extreme caution, two of Ibn Saud's major actions revealed his readiness to take calculated risks. One was his decision to move against Hasa in 1913, without the British commitment he had earlier sought. The other was his conquest of the Hejaz. In 1924 Ibn Saud reversed his former assessment and decided that Britain would not intervene against a Saudi onslaught on the Hejaz. His decision was based on the assumption that Husain, by adopting intransigent attitudes, failing to secure a treaty with Britain, and declaring himself caliph, had managed to alienate himself completely from the British, relieving them of any obligation toward him. As such an assumption still entailed a risk, Ibn Saud decided to have his troops (he himself was not at the scene) attack Taif first in order to test the British reaction. Only when his calculation about the British inaction proved justified did Ibn Saud move against Mecca and the rest of the Hejaz.[15]

Ibn Saud's conduct was also characterized by clear objectives and persistence. Despite Britain's repeated rejection of his overtures, he continued to adhere to his concept of British protection against the Ottomans as the only means for obtaining independence. Similarly, owing to the British rejection of his overtures, he consistently recognized the Ottomans' sovereignty over his territories and offered them his submission, despite his animosity toward the Porte.

Another salient feature in Ibn Saud's conduct was his desire to leave all options open and avoid any alliance with one power that might irreversibly alienate him from another. He refused to commit himself to the British side on the eve of World War I, as Mubarak had asked him to do, and instead hoped that "God will give the victory to those from whom advantage comes to us." Loyalty to his permanent interests rather than to any particular friends led him to desist from fighting the Ottomans although he wanted to support the British. Likewise, as much as he hated the Ottomans, he wished in late 1917 that they would win the war since, from the point of view of his self-interest, Sharif Husain, in alliance with Britain, posed a graver danger to the Saudi state. Major Keyes, the British political agent at Bahrain, was conscious of Ibn Saud's considerations, explaining that "he signed a treaty with the Turks, and as soon as he thought that they were going under he said it was only 'the name of a treaty.' I do not think that, if it appeared to him that the interests of his dynasty required it, he would hesitate a moment in treating his agreement with us as he treated the scrap of paper between him and Turkey."[16] Such a pattern, characteristic of his conduct during World War I, repeated itself during World War II, when Ibn Saud kept his bridges open to both Britain and Germany.

Ibn Saud's conduct also revealed a tendency to curb or quell overambitiousness lest he thereby jeopardize existing Saudi assets. This tendency was reflected in his forgoing the absorption of the gulf principalities into the Saudi state, even though his military superiority over these entities was unquestionable. This policy has persisted to the present day, although the British barrier, which had prevented such a Saudi absorption, disappeared from the area after 1971. Ibn Saud's tendency to repress ambition was also illustrated by his decision to conclude a peace agreement with Yemen in 1934 and not annex the country, even though he had defeated the Yemeni forces and the country was virtually defenseless. Finally, despite strong pressures from within his own community, Ibn Saud abstained from attacking Transjordan or Iraq following his final conquest of the Hejaz in late 1925. Such an attack would have been only natural in view of both the religious differences (Wahhabis against "deviationist" Muslims) and the dynastic sentiments (Saudis versus Hashemites), particularly after Ibn Saud's expulsion of the Hashemites from the Hejaz in 1925. Nevertheless, he refrained from attacking these two Hashemite states, ruled by Husain's sons, 'Abdallah and Faisal, because he perceived that the British, being Mandatory Power over Iraq and Transjordan, would have to confront the Saudis and defend both countries. Thus, simultaneous with his expulsion of the Hashemites from the Hejaz, Ibn Saud signed the Bahra and Hadda Agreements with the Hashemite-ruled Iraq and Transjordan, recognizing their independence and territorial integrity.[17]

Ibn Saud's conquest of Mecca and Medina, the holy cities of Islam, revealed yet another characteristic feature of Saudi foreign policy: the desire not to alienate the Islamic world. Saudi conduct after their conquest of the Hejaz in 1924–1925 was all the more remarkable when contrasted with their previous occupation of the area one hundred and twenty years earlier. In 1804, the Saudi conquest of Mecca and Medina had not only challenged the authority of the head of the Islamic community, the sultan, but also constituted an act of defiance against the whole Islamic world, for the Saudi-Wahhabi conquerors destroyed tombs, domes above tombs, and other objects of Muslim pilgrimage in Mecca and Medina that were anathema to their own doctrine. They even stopped the annual haj to the holy places, allowing only Wahhabis to perform the pilgrimage. In 1925, Ibn Saud adopted a diametrically opposed approach. He declared that the pilgrimage would continue unhindered; he promised free access to the holy places to all Muslims of all schools and sects, even those that were anathema to Wahhabism; and he vowed to guarantee the security of the holy places and the pilgrimage. Furthermore, in 1926, he convened in Mecca the Muslim World Conference, which was ostensibly intended to discuss the future status of the Hejaz. In reality, Ibn Saud endeavored through the conference to obtain international Islamic recognition of and legitimacy for his control of the holy places of Islam, as well as to prove that freedom and security were prevailing in the Hejaz.[18]

Ibn Saud was interested not only in securing his position in the Islamic world but also in having other powers, regardless of their religion or ideological persuasion, recognize his status and in broadening the range of his foreign relations. To that end, he established diplomatic relations even with the communist, godless-atheist Soviet Union, and in 1932 his son, Faisal, paid a visit to Moscow, in the course of which he met Stalin. In the 1930s, Ibn Saud inaugurated relations with the United States by granting oil concessions to American companies. From 1933 to 1939 he even tried to develop contacts with Hitler's Germany.[19]

One of the cornerstones of Saudi foreign policy throughout the twentieth century, introduced by Ibn Saud, was opposition to the establishment of any pan-Arab or pan-Islamic political formations. Ibn Saud refused to endorse any plans that aimed to recongregate the newly independent Arab countries into a larger unity. He rejected the formation of both a general Arab Union and a union of a limited number of Arab states. He was little influenced by the prounity propaganda of both the Arab nationalists in Syria and the Muslim Brothers in Egypt in the 1930s. He opposed plans for too strong an Arab League in 1945 and refused to be drawn into any scheme of integration, insisting that the separate existence of each Arab state be recognized. Even the restoration of the institution of the caliphate, an integral and central aspect of Islam which was indispensable for the preservation of the Islamic community, was rejected by Ibn Saud. He and his successors opposed all attempts aimed at the creation of larger Arab or Islamic unions, including Sharif Husain's vision of an Arab kingdom with himself as king of all Arabs, Husain's declaration of himself as caliph in 1924, the Hashemite-conceived unity schemes of the "Fertile Crescent" and "Greater Syria," the ambitions of King Faruq of Egypt to become the new caliph, and Nasser's drive for Arab unity. Ibn Saud rejected the idea not only when it envisaged another leader or another country as heading the projected union. In the period 1902–1918, he himself refused to assume an all-Arab role beyond the Saudi context in Arabia proper. Similarly he evinced no ambitions to set himself up as the caliph or sultan of an Islamic union. Ibn Saud's position contrasted with Sharif Husain's simultaneous aspiration to become the king of all Arabs, ruling over the whole of the Arabian Peninsula and the Fertile Crescent, and his subsequent assumption of the title of caliph.

The rationale for this Saudi position, which became a constant in Saudi foreign policy, consisted of two basic components. First, the Saudis realized that because of geography (remoteness of Arabia), demography (lack of manpower), and strategy (inherent military weakness), it was very unlikely that Saudi Arabia would become the leader of any projected union. If such a union, limited or extensive, were realized, it would in all probability be headed by one of the traditional centers in the Arab world—Cairo, Baghdad, or Damascus. The second reason for the Saudis' policy was their recognition that the circumstances of such a unity would not only pose a direct challenge to the political basis of the Saudi dynasty but also obliterate Saudi independence altogether and submit the kingdom to the authority of others. The Saudis' deep-seated anxiety on this score continued to determine their opposition to all unity plans to this day.

Underlying this anxiety is one of the most salient features of

Saudi foreign policy in the twentieth century: it is predicated on a defensive posture, motivated by past traumatic experience. Saudi policy-makers perceive the kingdom, and the peninsula as a whole, as the object of foreign invasions by militarily superior forces. They view the region as containing many adversaries, all hostile to Saudi Arabia, who are attempting to encroach, as they did in the past and will probably do in the future, on Saudi independence. The 1811–1818 Ottoman-Egyptian invasion, the 1838–1840 Egyptian expedition, the 1871 Ottoman conquest of Hasa, the Hashemites' attempts for three decades since 1916 to absorb the Saudi dominions, Egypt's involvement in the civil war in North Yemen during 1962–1967, and the new threats posed by Khomeini's Iran, are all manifestations of this pattern of encroachment. It is incumbent on the Saudi leadership, first and foremost, to protect the kingdom from such "invasions" by external adversaries, and ideally to prevent them altogether. The overriding goal of Saudi foreign policy is thus of a defensive nature: securing the independence and integrity of the state, as well as the position of the Saudi royal family, in the face of a chain of external enemies. Ibn Saud himself phrased this policy when explaining his refusal to assume a military role in the British effort during World War I: "I am a person who desired to remain quiet so that my state may not become impaired."[20] The predominant goal, as stipulated in the 1915 Saudi-British Treaty, was to secure the existing political assets—Nejd, Hasa, Qatif, and their dependencies—and not to entertain visions that transcended the limits of Saudi territories. Once again, Saudi policy contrasted with Sharif Husain's political and territorial ambitions, as stated in his correspondence with McMahon.

The course of Saudi foreign policy in the first two decades of the twentieth century not only influenced the direction of foreign policy in subsequent years but also shaped the kingdom's perception of and relations with the West in general. In this respect, it also set Saudi Arabia apart from the rest of the Arab world. The evolution of Saudi foreign policy was devoid of the strong, deepseated anti-Western sentiments prevalent in the other Arab countries, such as Egypt, Syria, and Iraq. These sentiments were nurtured by the long confrontation between the European Mandatory Power, Britain and France, which had come to control the Arab states after World War I, and the various national movements that emerged in the Arab world. The West was perceived as not only the major obstacle frustrating the realization of Arab aspirations for independence but also the cause of the fragmentation of the Arab world. In Saudi Arabia, in contrast, such sentiments were inexistent. Not only was Britain not viewed as an enemy curbing Saudi independence, but it was perceived as instrumental in obtaining Saudi freedom from the Ottomans. Saudi independence was achieved as the result of an alliance with Britain, not of a struggle against it.

The absence of anti-Western feelings, combined with the fact that Saudi Arabia has no legacy of Western occupation, had an impact on other features of the kingdom besides its foreign policy. This distinct legacy probably accounts for the fact that the process of modernization in Saudi Arabia was not characterized by the political, social, and religious upheavals that were prevalent in the rest of the Arab world. Their absence was all the more remarkable in view of the deep Islamic foundations of the Saudi state. One would have assumed that precisely in Saudi Arabia the strongest antagonism toward modernization would surface. The absence of an anti-Western legacy also accounts in all probability for the fact that it is much easier for Saudi Arabia than the rest of the Arab world to cultivate close relations with the United States.

Implications for the Third Saudi State

The new foreign policy of Ibn Saud had implications for the nature of the third Saudi state. Since the inception of the Wahhabi doctrine and the rise of the house of Saud in the first half of the eighteenth century, all three Saudi states have been based on two pillars, the religious Wahhabi and the dynastic Saudi. The relationship between these two cohesive forces of the Saudi state was described in the *Saudi Memorial* as one of an end and a means: "For two centuries the basis of the rule of the House of Saud has been the original creed of Islam, the return to which was led by Sheikh Ibn 'Abd al-Wahhab. In support of this movement the House of Saud has produced a series of great rulers."[21] In such a configuration, the central objective of the community was to disseminate the new religious doctrine and convert the population in the occupied areas to Wahhabism. The Saudi dynasty was to provide the military and political power necessary for waging the wars of occupation and proselytism.

This type of relationship ceased to exist in the third Saudi state. The transformation of Ibn Saud's foreign policy reflected a change in, if not a reversal of, the roles of the Saudi and Wahhabi components. To the extent that foreign policy constitutes the expression of national goals, the major goals of Ibn Saud were the reinstatement of the house of Saud in Arabia, the restoration of former dynastic dominions, and the consolidation of his own authority, not the expansion of the Saudi state in order to disseminate and impose the Wahhabi doctrine. Shakespear noted that "Ibn Saud was animated, first, by intense patriotism for his country and by a profound veneration for his religion as well as by a single-minded desire to do his best for his people by obtaining for them lasting peace and security." Keyes argued that "Ibn Saud was driven by a sense of patriotism," which "with him is entirely dynastic." And Hamilton, the political agent in Kuwait, claimed that Ibn Saud was motivated by "dreams of the restoration of the ephemeral Wahhabi empire."[22]

This distinction between dynastic-Saudi motivations and religious-Wahhabi considerations goes to the heart of the issue of expansion. As long as the raison d'être of the community was proselytism, which condoned unchecked pillage and plunder, no limits could be set for expansion, since the Wahhabi ideal could not conceive of expansion as being limited or confined to certain areas. Once, however, the major cohesive force of the community became the Saudi dynasty and its major goal focused on the retrieval of ancestral dominions, the territorial ambitions of the state could be qualified and modified by considerations of realpolitik. Thus, if the restoration of a former Saudi province might cause a confrontation with a superior force, it was preferable to forego the opportunity of extending Saudi rule and avoid the risks to existing Saudi territories involved in such a confrontation.

The decline of Wahhabism and the ascendance of the Saudi dynasty as the most cohesive force of the community attested to a new configuration of forces within the third Saudi state. But the relationship between the Wahhabi and Saudi, or the religious-ideological and political-pragmatic, components was much more complex, because the new approach was essentially conceived and pursued by only one man, Ibn Saud. Furthermore, on the domestic front, the traditional Wahhabi way of life did not lose ground; on the contrary, it was strengthened and reinforced by the establishment of the Ikhwan movement. And the internal Wahhabi flame was what enabled Ibn Saud to turn his entity into the strongest in Arabia and to extend Saudi rule over most of the peninsula. This inherent tension between a non-Wahhabi foreign policy which relied on a domestic Wahhabi spirit had existed since the Saudi revival in 1902. It surfaced, however, only on the few occasions when Ibn Saud's tactics, such as his agreements with the Ottomans and his siding with the British during World War I, were inconsistent with traditional Wahhabi attitudes. For the most part the tension remained subterranean, because until 1926 Ibn Saud's dynamism in restoring Saudi territories converged with traditional Wahhabi expansionism and satisfied the Ikhwan.

Once expansion came to an end in 1926, however, the inherent contradiction and the fundamentally divergent views of expansion erupted into a full-fledged confrontation between Ibn Saud, the exponent of the new policies, and the Ikhwan, who represented traditional Wahhabism. The 1929 confrontation, known as the Ikhwan rebellion, was essentially an overt manifestation of a fundamental dichotomy, which had characterized the third Saudi state from its very beginning. It represented more than a disagreement over the enforcement of the new boundaries.[23] It was an all-encompassing confrontation between two competing and conflicting currents, striving to steer the Saudi state along diametrically opposed lines. Ibn Saud's victory in the final showdown enabled him to continue to pursue a policy that he had initiated more than a quarter of a century earlier.

The Ikhwan rebellion in the late 1920s was not the last eruption of traditional Wahhabism against the Saudi ruling family. Traditional Wahhabism has lain dormant for the most part since 1929, in submission to the policy lines adopted by the royal family. It nevertheless manifested itself on several occasions in the late 1950s and early 1960s when the Saudi regime was perceived as seriously deviating from the right path of Wahhabism by introducing such innovations as television and education for girls. The most serious eruption occurred in November 1979 when hundreds of rebels took over the Grand Mosque of Mecca for two weeks and posed a major challenge to the royal family.[24] Paradoxically, this last confrontation attested to the success of Ibn Saud's new foreign policy. In 1926, when the Ikhwan formulated their grievances and listed their demands for Ibn Saud, one of their central articles was the accusation that he had abandoned the duty to wage continuous jihad against the "polytheists," and they called for a resumption of operations against Iraq and Transjordan. They also criticized Ibn Saud for sending his sons, Saud and Faisal, to Egypt and England, "infidel countries." Such accusations reflected their adherence to the traditional Wahhabi concepts of expansion and foreign policy. By 1979, however, even the rebels who attacked the Mecca Mosque did not raise the issue of continuing Wahhabi-Saudi expansion. Listing their grievances against the royal family in several pamphlets that they distributed during the attack, the rebels protested against the domestic Saudi policies and life-style and made no reference to the regime's failure to carry out a Wahhabi-anchored foreign policy. This omission illustrated Ibn Saud's success not only in introducing his new foreign policy and carrying it out during his lifetime but also in turning it into a legitimate, undisputed, entrenched phenomenon, which outlived Ibn Saud himself.

The primacy that Ibn Saud accorded to dynastic and political goals in formulating foreign policy resulted not only in the diminishing importance of Wahhabism but also in the gradual weakening of Islam in general as a determinant in Saudi foreign policy in the twentieth century. Rather than steering the course and direction of Saudi foreign policy, Islam became an effective means of providing it with ideological legitimacy in the eyes of the Saudis and other Arabs and Muslims. Islam enhanced the Saudi position and counterbalanced accusations that Saudi Arabia was too pro-Western. But while Islam has been a feature of Saudi foreign policy, it was not the interests of Islam that the foreign policy was designed to promote, but the interests of the Saudi dynasty.[25]

The third Saudi state owes its ability to survive, as distinct from its two predecessors, to two changes that Ibn Saud introduced into its fabric. One change concerned the internal structure of the community and focused on the transformation of "the true character of the volatile Bedouin society."[26] As Philby noted, Ibn Saud's task was not unsimilar to that of the Prophet, striving to transform the Bedouin's loyalty from the tribe to the community. For that purpose, Ibn Saud devised two new approaches. First, he married into all the major tribes under his control, turning them all in a way into Saudis and thereby creating a new focus of identity and loyalty. Second, he established the Ikhwan movement and made the Wahhabi doctrine serve as the cement transcending all previous tribal barriers.

The other change that Ibn Saud undertook was the transformation in foreign policy. A Wahhabi state along the lines of the first two Saudi states could not have survived for long in modern times. With uncontrolled expansion as its foundation and most cohesive force, such a state was bound to be checked and even crushed. Ibn Saud had the insight to grasp this reality and thus secure the survival of the state.

Contemporary Saudi Arabia remains in both theory and practice officially dedicated to the preservation of pure Islam as propounded by Muhammad Ibn 'Abd al-Wahhab.[27] But the propagation of Wahhabism is another matter. Not only is Saudi Arabia no longer dedicated in practice to the propagation of the Wahhabi doctrine, but even the theory has been obliterated in the twentieth century. Whether such a shift in foreign policy will contribute to the erosion of the internal preservation of the Wahhabi doctrine in the closing years of the twentieth century remains to be seen.

Appendixes A-C
Bibliography
Notes
Index

Treaty Between Ibn Saud and the Turks

Dated 4th Rajab 1332–15th May 1914.

(Original found among Turkish records at Basra)

Wali of the Vilayet of Basra. Suleiman Shafik bin Ali Kumali.

Article 1. This Treaty is signed and executed between the Wali and Commandant of Basrah, Suleiman Shafik Pasha, who is specifically empowered by Imperial Iradeh, and H. E. Abdul Aziz Pasha al-Saood Wali and Commandant of Nejd: This Treaty is relied on by the Imperial Government and consists of 12 articles, explaining secret matters mentioned in the Imperial Firman dated——with reference to the Vilayet of Nejd. The text of this Treaty shall be secret, and relied upon.

Article 2. The Vilayet of Nejd is to remain in charge of Abdul Aziz Pasha al-Saood so long as he is alive, according to the Imperial Firman.

After him it will go to his sons and grandsons by Imperial Firman, provided that he shall be loyal to the Imperial Government and to his forefathers, the previous Valis.

Article 3. A Technical Military Official shall be appointed by the said Wali and Commandant (i.e. Bin Saud) to live wherever he wishes: if he sees fit and necessary he may introduce Turkish Officers for the fundamental technical training of Local Troops, and their number shall depend upon the choice and wishes of the said Wali and Commandant (i.e. Ibn Saud).

Article 4. A number of soldiers and gendarmerie, as deemed fit by the Wali and Commandant aforesaid, shall be stationed at seaports such as Katif, and Ojair.

Article 5. All the business of the Customs, Taxes, Ports and Light houses shall be exercised subject to the international rights of Governments, and shall be conducted according to the principles of the Turkish Government under the direction of the said Wali and Commandant.

Article 6. Till the sources of the revenues reach a degree sufficient to meet the requirements of the Vilayet and the local expenditure and military dispositions according to the present circumstances and normal conditions of Nejd, the deficiency in the budget shall be met from the Customs, Posts, Telegraphs and Ports revenue; and if there is a surplus, it should be sent to the Porte with a report.

If the local revenue is sufficient to meet all expenses, the income of the Posts, Telegraphs and Customs shall be remitted to their respective Departments. Also as regards local incomes other than those mentioned above, if there is any surplus, 10 percent of it shall be sent to the Government Treasury.

Article 7. The Turkish flag shall be hoisted on all government buildings and places of importance on the sea and on the land, and also on boats belonging to the Vilayet of Nejd.

Article 8. Correspondence shall be conducted with the Marine Department for the regular supply of arms and ammunition.

Article 9. The said Wali and Commandant is not allowed to interfere with, or correspond about foreign affairs and international treaties, or to grant concessions to foreigners.

Article 10. All the correspondence of the Wali and Commandant shall be direct with the Imperial Ministeries of Interior and Marine, without intermediary.

Article 11. Post Offices shall be established in the Vilayet of Nejd, in order to facilitate communication; and arrangements shall be made to dispatch posts to the necessary places in a fitting manner; Turkish stamps shall be affixed to all letters and packages.

Article 12. If, God forbid, the Government should have to fight with a foreign power or if there should be any internal disturbance in any Vilayet and the Government asks the said Wali for a force to cooperate with its own forces it is incumbent on the Wali to prepare a sufficient force with provisions and ammunition, and to respond to the demand at once, according to his power and ability.

(Signed) Abdul Aziz,
          Wali of Nejd Wilayet, and Commander of its Army.

          Suleiman Shafik Bin Ali Kamali,
          Wali of Basrah Wilayet, and Commander of its Forces.

Appendix B

Drafts of the Anglo-Saudi Treaty

British draft (February 1915)

In the name of God the Merciful and Compassionate.

The High British Government on its own part, and Abdul Aziz-bin-Abdur Rahman-Bin-Faisal al-Saud, Ruler of Nejd, Al Hasa and Qatif, on behalf of himself, his heirs and successors and tribesmen, being desirous of confirming and strengthening the friendly relations which have for generations existed between the two parties, and with a view of consolidating their respective interests—the British Government have named and appointed Lt.-Colonel Sir Percy Cox, K.C.I.E., C.S.I., British Resident in the Persian Gulf, as their Plenipotentiary to conclude a Treaty for this purpose with Abdul Aziz-bin-Abdur Rahman-bin-Faisal al-Saud, the said Lt.-Colonel Sir Percy Cox, and Abdul Aziz-bin-Abdur Rahman-bin-Faisal al-Saud, hereafter known as "Bin Saud," have agreed upon and concluded the following articles:

Saudi draft (April 1915)

In the name of God the Merciful and Compassionate.

The High British Government on its own part, and Abdul Aziz-bin-Abdur Rahman-Bin-Faisal al-Saud, Ruler of Nejd, Al Hasa, Qatif, *Jubail, and the towns and ports belonging to them,* on behalf of himself, his heirs and successors and tribesmen, being desirous of confirming and strengthening the friendly relations which have for *a long time* existed between the two parties, and with a view to consolidating their respective interests—the British Government have named and appointed Lt.-Colonel Sir Percy Cox, K.C.I.E., C.S.I., British Resident in the Persian Gulf, as their Plenipotentiary to conclude a Treaty for this purpose with Abdul Aziz-bin Abdur Rahman-bin-Faisal al-Saud.

The said Lt.-Colonel Sir Percy Cox, and Abdul Aziz-bin-Abdur Rahman-bin-Faisal al-Saud, hereafter known as "Bin Saud," have agreed upon and concluded the following articles:

Significant differences between the two drafts are shown in italics.

I

The British Government do acknowledge and admit that Nejd, Al Hasa and Qatif, and their territories and ports on the shores of the Persian Gulf are the territory of Bin Saud and of his fathers before him, and do hereby recognize the said Bin Saud as the independent Ruler thereof, and after him his sons and descendants by inheritance, but the selection of the individual shall be *subject to the approval of the British Government after confidential consultation with them.*

I

The British Government do acknowledge and admit that Nejd, al Hasa, Qatif, *Jubail their dependencies and territories, which will be discussed and determined hereafter,* and their territories and ports on the shores of the Persian Gulf are the *countries* of Bin Saud and of his fathers before him and do hereby recognize the said Bin Saud as the independent Ruler thereof *and as absolute Chief of their tribes,* and after him his sons and dependents by inheritance, but the selection of the individual shall be according to the designation of his successor (by the living Ruler) *or by the calling for the votes of the subjects inhabiting those countries.*

II

In the event of *unprovoked* aggression by any Foreign Power on the territories of the said Bin Saud and his descendants, the British Government will aid Bin Saud *to such extent and in such manner as the situation may seem to them to require.*

II

In the event of aggression by any Foreign Power on the territories of the countries belonging to the said Bin Saud, and his descendants, the British Government will aid Bin Saud *in all circumstances and in any place.*

III

Bin Saud hereby agrees and promises to refrain from entering into any correspondence, agreement or Treaty with any Foreign Nation or Power and further to give immediate notice to the political authorities of the British Government of any attempt on the part of any other Power to interfere with the above territories.

III

Bin Saud hereby agrees and promises to refrain from entering into any correspondence, agreement or Treaty with any Foreign Nation or Power and further to give immediate notice to the political authorities of the British Government of any attempt on the part of any Power to interfere with the above territories.

IV

Bin Saud hereby undertakes *for ever* that he will not cede, *sell*, mortgage or otherwise dispose of the above territories or any part of them, or grant concessions within those territories to a Foreign Power or to the subjects of any Foreign Power without the consent of the British Government, whose advice he will unreservedly follow.

V

Bin Saud hereby promises to keep open the roads leading through the above territories to the Holy Places and to protect pilgrims on their way to and from the said shrines.

VI

Bin Saud undertakes as his fathers did before him to refrain from all aggression on, or interference with, the territories of Kuwait, Bahrain, Qatar and Oman Coast, or *other tribes and Chiefs* who are under the protection of the British Government, and the limits of whose territories shall be hereafter determined.

VII

The British Government and Bin Saud agree to conclude *so soon as this can conveniently be arranged*, a further detailed Treaty in regard to *other* matters jointly concerning them.

IV

Bin Saud hereby undertakes that he will not cede, mortgage, or otherwise dispose of the above territories or any part of them, or [grant] concessions within those territories to a Foreign Power or to the subjects of any Foreign Power without the consent of the British Government, whose advice he will unreservedly follow, *where his interests require it.*

V

Bin Saud hereby promises to keep open the roads leading *through his countries to the* Holy Shrines and to protect pilgrims on their *return* to the Holy Places.

VI

Bin Saud undertakes, as his fathers did before him to refrain from all aggression on or interference with the territories of Kuwait, Bahrain, *the Shaikhs of* Qatar and the Oman Coast, who are under the protection of the exalted Government and have Treaty relations and the limits of their territories shall be hereafter determined.

VII

The British Government and Bin Saud agree to conclude a further detailed Treaty in regard to matters jointly concerning the two parties.

(Signed)   Abdul Aziz- Bin-Abdur
Rahman-Bin-Faisal-
Bin Saud

Appendix C

The Anglo-Saudi Treaty, December 1915

In the Name of God the Merciful and Compassionate
Preamble

The High British Government on its own part, and Abdul Aziz-bin-Abdur Rahman-bin-Faisal Al-Saud, Ruler of Nejd, El Hassa, Qatif *and Jubail, and the towns and ports belonging to them,* on behalf of himself, his heirs and successors, and tribesmen, being desirous of confirming and strengthening the friendly relations which have *for a long time* existed between the two parties, and with a view of consolidating their respective interests—the British Government have named and appointed Lt.-Colonel Sir Percy Cox, K.C.S.I., K.C.I.E., British Resident in the Persian Gulf, as their Plenipotentiary, to conclude a treaty for this purpose with Abdul Aziz-bin-Abdur Rahman-bin-Faisal Al-Saud.

The said Lt.-Colonel Sir Percy Cox and Abdul Aziz-bin-Abdur Rahman bin-Faisal Al-Saud (hereafter known as "Bin Saud"), have agreed upon and concluded the following articles:

I

The British Government do acknowledge and admit that Nejd, El Hassa, Qatif *and Jubail,* and their *dependencies and* territories, *which will be discussed and determined hereafter,* and their ports on the shores of the Persian Gulf are the *countries* of Bin Saud and of his fathers before him, and do hereby recognize the said Bin Saud as the independent Ruler thereof *and absolute Chief of their tribes,* and after him his sons and descendants by inheritance; but the selection of the individual shall be *in accordance with the nomination (i.e., by the living Ruler) of his successor; but with the proviso that he shall not be a person antagonistic to the British government in any respect; such as, for example, in regard to the terms mentioned in this treaty.*

The resolution of significant differences between the two drafts is shown in italics.

II

In the event of [*"unprovoked"* omitted] aggression by any foreign Power on the territories of the countries of the said Bin Saud and his descendants *without reference to the British Government and without giving her an opportunity of communicating with Bin Saud* and composing the matter, the British Government will aid Bin Saud to such extent and in such a manner as the *British government after consulting Bin Saud may consider most effective for protecting his interests and countries.*

III

Bin Saud hereby agrees and promises to refrain from entering into any correspondence, agreement, or treaty with any foreign nation or Power, and, further, to give immediate notice to the political authorities of the British Government of any attempt on the part of any other Power to interfere with the above territories.

IV

Bin Saud hereby undertakes that he will *absolutely* not cede, sell, mortgage, *lease*, or otherwise dispose of the above territories or any part of them, or grant concessions within those territories to any foreign Power or to the subjects of any foreign Power, without the consent of the British Government.

    And that he will follow her advice unreservedly provided that it be not damaging to his own interests.

V

Bin Saud hereby *undertakes* to keep open *within his territories the roads leading to the Holy Places*, and to protect pilgrims on their *passage* to and from the Holy Places.

VI

Bin Saud undertakes, as his fathers did before him, to refrain from all aggression on or interference with the territories of Kuwait, Bahrein, *and of the Sheikhs of* Qatar and the Oman Coast ["other tribes and chiefs" omitted] who are under the protection of the British Government, *and who have treaty relations with the said Government;* and the limits of their territories shall be hereafter determined.

Appendix C

VII

The British Government and Bin Saud agree to conclude [words in original draft omitted] a further detailed treaty in regard to ["other" omitted] matters concerning the two parties.

Dated 18th Safar 1334, corresponding to 26th December, 1915,

(Signed and sealed)   Abdul Aziz Al-Saud

                         P. Z. Cox, Lt.-Colonel, British Resident in the Persian Gulf

(Signed)   Chelmsford, Viceroy and Governor-General of India

Bibliography

Primary Sources

GREAT BRITAIN

Admiralty, Geographical Section. *A Handbook of Arabia*. London: H. M. Stationary Office, 1920.

———, Naval Intelligence Division, Geographical Handbook Series. *Iraq and the Persian Gulf*. London: H. M. Stationary Office, 1944.

———, *Western Arabia and the Red Sea*. London: H. M. Stationary Office, 1946.

Commonwealth Relations Office: India Office Records, London. Political and Secret Correspondence with India, 1875–1911 (L/P&S/7).

———. Departmental Papers, Political and Secret Separate Files, 1902–1931 (L/P&S/10).

———. Departmental Papers, Political and Secret Annual Files, 1902–1930 (L/P&S/11).

———. Political and Secret Correspondence, Residency Files: Bushire (1), Bahrain (2,3), Kuwait (5) (R/15/1,2,3,5).

Foreign Office. *The Arab Bulletin*. Cairo: The Arab Bureau, 1915–1919.

———. *Arbitration Concerning Buraimi and the Common Frontier Between Abu Dhabi and Sa'udi Arabia: Memorial submitted by the Government of the United Kingdom of Great Britain and Northern Ireland*. London: H. M. Stationary Office, 1955.

———. *British Documents on the Origins of the War, 1898–1914*, ed. George P. Gooch and Harold Temperly, 11 vols. London: H. M. Stationary Office, 1926–1938.

———. *The Official History of the Campaign in Mesopotamia*, 4 vols. London: H. M. Stationary Office, 1921.

———, Confidential Print. Robin Bidwell. *The Affairs of Kuwait, 1896–1905*. London: Frank Cass, 1971.

———, Confidential Print. Robin Bidwell. *The Affairs of Arabia, 1905–1906*. London: Frank Cass, 1971.

———, Historical Section. *Peace Handbook*, vol. 11, Arabia; vol. 13, Persian Gulf. London: H. M. Stationary Office, 1920.

Philby, St. John B. Private Papers Collection (St. Anthony's College, Middle East Center, Oxford University).

Public Record Office. Foreign Office files, series 78 (until 1905).

———. Foreign Office files, series 371 (1905 on).

———. Foreign Office files, series 406, Confidential Print (Eastern Affairs).

———. Foreign Office files, series 424, Confidential Print (Turkey).

INDIA

Aitchinson, C. U. *A Collection of Treaties, Engagements, and Sanads Relating to India and Neighbouring Countries.* Delhi: Manager of Publications, 1933.

Lorimer, John Gordon. *Gazetteer of the Persian Gulf, Oman, and Central Arabia.* Calcutta: Government Printing House, 1908–1915.

Saldanha, J. A. *Précis of Correspondence Regarding the Affairs of the Persian Gulf, 1801–1853.* Calcutta: Government Printing House, 1906.

———. *Précis of Najd Affairs, 1804–1904.* Calcutta: Government Printing House, 1904.

——— *Précis of Turkish Arabia Affairs, 1801–1905.* Calcutta: Government Printing House, 1906.

———. *Précis of Turkish Expansion on the Arab Littoral of the Persian Gulf, and Hasa and Qatif Affairs.* Calcutta: Government Printing House, 1904.

SAUDI ARABIA

Memorial of the Government of Saudi Arabia: Arbitration for the Settlement of the Territorial Dispute Between Muscat and Abu-Dhabi on One Side and Saudi Arabia on the Other. 3 vols. Cairo: al-Maaref Press, 1955.

al-Rashid, Ibrahim. *Documents on the History of Saudi Arabia.* Salisbury, N.C.: Documentary Publications, 1970.

Secondary Sources

'Abdallah, Ibn Husain. *Memoirs of King 'Abdallah of Transjordan,* ed. Philip Graves. London: Cape, 1950.

Almana, Mohammed. *Arabia Unified: A Portrait of Ibn Saud.* London: Hutchinson, 1980.

al-Alusi, Mahmud Shukri. *Ta'rikh Najd* [The History of Najd]. Cairo: Matba'a al-Salafiyya, 1929.

Anderson, Irvine H. *ARAMCO, the United States, and Saudi Arabia: A Study of the Dynamics of Foreign Policy, 1933–1950.* Princeton: Princeton University Press, 1981.

Anderson, Matthew S. *The Eastern Question, 1774–1923: A Study in International Relations.* London: Macmillan, 1974.

Antonius, George. *The Arab Awakening.* New York: Putnam, 1938.

Arif, Muhammad Ibn Ahmad. *The Hijaz Railway and the Muslim Pilgrimage,* ed. Jacob M. Landau. Detroit: Wayne State University Press, 1971.

Armstrong, Harold C. *Lord of Arabia, Ibn Saud: An Intimate Study of a King.* London: Penguin, 1934.

Assah, Ahmad. *Mu'jiza fawqa al-rimal* [Miracle on the Sand]. Beirut: n.p., 1965.

'Attar, Ahmad 'Abd al-Ghafur. *Saqr al-jazira* [The Hawk of the Peninsula]. Beirut: Matba'at al-Hurriyya, 1973.

Bari, M. A. "The Early Wahhabis, Some Contemporary Assessments," *Proceedings of the International Congress of Orientalists, 1967* (1971): 264–266.

Belhaven, Lord. *The Uneven Road*. London: Murray, 1955.

Bell, Gertrude. *The Arab War: Confidential Information for General Headquarters*. London: Golden Cockerel Press, 1940.

———. *The Desert and the Sown*. New York: Dutun, 1907.

———. *The Letters of Gertrude Bell*, ed. Lady Bell. London: Benn, 1927.

———. *Review of the Civil Administration of Mesopotamia*. London: H. M. Stationary Office, 1920.

Benoist-Méchin, Jacques. *Arabian Destiny*. London: Elek, 1957.

Bray, N. N. E. *A Paladin of Arabia: The Biography of G. E. Leachman*. London: Unicorn Press, 1936.

———. *Shifting Sands*. London: Unicorn Press, 1934.

Bullard, Reader. *Britain and the Middle East*. London: Hutchinson, 1964.

———. *The Camels Must Go*. London: Faber, 1951.

Burgoyne, Elizabeth. *Gertrude Bell: From Her Personal Papers*. London: Benn, 1961.

Busch, Briton Cooper. *Britain and the Persian Gulf, 1894–1914*. Berkeley: University of California Press, 1967.

———. "Britain and the Status of Kuwait, 1894–1899," *Middle East Journal* 21 (1967): 187–198.

———. *Britain, India, and the Arabs, 1914–1921*. Berkeley: University of California Press, 1971.

Butterfield, Paul K. *The Diplomacy of the Baghdad Railway, 1890–1914*. Ph.D. dissertation, Goettingen, 1932.

Carruthers, Douglas. "Captain Shakespear's Last Journey," *Journal of the Royal Geographical Society* 59 (1922): 321–334, 401–418.

Chapman, M. K. *Great Britain and the Baghdad Railway, 1888–1917*. Northhampton: Smith College Press, 1948.

Clayton, Gilbert. "Arabia and the Arabs," *International Affairs* 8 (1929): 8–20.

———. *An Arabian Diary, Sir Gilbert Clayton*, ed. Robert O. Collins. Berkeley: University of California Press, 1969.

DeGaury, Gerald. "Arabia and the Future," *Journal of the Royal Asian Society* 31 (1944).

———. *Arabia Phoenix*. London: Harrap, 1946.

———. "The End of Arabian Isolation," *Foreign Affairs* 25 (1946): 82–89.

Dickson, Harold R. P. *The Arab of the Desert: A Glimpse into Badawin Life in Kuwait and Saudi Arabia*. London: Allen and Unwin, 1949.

———. *Kuwait and Her Neighbours*. London: Allen and Unwin, 1956.

Djemal, Pasha. *Memories of a Turkish Statesman, 1913–1919*. London: 1929.

Ghaith, Abdul Hakim. *The Marching Caravan: The Story of Modern Saudi Arabia*. Jedda: al-Madina al-Munawara, 1967.

Gibb, H. A. R. *Modern Trends in Islam*. Chicago: Chicago University Press, 1947.

Glubb, J. B. *War in the Desert*. London: Hodder and Stoughton, 1960.

Goldberg, Jacob. "Captain Shakespear and Ibn Saud: A Balanced Reappraisal," *Middle Eastern Studies* 21 (1985): 74–88.

———. "The Origins of British-Saudi Relations: The 1915 Anglo-Saudi Treaty Revisited," *Historical Journal* 28 (1985), pp. 693–703.

———. "Philby as a Source for Early Twentieth Century Saudi History— A Critical Examination," *Middle Eastern Studies* 21 (1985): 223–243.

———. "The 1913 Saudi Occupation of Hasa Reconsidered," *Middle Eastern Studies* 18 (1982): 21–29.

———. "The 1914 Saudi-Ottoman Treaty—Myth or Reality?" *Journal of Contemporary History* 19 (1984): 289–314.

Goldrup, Lawrence P. "Saudi Arabia, 1902–1932: The Development of a Wahhabi Society." Ph.D. dissertation, University of California, Los Angeles, 1971.

Graves, Philip. *The Life of Sir Percy Cox*. London: Hutchinson, 1941.

Habib, John S. *Ibn Saud's Warriors of Islam: The Ikhwan of Najd and Their Role in the Creation of the Saudi Kingdom, 1910–1930*. Leiden: E. J. Brill, 1978.

Hamza, Fu'ad. *Qalb jazirat al-'Arab* [The Heart of the Arabian Peninsula]. Riyadh: Maktabat al-Nasr al-Haditha, 1933.

Harrison, Paul W. *The Arab at Home*. London: Hutchinson, 1924.

———. *Doctor in Arabia*. New York: John Day, 1940.

———. "Al-Riadh, The Capital of Nejd," *Moslem World* 8 (1918): 412–419.

Helms, Christine M. *The Cohesion of Saudi Arabia*. London: Croom Helm, 1981.

Hirszowicz, Lukasz. *The Third Reich and the Arab East*. London: Routledge, 1966.

Hitti, Philip. *Makers of Arab History*. New York: St. Martin's Press, 1968.

Hogarth, David George. *A History of Arabia*. Oxford: Clarendon Press, 1922.

———. "Wahhabism and British Interests," *International Affairs* 4 (1925): 70–81.

Holden, David, and Richard Johns. *The House of Saud*. New York: Holt, Rinehart, Winston, 1981.

Holt, P. M. *Egypt and the Fertile Crescent, 1516–1922*. Ithaca: Cornell University Press, 1966.

Hopwood, Derek, ed. *The Arabian Peninsula*. London: Allen and Unwin, 1972.

Howarth, David. *The Desert King: Ibn Saud and His Arabia*. London: Collins, 1964.

Hurewitz, J. C. *Diplomacy in the Near and Middle East, A Documentary Record: 1535–1914*. London: Van Nostrand, 1956.

Ibn Hadhlul, Sa'ud. *Ta'rikh muluk al-Sa'ud* [The History of the Saudi Kings]. Riyadh: 1961.

Ibn 'Isa. *Ta'rikh Najd* [The History of Najd]. Riyadh: Dar al-Yamama, 1966.

Iqbal, Sheikh Muhammad. *Emergence of Saudi Arabia: A Political Study of King Abd al-Aziz ibn Saud, 1901–1953.* Kashmir: Shrinagar, 1977.

Jacob, Harold F. *The Kings of Arabia: The Rise and Set of the Turkish Sovereignty in the Arabian Peninsula.* London: Mills and Boon, 1923.

Kedourie, Elie. *England and the Middle East, 1914–1921: The Destruction of the Ottoman Empire.* London: Bowes, 1956.

———. *In the Anglo-Arab Labyrinth: the McMahon-Husayn Correspondence and its Interpretations, 1914–1939.* London: Cambridge University Press, 1976.

———. "The Surrender of Medina," *Middle Eastern Studies* 13 (1977): 124–143.

Kelly, J. B. *Britain and the Persian Gulf, 1795–1880.* London: Oxford University Press, 1968.

———. *Eastern Arabia Frontiers.* London: Faber, 1964.

———. "Mehemet Ali's Expedition to the Persian Gulf, 1837–1840," *Middle Eastern Studies* 1 (1965): 350–381; 2 (1965): 31–65.

———. "Salisbury, Curzon, and the Kuwaiti Agreement of 1899," in K. Bourne and D. C. Watt, *Studies in International History.* Hamden, Conn.: Archon, 1967.

al-Khatib, Syed Abdul Hamid. *Harbinger of Justice: A Biography of Ibn Saud.* Karachi: al-Arab Printing Press, 1951.

Kheirallah, George. *Arabia Reborn.* Albuquerque: University of New Mexico Press, 1952.

Kirk, G. L. "Ibn Saud Builds an Empire," *Current History* 40 (1934): 291–297.

Klieman, Aaron S. *Foundations of British Policy in the Arab World: The Cairo Conference of 1921.* Baltimore: The Johns Hopkins University Press, 1970.

Kumar, Ravindar. "Abdul-Aziz al-Saud and the Genesis of Saudi Arabia (1901–1907)," *Bengal Past and Present* 79–80 (1960): 60–66, 83–89.

———. *India and the Persian Gulf Region, 1858–1907.* New York: Asia Publishing Press, 1965.

Lacey, Robert. *The Kingdom.* London: Hutchinson, 1981.

Leachman, G. E. "A Journey Through Central Arabia," *Journal of the Royal Geographical Society* 43 (1914): 500–520.

Lebkicher, Roy. *The Arabia of Ibn-Saud.* New York: Russel Moore, 1952.

Lenczowski, George. *The Middle East in World Affairs.* Ithaca: Cornell University Press, 1962.

Lewis, C. C. "Ibn Saud and the Future of Arabia," *International Affairs* 12 (1933): 518–534.

Malone, J. J. "Saudi Arabia," *Muslim World* 56 (1966): 290–295.

Marlowe, John. *The Persian Gulf in the Twentieth Century.* London: Cresset Press, 1962.

Monroe, Elizabeth. *Britain's Moment in the Middle East, 1914–1956*. London: Chatto and Windus, 1963.

———. *Philby of Arabia*. London: Faber, 1973.

Montgomery, J. A. "Arabia Today," *Journal of the American Oriental Society* 47 (1927): 97–132.

Morris, James. *The Hashemite Kings*. London: Faber, 1959.

al-Mukhtar, Salah al-Din. *Ta'rikh al-mamlaka al-'Arabiyya al-Sa'udiyya fi madiha wa khadiriha* [The History of the Kingdom of Saudi Arabia in the Past and Present]. Beirut: Dar Maktabat al-Hayat, 1957.

Musil, Alois. "Kulturpolitischer Bericht aus Arabien," *Osterreichische Monatsschrift fur den Orient* 40 (1914): 161–162, 245–246.

———. *Northern Nejd*. New York: American Geographical Society, 1928.

———. "Religion and Politics in Arabia," *Foreign Affairs* (1928).

Pelly, Lewis. "A Visit to the Wahabee Capital, Central Arabia," *Journal of the Royal Geographical Society* 35 (1865).

Philby, St. John B. *Arabia*. London: Benn, 1930.

———. *Arabia of the Wahhabis*. London: Constable, 1928.

———. "Arabia Today," *International Affairs* 14 (1935): 619–634.

———. *Arabian Days*. London: Hale, 1948.

———. *Arabian Jubilee*. London: Hale, 1952.

———. *Forty Years in the Wilderness*. London: Hale, 1957.

———. *The Heart of Arabia*. London: Constable, 1922.

———. *Report on Najd Mission, 1917–1918*. Baghdad: Government Press, 1918.

———. *Saudi Arabia*. London: Benn, 1955.

———. "The Triumph of the Wahhabis," *Journal of the Royal Asian Society* 13 (1926).

Piscatori, James. "Islamic Values and National Interest: The Foreign Policy of Saudi Arabia," in Adeed Dawisha, ed. *Islam in Foreign Policy*. London: Cambridge University Press, 1983.

Plass, Jens B. *England zwischen Russland und Deutschland: Der Persian Golf in der Britischen Vorkriegspolitik, 1899–1907*. Hamburg: Gesellschaft fur Volkerrecht und Auswartige Politik, 1966.

Powell, Alexander E. *The Struggle for Power in Moslem Arabia*. London: John Long, 1925.

al-Rashid, 'Abd al-'Aziz. *Ta'rikh Kuwait* [The History of Kuwait]. Beirut: Dar Maktabat al-Hayat, n.d.

Rentz, George. "The Ikhwan," *Encyclopedia of Islam*, III, 1064.

———. "Literature on the Kingdom of Saudi Arabia," *Middle East Journal* 4 (1950): 244–248.

———. "Muhammad ibn 'Abd al-Wahhab (1703/4–1792) and the Beginnings of the Unitarian Empire in Arabia." Ph.D. dissertation, University of California, Berkeley, 1948.

———. "Philby as a Historian of Arabia," in *Studies in the History of Arabia*, vol. 1: *Sources for the History of Arabia*. Riyadh, 1977.

Rihani, Ameen. *Around the Coasts of Arabia*. London: Constable, 1930.

———. *Ibn Sa'oud of Arabia: His People and His Land*. London: Constable, 1928.

———. *Ta'rikh Najd al-hadith wa mulhaqatihi* [The Modern History of Najd and Its Dependencies]. Beirut: al-Matba'a al-'Ilmiyya, 1928.

Sa'id, Amin. *Ta'rikh al-dawla al-Sa'udiyya* [The History of the Saudi State]. Beirut: Dar al-Kitab al-'Arabi, 1964.

Sanger, Richard H. *The Arabian Peninsula*. Ithaca: Cornell University Press, 1954.

Shaw, Stanford. *History of the Ottoman Empire and Modern Turkey*. New York: Cambridge University Press, 1977.

Silverfarb, Daniel. "The Anglo-Najd Treaty of December 1915," *Middle Eastern Studies* 16 (1980): 167–177.

———. "British Relations with Ibn Saud of Najd, 1914–1919." Ph.D. dissertation, University of Wisconsin, 1972.

———. "The Philby Mission to Ibn Sa'ud, 1917–1918," *Journal of Contemporary History* 14 (1979): 269–286.

Smalley, W. F. "The Wahhabis and Ibn Saud," *Moslem World* 22 (1932): 227–246.

Smith, Wilfred C. *Islam in Modern History*. Princeton: Princeton University Press, 1957.

Stavrianos, Leften S. *The Balkans, 1815–1914*. New York: Holt, Rinehart, Winston, 1963.

Stitt, George. *A Prince of Arabia: The Emir Shereef Ali Haider*. London: Allen and Unwin, 1948.

Storrs, Ronald. *Orientations*. London: Nicholson and Watson, 1937.

Toynbee, A. J. "A Problem of Arabian Statesmanship," *International Affairs* 8 (1929): 367–375.

———. "The Rise of the Wahhabi Power," *Survey of International Affairs* 1 (1925).

Troeller, Gary. *The Birth of Saudi Arabia: Britain and the Rise of the House of Sa'ud*. London: Frank Cass, 1976.

———. "Ibn Saud and Sharif Husain: A Comparison in Importance in the Early Years of the First World War," *Historical Journal* 14 (1971).

Van der Meulen, Daniel. *The Wells of Ibn Saud*. New York: Praeger, 1957.

Wahba, Hafiz. *Arabian Days*. London: Barker, 1964.

———. *Jazirat al-'Arab fi'l qarn al-'ishrin* [The Arabian Peninsula in the Twentieth Century]. Cairo: Matba'at Lajnat al-Ta'lif wa al-Tarjama wa al-Nashr, 1935.

———. *Khamsun 'am fi jazirat al-'Arab* [Fifty years in the Arabian Peninsula]. Cairo: 1960.

———. "Wahhabism in Arabia: Past and Present," *Journal of the Royal Asian Society* 16 (1929).

Watt, D. C. "The Foreign Policy of Ibn Saud 1936–1939," *Journal of the Royal Asian Society* 50 (1963): 152–160.

Williams, Kenneth. *Ibn Saud: The Puritan King of Arabia*. London: Cape, 1933.

Wilson, Arnold T. *Loyalties Mesopotamia, 1914–1917*. London: Oxford University Press, 1930.

———. *Mesopotamia, 1917–1920: A Clash of Loyalties. A Personal and Historical Record*. London: Oxford University Press, 1931.

Winder, R. Bayly. *Saudi Arabia in the Nineteenth Century*. London: Macmillan, 1965.

Winstone, Harry V. F. *Captain Shakespear: A Portrait*. London: Cape, 1976.

Zirikli, Khayr al-Din. *Shibh al-jazira fi 'ahd al-malik 'Abd al-'Aziz* [The Peninsula at the Time of King 'Abd al-'Aziz]. Beirut: Dar al-Qalam, 1970.

Notes

Introduction

1. See e.g. Ravinder Kumar, *India and the Persian Gulf Region, 1858–1907* (London, 1965); Briton C. Busch, *Britain and the Persian Gulf, 1894–1914* (Berkeley, 1967); Busch, *Britain, India, and the Arabs, 1914–1921* (Berkeley, 1971); Gary Troeller, *The Birth of Saudi Arabia* (London, 1976); Christine M. Helms, *The Cohesion of Saudi Arabia* (London, 1981).

2. Ibid., pp. xviii, xv; Kumar, *India*, p. 118.

3. Hafiz Wahba, *Arabian Days* (London, 1964), p. 166; Sir Percy Cox, quoted in *Journal of the Royal Central Asian Society* 14 (1927): 40.

4. St. John B. Philby, "The Triumph of the Wahhabis," *Journal of the Royal Central Asian Society* 14 (1927): 294; Philby, "Arabia Today," *International Affairs* 14 (1935): 619–634; Jacob Goldberg, "Philby as a Source for Early Twentieth Century Saudi History—A Critical Examination," *Middle Eastern Studies*, vol. 21 (1985): 223–243; David George Hogarth, quoted in *Journal of the Royal Central Asian Society* 13 (1926): 314–315.

1. The Former Saudi States

1. P. M. Holt, *Egypt and the Fertile Crescent, 1516–1922* (Ithaca, 1966), ch. 1.

2. St. John B. Philby, *Saudi Arabia* (London, 1955), p. 33.

3. G. S. Rentz, "Muhammad ibn 'Abd al-Wahhab (1703/4–1792) and the Beginnings of the Unitarian Empire in Arabia," Ph.D. diss., University of California, Berkeley, 1948; *Encyclopedia of Islam* (Leiden, 1913–1938), III, 951–955.

4. Philby, *Saudi Arabia*, pp. 34–35.

5. In Philby's words, "The dominant factor was not the alarums and excursions of kings but the incubation of an idea." *Saudi Arabia*, p. 33.

6. Ibid., chs. 2–3; J. G. Lorimer, *Gazetteer of the Persian Gulf, Oman, and Central Arabia* (Calcutta, 1908–1915), I, 1053–1056.

7. Ibid., pp. 1057–1058.

8. Ibid., pp. 1059–1060; Philby, *Saudi Arabia*, p. 93.

9. Ibid., p. 83; Lorimer, *Gazetteer*, pp. 1054–1055, 1067–1069.

10. Quoted in W. F. Smalley, "The Wahhabis and Ibn Saud," *Moslem World* 22 (1932): 234.

11. Philby, *Saudi Arabia*, ch. 4; Lorimer, *Gazetteer*, pp. 1078–1080.

12. J. B. Kelly, *Eastern Arabia Frontiers* (London, 1964), pp. 53–54; Lorimer, *Gazetteer*, p. 1074.

13. J. B. Kelly, *Britain and the Persian Gulf, 1795–1880* (London, 1968), ch. 3; Lorimer, *Gazetteer*, pp. 1076–1077; Kelly, *Arabia*, p. 58.

14. Philby, *Saudi Arabia*, ch. 5.

15. Lorimer, *Gazetteer*, pp. 1070–1073, 1082–1090.

16. R. Bayly Winder, *Saudi Arabia in the Nineteenth Century* (London, 1965), p. 6; Troeller, *Saudi Arabia*, p. 14; Philby, *Saudi Arabia*, p. 2; David Holden and Richard Johns, *The House of Saud* (New York, 1981), p. 22.

17. J. A. Saldanha, *Précis of Correspondence Regarding the Affairs of the Persian Gulf, 1801–1853* (Calcutta, 1906), p. 93.

18. Lorimer, *Gazetteer*, pp. 1091–1093.

19. Philby, *Saudi Arabia*, ch. 6; Winder, *Saudi Arabia*.

20. Lorimer, *Gazetteer*, p. 1094.

21. Ibid., pp. 1094–1098; Kelly, *Arabia*, p. 62; Saldanha, *Persian Gulf*, pp. 172–173, 180.

22. Philby, *Saudi Arabia*, ch. 7; Lorimer, *Gazetteer*, pp. 1097–1098.

23. J. B. Kelly, "Mehemet Ali's Expedition to the Persian Gulf, 1837–1840," *Middle Eastern Studies* 1 (1965): 350–381; 2 (1966): 35–61.

24. Lorimer, *Gazetteer*, pp. 1097–1098, 1103; Kelly, "Mehemet Ali," pp. 353–356; Saldanha, *Persian Gulf*, p. 201.

25. Lorimer, *Gazetteer*, p. 1106.

26. Ibid., pp. 1106–1108.

27. Philby, *Saudi Arabia*, p. 190.

28. Kelly, *Arabia*, pp. 68, 62; Lorimer, *Gazetteer*, p. 1117. In May 1835, Britain and the chiefs of the Pirate Coast had signed the Maritime Truce agreement by which the trucial system was born, stipulating for the end of all armed activities in Persian Gulf waters and along the coasts. The truce was renewed annually until 1843, when it was signed for a ten-year period. In 1853 a permanent Treaty of Peace in Perpetuity was concluded, to be enforced by the British government. Kelly, *Britain*, ch. 9; J. C. Hurewitz, *Diplomacy in the Near and Middle-East* (London, 1956), I, 143–144.

29. Kelly, *Arabia*, pp. 74–78; Lorimer, *Gazetteer*, p. 1112.

30. Kelly, *Arabia*, pp. 79–80; Lorimer, *Gazetteer*, p. 1112; Winder, *Saudi Arabia*, p. 218; Saldanha, *Persian Gulf*, pp. 16–17.

31. Lorimer, *Gazetteer*, pp. 1112–1113.

32. Lewis Pelly, "A Visit to the Wahabee Capital, Central Arabia," *Journal of the Royal Geographical Society* 35 (1865): 169–190; Lorimer, *Gazetteer*, pp. 1118–1120.

33. Ibid., pp. 1122–1123.

34. Philby, *Saudi Arabia*, ch. 8.

35. Hurewitz, *Diplomacy*, I, 172; Lorimer, *Gazetteer*, pp. 1123–1124.

36. Lorimer, *Gazetteer*, p. 1117; Kelly, *Britain*, ch. 12. Cf. Troeller, *Saudi Arabia*, p. xvi.

37. Philby, *Saudi Arabia*, ch. 8.

38. Lorimer, *Gazetteer*, p. 1128; Kumar, *India*, p. 113.

39. Kelly, *Britain*, ch. 15.

40. Lorimer, *Gazetteer*, pp. 1129–1133.

41. Ibid., p. 1097; Winder, *Saudi Arabia*, pp. 69, 104–105; Lorimer, *Gazetteer*, pp. 1162–1173.

42. Ibid., pp. 1135–1139.

43. The Saudi chronicler Ibn Bishr, quoted in Winder, *Saudi Arabia*, p. 48.

44. Saldanha, *Persian Gulf*, p. 180; Winder, *Saudi Arabia*, p. 82; Kelly, *Arabia*, pp. 72–74.

2. The Molding of a Statesman

1. St. John B. Philby, *Arabian Jubilee* (London, 1952), pp. 5–6; H. C. Armstrong, *Lord of Arabia: Ibn Saud, An Intimate Study of a King* (London, 1934), pp. 27–34. According to Robert Lacey, *The Kingdom* (London, 1981), p. 561, Ibn Saud was born in 1876 and was fifteen years old.

2. Philby, *Jubilee*, p. 6; Armstrong, *Ibn Saud*, pp. 20–21; J. Benoist-Méchin, *Arabian Destiny* (London, 1957), p. 59; Abdul Hamid al-Khatib, *Harbinger of Justice: A Biography of Ibn Saud* (Karachi, 1951), p. 29.

3. Armstrong, *Ibn Saud*, pp. 38–39; Benoist-Méchin, *Destiny*, p. 70.

4. Armstrong, *Ibn Saud*, p. 30; Van der Meulen, *The Wells of Ibn Saud* (New York, 1957), pp. 41, 44; Philby, *Jubilee*, p. 9; Lorimer, *Gazetteer*, p. 1140.

5. Ibid., pp. 1014–1016; 'Abd al-'Aziz al-Rashid, *Ta'rikh Kuwait* (Beirut, n.d.), pp. 108–109; H. R. P. Dickson, *Kuwait and Her Neighbours* (London, 1956), pp. 136–137.

6. Al-Rashid, *Kuwait*, pp. 119–121; Dickson, *Kuwait*; Ameen Rihani, *Around the Coasts of Arabia* (London, 1930), pp. 246–248; Armstrong, *Ibn Saud*, p. 40.

7. Philby, *Jubilee*, p. 6; Van der Meulen, *Ibn Saud*, p. 44; Armstrong, *Ibn Saud*, pp. 40, 44; 'Abd al-Latif Ibn 'Abd al-Majid, quoted in George Kheirallah, *Arabia Reborn* (Albuquerque, 1952), pp. 74–75; Benoist-Méchin, *Arabian Destiny*, p. 72.

8. Armstrong, *Ibn Saud*, p. 43; Van der Meulen, *Ibn Saud*, p. 46.

9. Busch, *1894–1914*, pp. 114–132.

10. Ibid., pp. 189–193.

11. Ibid., p. 25. See also Kumar, *India*.

12. Armstrong, *Ibn Saud*, p. 44.

13. Lorimer, *Gazetteer*, pp. 1018, 1020; India Office (IO) to Foreign Office (FO), April 7, 1897, FO 406/14, p. 9. See also Busch, *1894–1914*, p. 98.

14. Ibid., pp. 99–103; Lorimer, *Gazetteer*, pp. 1018–1022; al-Rashid, *Kuwait*, pp. 128–130.

15. Busch, *1894–1914*, pp. 103–108; Lorimer, *Gazetteer*, pp. 1022–1023, 1049–1050; Hurewitz, *Diplomacy*, I, 218–219. See also J. B. Kelly, "Salisbury, Curzon and the Kuwaiti Agreement of 1899," in *Studies in International History*, ed. K. Bourne and D. C. Watt (London, 1967); Busch, *1894–1914*, pp. 109–113.

16. Ibid., p. 188.

17. Lorimer, *Gazetteer*, pp. 1024–1028.

18. Philby, *Saudi Arabia*, p. 238; Philby, *Jubilee*, pp. 9–10.

19. Busch, *1894–1914*, pp. 199–205, 211–212; Lorimer, *Gazetteer*, pp. 1029–1030; Troeller, *Saudi Arabia*, pp. 19–20; Wahba, *Arabian Days*, p. 124.

20. Fuad Hamza, *Qalb jazirat al-'Arab* (Riyadh, 1933), p. 364.

21. Ahmad Assah, *Mu'jiza fawqa al-rimal* (Beirut, 1965), pp. 45–46. Cf. Kumar, *India*, p. 200.

22. Philby, *Jubilee*, p. 8.

3. *Recognition of Ottoman Sovereignty, 1902–1912*

1. Busch, *1894–1914*, p. 256.

2. Cf. Troeller, *Saudi Arabia*, pp. xviii–xix, xx–xxi, 12, 243.

3. Winder, *Saudi Arabia*, pp. 240–241.

4. Philby, *Jubilee*, pp. 10–11; David Howarth, *The Desert King: Ibn Saud and His Arabia* (London, 1964), pp. 13–23; Kemball (gulf resident) to Government of India (GI), March 2, 1902, FO 406/16, pp. 73–74; Robin Bidwell, *The Affairs of Kuwait* (London, 1971), I, xv; Wratislaw (consul, Basra) to O'Conor (ambassador, Constantinople), March 22, 1902, FO 406/16, p. 79; Lorimer, *Gazetteer*, p. 1144.

5. Wratislaw to O'Conor, in O'Conor to FO, March 20; Ibn Rashid to the Grand Vezir, 21 Dhu al-Qa'da 1319 [March 2, 1902], FO 406/16, pp. 52, 89.

6. Wratislaw to O'Conor in O'Conor to FO, March 25, 31, 1902, FO 406/16, pp. 60, 83.

7. Mubarak to Kemball, 20 Shawwal 1319 [January 31]; Kemball to GI, February 19, 1902, FO 406/16, pp. 62, 71.

8. 'Abd al-Rahman to Kemball, 5 Safar 1320 [May 14, 1902], FO 406/16, p. 102; Lorimer, *Gazetteer*, p. 1157. Cf. *Memorial of the Government of Saudi Arabia* (Cairo, 1955), I, 294.

9. Kemball to GI, May 23; GI to Kemball, June 23; Wratislaw to O'Conor, July 31; O'Conor to FO, September 9; FO to IO, September 19; GI to Kemball, September 24, 1902, FO 406/16, pp. 101–102, 107, 113, 124.

10. Lorimer, *Gazetteer*, pp. 1145–1146.

11. News Agent, Kuwait to Kemball, March 8, FO 406/17, p. 29; Jens Plass, *England zwischen Russland und Deutschland: Der Persian Golf in der Britischen Vorkriegspolitik, 1899–1907* (Hamburg, 1966), p. 324; Kemp to Rear-Admiral Drury, March 14, 1903, FO 406/17, p. 27.

12. Kemp to Kemball, in Kemball to GI, March 16, 1903, FO 406/17, p. 28; Lorimer, *Gazetteer*, p. 1146.

13. Kemp to Drury, March 14, 1903, FO 406/17, p. 27.

14. Gaskin (agent, Bahrain) to Kemball, November 7, India Office Records, Persian Gulf Residency (R) 15/5/24, pp. 32–34; Minute by Dane, July 23, 1903, quoted in Busch, *1894–1914*, p. 227n.

15. Minute by Dane, December 15, 1903, quoted in Kumar, *India*, p. 201; GI to Kemball, January 6, 1904, R/15/5/24, p. 35; Lorimer, *Gazetteer*, p. 1158; Kemball to GI, February 5; IO to GI, February 8, 1904, FO 78/5488.

16. GI to IO, March 24, 1904; Robin Bidwell, *The Affairs of Arabia* (London, 1971), I, xxxv.

17. Lorimer, *Gazetteer*, p. 1146; St. John B. Philby, *Arabia* (London, 1930), p. 175; Ibn Saud to Mubarak, 10 Muharram 1322 [March 27]; Devey (consul, Jidda) to O'Conor, April 22, 1904, FO 406/18, p. 31.

18. Wratislaw to de-Bunsen (embassy, Constantinople), June 22, July 3; Wratislaw to O'Conor, August 15, 1902, FO 406/16, pp. 106, 105, 119; Bidwell, *Kuwait*, I, xxi; Bidwell, *Arabia*, I, xxvii.

19. Sayyid Talib, "Memorandum on Najd Affairs," in O'Conor to FO, August 26, FO 78/5488; Ibn Rashid to Grand Vezir, January 7, 1904, R/15/5/24, p. 41.

20. Crow (consul, Basra) to Kemball, April 17; GI to IO, April 28; Crow to O'Conor, April 27, 1904, FO 406/18, pp. 26, 27, 35.

21. Ibn Saud to Cox and Mubarak, May 2, in GI to IO, May 20, 1904, FO 406/18, p. 32.

22. Cox to GI, May 16; GI to IO, April 28, May 20; O'Conor to FO, April 13, 1904, FO 406/18, pp. 32, 27, 21–22.

23. Cf. Kumar, *India*, p. 203; Troeller, *Saudi Arabia*, p. 22.

24. FO to O'Conor, May 10, 21; O'Conor to FO, May 16, 23, GI to IO, May 29, 1904, FO 406/18, pp. 29, 33, 34, 34*, 44.

25. O'Conor to FO, May 16; Memorandum by E. C. Blech, in O'Conor to FO, May 24, GI to IO, May 29, 1904, FO 406/18, pp. 34, 36–42, 44. Cf. Troeller, *Saudi Arabia*, p. xviii.

26. Maunsell to O'Conor, August 9, 1904, FO 406/18, p. 59.

27. FO 406/18, pp. 63, 76, 85; Lorimer, *Gazetteer*, p. 1147; Howarth, *Ibn Saud*, pp. 45–50; Hamza, *Qalb*, p. 366; Knox to Cox, August 26, 1904, FO 406/18, p. 92.

28. Knox to Cox, October 17, 1904, FO 406/25, p. 2; Lorimer, *Gazetteer*, p. 1148; Philby, *Jubilee*, p. 18; Wahba, *Arabian Days*, p. 164.

29. Armstrong, *Ibn Saud*, p. 82; Benoist-Méchin, *Arabian Destiny*, p. 96.

30. 'Abd al-Rahman to Fakhri Pasha, n.d., in Fakhri to Grand Vezir, October 8, 1904, FO 406/18, p. 85.

31. Grand Vezir to Minister of Interior, October 17, FO 406/18, p. 85; Monahan to Townley, December 29, 1904, FO 406/20, pp. 6–7.

32. Ibn Saud to Sultan and to Wali of Basra, November 16, quoted in Monahan to Townley, December 29, 1904, FO 406/20, pp. 6–7; February 18, 24, 1905, FO 406/21, pp. 13, 29–30.

33. Newmarch to Townley, November 28, December 26, 1904; Townley to FO, January 2, 1905, FO 406/20, pp. 9, 56–57, 74–75, 7; Monahan to Townley, February 24, 1905, FO 406/21, p. 29; Benoist-Méchin, *Arabian Destiny*, p. 96; Ibn Saud to Sultan, December 10, 1904, quoted in Husain (consulate, Jidda) to Townley, January 3, 1905, FO 406/20, p. 73, see also p. 82.

34. Knox to Cox, January 17, in GI to IO, January 23, 1905, FO 406/20, p. 69; IO to GI, December 30, 1904, FO 406/25, p. 3; FO to Townley, January 4; Lansdowne to Musurus (Ottoman ambassador, London), January 13; Lansdowne to Townley, January 11, FO 406/20, pp. 4, 32, 31; Knox to Cox, January 27, in Cox to GI, February 5; Mubarak to Cox, January 27, 1905, FO 406/21, p. 70.

35. Mubarak to Mukhlis, in Monahan to Townley, January 22, 1905, FO 406/20, p. 75.

36. 'Abd al-Rahman to Sultan, January 28, in Townley to FO, January 31, 1905, FO 406/20, pp. 81–82.

37. Townley to FO, February 12, 14, 17, FO 406/20, pp. 131, 142, 138; Persian Gulf summary of events, FO 406/21, pp. 89–90; Knox to Cox, February 28; Crow to O'Conor, May 19, FO 406/22, pp. 47, 75; Lorimer, *Gazetteer*, pp. 1150–1153; O'Conor to FO, March 27, 1905, FO 406/21, p. 60. Cf. Philby, *Jubilee*, p. 19.

38. Benoist-Méchin, *Arabian Destiny*, pp. 96–98; Armstrong, *Ibn Saud*, pp. 82–83.

39. Townley to FO, February 7, 14, FO 406/20, pp. 134, 142; Newmarch to O'Conor, April 15; Faizi to Wali of Basra, quoted by Crow to O'Conor, May 8, 1905, FO 406/22, pp. 43, 39, 54–55.

40. 'Abd al-Rahman Ibn Saud to Agah Pasha (of the imperial household), April 4, quoted in Crow to O'Conor, April 22, 1905, FO 406/22, p. 30.

41. Amir Ibn Sha'ban (chief of Bani Hajir) to Zaid Ibn Khalifa (chief of Abu Dhabi); n.d.; Diary of Persian Gulf Political Residency, October 5; Khalid Ibn 'Abdallah al-Suwaidi to Zaid Ibn Khalifa, 27 Jumada al-Thani 1323 [August 29, 1905], FO 406/27, pp. 39, 41.

42. Ibn Saud to Maktum Ibn Hashar (chief of Dubai), 20 Jumada al-Thani 1323 [August 22, 1905], FO 406/27, p. 40. See also R/15/1/556, pp. 1–10.

43. Residency Agent (Sharja) to Cox, October 5; Trevor (acting resident) to GI, October 29, 1905; Cox to GI, February 4, 1906, FO 406/27, pp. 40, 58.

44. Cox to Knox, January 17; O'Conor to FO, March 20; GI to IO, January 11, 1906; GI to Cox, December 5, 1905, FO 406/27, pp. 92, 37, 42.

45. GI to IO, January 11; IO to FO, February 22, 1906, FO 406/27, pp. 37, 36.

46. O'Conor to FO, March 20; FO to IO, March 31, FO 406/27, pp. 92, 93; IO to Viceroy, April 13, 1906, FO 406/28, p. 22.

47. Knox to Cox, January 19, FO 406/27, p. 59; February 3, 1906, FO 406/28, p. 6.

48. Ibn Saud to Mubarak, n.d., in Knox to Cox, February 25, 1906, FO 406/28, p. 49. Cf. *Memorial*, I, 303.

49. Cf. Helms, *Saudi Arabia*, p. 24.

50. FO 406/22, pp. 1–5, 77–78; 406/23, p. 22; 406/24, pp. 47–50, 80; 406/27, pp. 3, 5; Lorimer, *Gazetteer*, pp. 1042, 1156.

51. Prideaux to Cox, February 12, in Cox to GI, February 23, 1906, FO 406/28, p. 6.

52. Ibn Saud to Sultan, 24 Dhu al-Hijja 1323 [February 18, 1906], FO 406/28, pp. 7–8.

53. Qa'im-maqam of Qatif to Wali of Basra, in O'Conor to FO, November 14, 1905, FO 406/24, p. 56.

54. Cox to GI, April 25; Husain to O'Conor, April 28, May 13, FO 406/28, pp. 23, 66–67; Husain to O'Conor, July 18, 1906, FO 424/210, pp. 64–65.

55. Lorimer, *Gazetteer*, p. 1160; Plass, *England*, p. 360.

56. Husain to O'Conor, June 19, FO 406/29, p. 5; O'Conor to FO, July 3, FO 371/153, no. 23214; Husain to O'Conor, August 22, 1906, FO 424/210, pp. 91–92; Lorimer, *Gazetteer*, p. 1154.

57. Knox to Cox, August 28, September 18, 1906, FO 371/345, no. 10143/2, 7; Lorimer, *Gazetteer*, p. 1160.

58. Cox to GI, September 16, FO 371/345, no. 10143/2; Philip Graves, *The Life of Sir Percy Cox* (London, 1941), pp. 104–105; IO to Viceroy, November 9, 1906, FO 424/210, p. 146.

59. O'Conor to FO, October 30, 1906, FO 371/155, no. 32066; Lorimer, *Gazetteer*, pp. 1154-1155.

60. FO 371/345, no. 10143/12-13, 15–16; Cf. *Memorial*, I, 303.

61. Prideaux to Cox, November 17; Knox to Cox, November 20, 1906, FO 371/345, no. 10143/11, 13.

62. Cox to GI, November 24, 1906, FO 371/345, no. 10143/10.

63. Minute by R. E. Holland (Foreign Department, GI), January 22, quoted in Kumar, *India*, p. 209; GI to IO, February 21, 1907, FO 371/345, no. 10143.

64. O'Conor to FO, May 1, June 11, 1906, FO 406/28, pp. 23, 66; April 1, 1907, FO 371/345, no. 11067.

65. FO to IO, April 16; IO to GI, May 3, 1907, FO 371/345, nos. 11067, 10143.

66. Arif Muhammad Ibn Ahmad, *The Hijaz Railway and the Muslim Pilgrimage*, ed. Jacob M. Landau (Detroit, 1971); Paul K. Butterfield, *The Diplomacy of the Baghdad Railway, 1890–1914* (Goettingen, 1932); and M. K. Chapman, *Great Britain and the Baghdad Railway, 1884–1914* (Northampton, 1948); Cox to GI, quoted in Howarth, *Ibn Saud*, p. 78.

67. Shakespear to Trevor, March 9, 1910, FO 424/223, pp. 49–50; Harry V. F. Winstone, *Captain Shakespear: A Portrait* (London, 1976), p. 84.

68. Cox to GI, April 20, 1911, FO 424/227, p. 51.

69. Cf. Helms, *Saudi Arabia*, p. 277.

70. Shakespear to Cox, April 8, FO 424/227, pp. 52–54; March 18, R/15/5/27, p. 1; Winstone, *Shakespear*, pp. 100–104; Cox to GI, July 23, 1911,

India Office Records, Letters, Political and Secret (L/P&S) 7/251, file 1419, and R/15/5/27, p. 25.

71. IO to FO, June 7; FO to IO, July 28, 1911, L/P&S/7/251, files 899, 3955.

72. Ibn Saud to Shakespear, 20 Shawwal 1329 [October 23, 1911]; Shakespear to Ibn Saud, March 11; Ibn Saud to Shakespear, 22 Rabi' al-Thani 1330 [April 12, 1912], R/15/5/27, pp. 28, 30, 33.

4. Saudi-Ottoman-British Ambiguities, 1913–1914

1. Shakespear to Cox, May 15, 1913, FO 424/238, p. 210.

2. Cf. Philby, *Saudi Arabia*, pp. 265–266; Dickson, *Kuwait*, pp. 149–150; Great Britain, Admiralty, Geographical Section, *A Handbook of Arabia* (London, 1920), p. 355; Helms, *Saudi Arabia*, p. 282; Philby, *Jubilee*, p. 35; Gilbert Clayton, *An Arabian Diary, Sir Gilbert Clayton*, ed. Robert O. Collins (Berkeley, 1969), p. 19.

3. Shakespear to Cox, May 15, 1913, FO 424/238, p. 211.

4. Armstrong, *Ibn Saud*, p. 63.

5. Shakespear to Cox, April 8, 1911, FO 424/227, pp. 52–54.

6. Stanford Shaw, *History of the Ottoman Empire and Modern Turkey* (New York, 1977), II, 289–298; Leften S. Stavrianos, *The Balkans, 1815–1914* (New York, 1963), pp. 112–118; Armstrong, *Ibn Saud*, pp. 76–77.

7. G. E. Leachman, "A Journey through Central Arabia," *Journal of the Royal Geographical Society* 43 (May 1914): 500–520; Shakespear to Ibn Saud, December 17, 1912; Ibn Saud to Shakespear, 29 Muharram 1331 [January 6], R/15/5/27, pp. 39, 41–42; Shakespear to Cox, May 15, 1913, FO 424/238, p. 210; Armstrong, *Ibn Saud*, pp. 76–77; Ahmad 'Abd al-Ghafur 'Attar, *Saqr al-jazira* (Beirut, 1973), pp. 393–409.

8. Reports by Political Agent, Bahrain, FO 424/238, pp. 93, 116, 212; *Times*, May 23; Crow to Cox, in Cox to FO, May 10; Political Agent (Bahrain) to Cox, June 1, in Cox to GI, June 5, 1913, FO 424/238, pp. 109, 146.

9. Ibn Saud to Wali of Basra, reported by Political Agent (Bahrain) to Cox, May 26, in Cox to GI, May 30, FO 424/238, p. 130; Crow to Lowther (ambassador, Constantinople), May 18, in Lowther to FO, June 17, 1913, FO 371/1820, E28326/22076/44. Cf. Helms, *Saudi Arabia*, p. 285.

10. Ibn Saud to Cox, 8 Rajab 1331 [June 13, 1913], FO 424/239, p. 160.

11. Busch, *1894–1914*, pp. 322–347.

12. Cox to GI, May 26; GI to IO, May 31, 1913, FO 424/238, pp. 210, 146.

13. Minute by McMahon, May 28, quoted in Busch, *1894–1914*, p. 341; IO to FO, June 4; GI to IO, May 31, 1913, FO 424/238, pp. 145–146.

14. FO to IO, June 7; IO to GI, June 10; FO to IO, June 18, 1913, FO 424/238, pp. 152, 174, 191.

15. GI to IO, July 1; FO to IO, July 2; IO to GI, July 3; Cox to GI, July 11; FO to IO, July 15, FO 424/239, pp. 20, 22, 39, 56, 64; Cox to Ibn Saud, July 9 (sent on July 17), 1913, R/15/2/31, p. 14.

16. Political Agent (Bahrain) to Cox, in Cox to GI, July 11, 1913, FO 424/239, p. 56.

17. Cox to GI, July 30, R/15/2/31, p. 43; GI to IO, August 1, FO 424/239, p. 115; Ibn Saud to Shakespear, 20 Sha'ban [July 26], R/15/5/27, p. 94; Ibn Saud to Cox, 4 Ramadan 1331 [August 7], in GI to IO, September 5, 1913, L/P&S/10/384, p. 35.

18. GI to IO, August 2, 1913, FO 424/239, p. 115.

19. Cox to GI, August 7; GI to IO, August 10, 1913, FO 424/239, pp. 133–134.

20. George P. Gooch and Harold Temperley, ed., *British Documents on the Origins of the War, 1898–1914* (London, 1926), vol. 10, pt. 2, pp. 190–194; FO to IO, August 16, 1913, FO 424/239, p. 138.

21. Minute by Parker, August 14, 1913, FO 371/1820, E37510/22076/44.

22. Report by Parker, FO 424/239, p. 138.

23. FO to IO, August 16; IO to GI, August 21, FO 424/239, pp. 138, 179; Cox to Ibn Saud, September 11, 1913, FO 424/240, p. 30.

24. Trevor to Resident, December 20, 1913, FO 424/251, p. 112, and R/15/2/31, p. 73.

25. IO and FO letters, August 13, 1913, FO 424/239, p. 133.

26. Trevor to Resident, December 20, FO 424/251, p. 112; Ibn Saud to Cox, 25 Shawwal 1331 [September 27, 1913], in GI to IO, October 26, 1913, FO 424/240, p. 41.

27. Cox to GI in GI to IO, October 26; IO to FO, October 29; FO to IO, October 31, 1913, FO 424/240; pp. 41, 46.

28. IO to GI, August 21, 1913, FO 424/239, p. 179.

29. Cox, "Memorandum as Regards Bin Saud"; Cox to GI, December 2, 1913, L/P&S/10/385, pp. 255–256.

30. Trevor to Resident, December 20, 1913, FO 424/251, pp. 107–114.

31. Lorimer to GI, January 4, 1914, FO 424/251, pp. 108–109.

32. FO to Mallet (ambassador, Constantinople), March 26, FO 371/2123, E13135/1990/44; April 1, 1914, FO 424/252, p. 1. See also Graves, *Percy Cox*, p. 173.

33. FO Memorandum, March 9, 1914, FO 424/251, pp. 223–224. The Anglo-Turkish Convention Respecting the Boundaries of Aden was ratified on June 5, 1914. *British Documents*, vol. 10, pt. 2, pp. 340–341; Minute by Hirtzel (Political and Secret Department, IO), March 16, 1904, L/P&S/10/385, p. 227.

34. Cf. Daniel Silverfarb, "The Anglo-Najd Treaty of December 1915," *Middle Eastern Studies* 16 (1980): 167–177.

35. 'Arif Ibn Yusuf (wali of Syria and 'Umar Fawzi's father) to Mubarak, 12 Rabi' al-Awwal [February 9]; 'Umar Fawzi to Mubarak, 21 Rabi' al-Thani 1332 [March 9]; Grey (agent, Kuwait) to Knox, April 2, FO 371/2123, E21167/1990/44; Shakespear, "Note on Ibn Rashid's Affairs," May 21; Knox to GI, March 15; Grey to Knox, April 2, FO 371/2124, E29736, E12320, E21167/1990/44; Minute by Parker on meeting with Hakki, March 7, 1914, FO 424/251, pp. 215–216.

36. Douglas Carruthers, "Captain Shakespear's Last Journey," *Journal of the Royal Geographical Society* 59 (1922): 321–334, 401–418; Winstone, *Shakespear*, pp. 145–184; Ibn Saud to Trevor, 1 Rabi' al-Thani 1332 [February 26]; Shakespear to IO, June 26, 1914, FO 424/252, pp. 39, 171–174.

37. IO to GI, March 16, FO 371/2123, E12320/1990/44; Trevor to Ibn Saud, March 21, 1914, FO 424/252, p. 61.

38. Enver, Shafiq, and Talib to Mubarak, n.d., FO 371/2123, E21167/1990/44.

39. Ibn Saud to Mubarak and Talib, n.d., in Grey to Knox, April 7, 11, FO 371/2123, E21167/1990/44; Ibn Saud to Trevor, 6 Jumada al-Awwal 1332 [April 2]; Trevor to Ibn Saud, April 6, 1914, FO 371/2124, E22424/1990/44.

40. Talib to Mubarak, 15 Jumada al-Awwal [April 11]; Ibn Saud to Mubarak, 20 Jumada al-Awwal 1332 [April 16, 1914], FO 371/2124, E24823/1990/44.

41. Ibn Saud to Trevor, 22 Jumada al-Awwal 1332 [April 18, 1914], FO 371/2124, E24823/1990/44.

42. FO to Mallet, March 26; Mallet to FO, March 29, FO 424/251, pp. 286, 294; FO 424/252, p. 4.

43. Mallet to FO, March 27, 1914, FO 371/2123, E13605/1990/44.

44. Minute by Hirtzel, April 2, L/P&S/10/385, p. 199; FO to IO, April 1, 3; IO to GI, April 7, 1914, FO 424/252, pp. 2, 5–6, 30.

45. Grey to Knox, April 29, 1914, FO 371/2124, E24823/1990/44.

46. Shakespear to Cox, January 4, 1915, FO 371/2479, p. 338; Grey to Knox, May 6; Crow to Mallet, May 2, FO 371/2124, E26063/1990/44; Knox to GI, in GI to IO, May 10, FO 371/2123, E21050/1990/44; Crow to Mallet, May 8, FO 371/2123, E20672/1990/44; May 16, 1914, FO 424/252, p. 159.

47. Minute by Parker, March 7, FO 424/251, pp. 215–216; Mallet to FO, May 1, FO 371/2123, E19291/1990/44; May 12, FO 424/252, pp. 102–104; Hakki to Parker, May 21, 1914, FO 371/2124.

48. IO to FO, May 27; FO to IO, June 4, 1914, FO 424/252, pp. 136, 142–143.

49. FO, *Arbitration Concerning Buraimi and the Common Frontier Between Abu Dhabi and Sa'udi Arabia: Memorial Submitted by the Government of the United Kingdom of Great Britain and Northern Ireland* (London, 1955), II, annex A, no. 8; Amin Sa'id, *Ta'rikh al-dawla al-Sa'udiyya* (Beirut n.d.), II, 58–60; Jacob Goldberg, "The 1914 Saudi-Ottoman Treaty—Myth or Reality?" *Journal of Contemporary History* 19 (1984); 289–314; Mallet to FO, July 9, FO 424/253, p. 13; Enver to Ibn Saud, n.d., FO 371/2124, E34347/1990/44; Porte to Ibn Saud, 24 Ramadan 1332 [August 17, 1914], R/15/2/31, p. 199.

50. Bullard to Knox, June 23, Grey to Knox, June 26, Keyes to Knox, June 30, July 4, 1914, R/15/2/31, p. 158, FO 371/2124, E34347/1990/44, and R/15/2/31, p. 156.

51. Keyes to Knox, August 26, 1914, R/15/2/31, p. 190.

52. Knox to Cox, September 15, 1914, R/15/2/31, p. 304.

53. Report by Grey on meeting with Mubarak, quoted in Crow to Mallet, April 7, 1914, FO 424/252, p. 95.

54. *Memorial*, I, 393, 398; Cox to GI, January 26, 1915, FO 371/2479, p. 322b.

55. Shakespear to Cox, January 4, 1915, FO 371/2479, p. 338.

5. Independence and British Protection, 1914–1915

1. Busch, *1914–1921*, p. 10; Knox to GI, August 20, 1914, L/P&S/10/462, p. 166; Gertrude Bell to Wyndham Deeds, in Elizabeth Burgoyne, *Gertrude Bell: From Her Personal Papers* (London, 1961), p. 14.

2. British Commander of General Staff, India, to War Office, January 19, 1915, FO 371/2479, p. 274; Howarth, *Ibn Saud*, pp. 84–85; Philby, *Jubilee*, p. 40; Armstrong, *Ibn Saud*, p. 93.

3. Knox to GI, September 27, in GI to IO, September 28, 1914, L/P&S/10/387, p. 200; Philby, *Jubilee*, p. 40.

4. Jacob Goldberg, "Captain Shakespear and Ibn Saud: A Balanced Reappraisal," *Middle Eastern Studies* 22 (1986): 74–88; Minutes by G. R. Clerk and E. Crowe (FO), October 2, 3, FO 371/2139; Arab Bureau to GI, September 21, R/15/2/31, p. 206; Minutes of IO, September 22, L/P&S/10/387, p. 206; IO to Shakespear, October 5, L/P&S/10/387, pp. 186–187; Mallet to FO, September 4, 1914, FO 371/2139.

5. Knox to Ibn Saud, October 5, FO 371/2140; Knox to Keyes, October 5, R/15/2/31, p. 212; Mubarak to Ibn Saud, 25 Dhu al-Qa'da 1332 [October 14, 1914], L/P&S/10/387, pp. 164–167; Arnold T. Wilson, *Loyalties Mesopotamia, 1914–1917* (London, 1930), p. 30.

6. Ibn Saud to Knox, 4 Dhu al-Hijja [October 24]; Ibn Saud to Shakespear, 15 Dhu al-Hijja 1332 [November 4, 1914], FO 371/2479, pp. 258, 256; Howarth, *Ibn Saud*, pp. 84–85.

7. Declaration of war, November 5, 1914, FO 371/2145; Busch, *1914–1921*, p. 4; Proclamations by Knox, October 31, November 1, 1914, in Wilson, *1914–1917*, pp. 309–310.

8. Knox to Ibn Saud, November 3, FO 371/2140; Shakespear to Ibn Saud, November 8, 1914, FO 371/2479, p. 259.

9. Grey to Resident, November 21, 1914, L/P&S/10/387, pp. 129–130.

10. Ibn Saud to Knox; Ibn Saud to Shakespear, 10 Muharram 1333 [November 28, 1914], FO 371/2479, pp. 305a, 292; Hurewitz, *Diplomacy*, II, 4.

11. Cox to GI, November 29; Cox to Viceroy, November 22, 1914, L/P&S/10/387, pp. 141–142; Graves, *Percy Cox*, p. 182.

12. Shakespear to Cox, November 20, December 7, 1914, January 4, 1915, Shakespear to Ibn Saud, November 20, 1914; Ibn Saud to Cox, 15 Safar 1333 [January 2]; Shakespear to Cox, January 4, 1915, FO 371/2479, pp. 237, 291b, 338, 240, 341a, 338; Graves, *Percy Cox*, p. 187; Philby, *Jubilee*, p. 41.

13. Ibn Saud to Cox, 17 Muharram 1333 [December 5]; Cox to Ibn Saud, December 17, 1914, FO 371/2479, pp. 320a, 320.

14. Report by Shakespear to Cox, January 4, 1915, FO 371/2479, pp. 338–340.

15. Ibn Rashid played a threefold role: he was one of the reasons for Ibn Saud's reluctance to advance to Mesopotamia; he served as an excuse for Ibn Saud's inability to support the Ottomans; and he proved an indirect means by which Ibn Saud could support the British. Philby, *Jubilee*, p. 41; Djemal Pasha, *Memories of a Turkish Statesman, 1913–1919* (London, 1929), p. 165.

16. Shakespear to Cox, January 4, FO 371/2479, p. 340; January 19, 1915, L/P&S/10/388, pp. 190–193.

17. Cox to Ibn Saud; Cox to GI, January 16, 1915, FO 371/2479, pp. 308a, 307. See also Graves, *Percy Cox*, p. 187.

18. GI to Cox, January 21, 1915, FO 371/2479, p. 319.

19. IO to GI, January 23; Viceroy to IO, January 25, 1915, FO 371/2479, pp. 287, 275–276.

20. IO to FO, January 30, 1915, FO 371/2479, pp. 271–273.

21. Minutes of FO, January 31, February 1; FO to IO, February 2; GI to Cox, February 6, 1915, FO 371/2479, pp. 270, 281, 342a.

22. Cox to GI, February 16; Shakespear to Cox, January 16, in Cox to GI, January 29, 1915, FO 371/2479, pp. 316, 338; Philby, *Saudi Arabia*, p. 272; Gertrude Bell, *Review of the Civil Administration of Mesopotamia* (London, 1920), p. 25; Winstone, *Shakespear*, pp. 206–212; Ibn Saud to Cox, 19 Rabi' al-Awwal 1333 [February 4]; Grey to Cox, February 17, 1915, FO 371/2479, pp. 367, 365–366.

23. Gary Troeller, "Ibn Saud and Sharif Husain: A Comparison in Importance in the Early Years of the First World War," *Historical Journal* 14 (1971). Cf. Howarth, *Ibn Saud*, p. 87; Clayton, *Arabian Diary*, p. 23; Philby, *Saudi Arabia*, p. 272; Philby, *Arabia*, pp. 233–234; Philby, *Arabian Days* (London, 1948), p. 157; St. John B. Philby, *The Heart of Arabia* (London, 1922), I, 386; Busch, *1914–1921*, p. 233.

24. Ibn Saud to Cox, 19 Rabi' al-Awwal 1333 [February 4]; Cox to GI, February 24; GI to Cox, February 28; Cox to Ibn Saud, February 24, 1915, FO 371/2479, pp. 369, 373, 374.

25. Ibn Saud to Cox; Ibn Saud to Viceroy, 9 Jumada al-Thani 1333 [April 24, 1915], L/P&S/10/387, p. 43.

26. Cox to GI, June 24, 26; Cox to Ibn Saud, June 26, L/P&S/10/387, pp. 49, 45; Minute by Langley, August 12; FO to IO, August 16; Viceroy to Cox, August 18; Viceroy to Ibn Saud, August 26, 1915, FO 371/2479, pp. 382, 389, 395, 396.

27. Philby, *Jubilee*, p. 42; Bell, *Mesopotamia*, p. 25; Armstrong, *Ibn Saud*, pp. 97–98; Dickson, *Kuwait*, p. 250; Ibn Saud to Viceroy, 7 Dhu al-Hijja 1333 [October 16], FO 371/2769, E41435/4650/44; Keyes to Cox, December 4, R/15/2/32, p. 153; Grey to Cox, July 23, R/15/1/480, pp. 36–37; Philby, *Jubilee*, p. 42; Armstrong, *Ibn Saud*, p. 98; Ibn Saud to Cox, 14

Ramadan [July 27]; Cox to Ibn Saud, September 15, 1915, FO 371/2479, p. 400.

28. Salih al-Sharif al-Hasani to Ibn Saud, 2 Ramadan 1333 [July 15, 1915], FO 371/2769, E41435/4650/44.

29. Ibn Saud to Cox; Cox to GI, September 15; Viceroy to IO, October 7; IO to FO, October 14; FO to IO, October 18; IO to Viceroy, October 25, FO 371/2479, pp. 401–404, 406, 399, 408, 411; Ibn Saud to Cox, 30 Dhu al-Qa'da [October 10], R/15/1/480, pp. 40–41; Philby, *Jubilee*, p. 42; Busch, *1914–1921*, p. 246; Armstrong, *Ibn Saud*, p. 98; Ibn Saud to Viceroy, 7 Dhu al-Hijja 1333 [October 16, 1915], FO 371/2769, E41435/4650/44.

30. Keyes to Cox, December 4, 1915, R/15/2/32, p. 152; Graves, *Percy Cox*, p. 197; Busch, *1914–1921*, p. 246; al-Rashid, *Kuwait*, pp. 198–200.

31. Howarth, *Ibn Saud*, p. 88; Clayton, *Arabian Diary*, p. 23.

32. Reports by Cox, December 26, 1915, R/15/2/32, p. 211; January 3, 10, 1916, FO 371/2769, E38086, E136744/4650/44.

33. Viceroy in Council to IO, L/P&S/10/387, pp. 328–329. Cf. Philby, "Triumph," p. 302. See also Silverfarb, "Anglo-Najd Treaty."

34. FO, Political Intelligence Department, "Memorandum on British Commitments to King Husain," L/P&S/10/635, p. 79; FO, Political Intelligence Department, "Memorandum on British commitments to Ibn Saud," L/P&S/10/390, p. 254; McMahon to FO, February 29, 1916, FO 371/2769, E45854/4650/44.

35. Hurewitz, *Diplomacy*, I, 194, 209, 208, 218; II, 22.

36. Cox to GI, December 27; Minute by Oliphant, December 31, 1915; FO 371/2479, pp. 426, 424; Viceroy to IO, February 8, 1916, 371/2769, E26095/4650/44; Hogarth to Viceroy, April 11, 1915, quoted in Busch, *1914–1921*, p. 235.

37. Hurewitz, *Diplomacy*, II, 12–17; FO, "Memorandum on Ibn Saud," L/P&S/10/390, p. 254.

38. Jacob Goldberg, "The Origins of British-Saudi Relations: The 1915 Anglo-Saudi Treaty Revisited," *Historical Journal* 28 (1985), pp. 693–703. Cf. Silverfarb, "Anglo-Najd Treaty," p. 167; Troeller, *Saudi Arabia*, p. 90; Busch, *1914–1921*, p. 236.

6. Between the Hammer and the Anvil, 1916–1918

1. IO, "Memorandum on the Relations Between the 'Ajman and the Recent History of the Latter," July 25, 1916, L/P&S/10/387, pp. 333–338; Philby, *Jubilee*, pp. 45, 52, 61–63; al-Rashid, pp. 198–202; Dickson, *Kuwait*, pp. 150–153, ch. 10; Busch, *1914–1921*, p. 246.

2. FO, *The Official History of the Campaign in Mesopotamia* (London, 1921).

3. Ibn Husain 'Abdallah, *Memoirs of King 'Abdallah of Transjordan* (London, 1950), pp. 72–73; Troeller, *Saudi Arabia*, pp. 37–39; Philby, *Jubilee*, pp. 26–27; IO, "Arabia: The Hejaz-Nejd Feud," L/P&S/10/390, p. 200;

Shakespear to Cox, November 6, 1910, R/15/5/25, pp. 93, 101; Note by Cox on Ibn Saud, December 26, 1915, R/15/2/32/ p. 211.

4. Philby, "Report on the Operations of the Najd Mission," L/P&S/10/ 390, pp. 132–153; Monroe, *Philby*, p. 70; Troeller, *Saudi Arabia*, p. 105.

5. General Headquarters (Basra) to GI, July 9; Cox to Ibn Saud, June 25, 1916, FO 371/2769, E136744, E180581/4650/44.

6. Ibn Saud to Cox, 19 Ramadan 1334 [July 20, 1916], FO 371/2776. The India Office detected his awareness and instructed Cox to discourage any Saudi attempt "to play off Egyptian against Indian authorities." IO to GI, October 27, 1916, FO 371/2769, E218206/4650/44.

7. Husain to Ibn Saud, n.d.; Ibn Saud to Husain, 13 Shawwal 1334 [August 13, 1916], FO 371/3044, p. 413.

8. Ibn Saud to Cox, 15 Shawwal, 4 Dhu al-Qa'da 1334 [August 15, September 3, 1916], FO 371/2776.

9. 'Ali Haider to Ibn Saud, 14 Shawwal 1334 [August 14], FO 371/ 3047, p. 21; George Stitt, *A Prince of Arabia: The Emir Shereef Ali Haider* (London, 1948), p. 17; Ibn Saud to Cox, 13 Dhu al-Qa'da 1334 [September 12, 1916], FO 371/3047, p. 20.

10. Cox to GI, September 8; Cox to Arab Bureau, September 27, 1916, FO 371/2769, E180581/4650/44.

11. FO to McMahon (Cairo), September 23; IO to GI, September 19; GI to IO, September 30, FO 371/2769, E187737, E180581, E196560/4650/ 44; Minute by Hirtzel, October 17, 1916, L/P&S/10/387, p. 268; IO to GI, October 27, 1916, FO 371/2769, E218206/4650/44.

12. Cox to Ibn Saud, October 18, 1916, FO 371/2781, E244263/201201/ 44.

13. Husain to Ibn Saud, 6 Dhu al-Qa'da 1334 [September 5, 1916], FO 371/2781, E244263/201201/44.

14. Ibn Saud to Cox, 24 Dhu al-Hijja 1334 [October 22]; Cox to GI, October 29, 1916, FO 371/3044, p. 416.

15. Cox to GI, November 13, 21, 1916, FO 371/2769, E224780, E236884/ 4650/44.

16. George Antonius, *The Arab Awakening* (New York, 1938), p. 213.

17. Cox to GI, November 13; IO to GI and Cox, November 15, 1916, FO 371/2769, E224780, E230491/4650/44.

18. Graves, *Percy Cox*, p. 214; Wilson, *1914–1917*, p. 160; Cox to Ibn Saud, November 20, 1916, FO 371/3044, p. 418.

19. Gertrude Bell, "A Ruler of the Desert," in FO 371/3046, reprinted in Burgoyne, *Bell*, pp. 48–51; Cox to GI, November 21, 1916, FO 371/2769, E236884/4650/44; FO, "Memorandum on Relations with Ibn Saud," January 1, 1917, FO 371/3044, E35392/1458/44; Graves, *Percy Cox*, p. 214; Ibn Saud to Cox, 23 Muharram 1335 [November 20, 1916], FO 371/3044, p. 419.

20. Philby, *Jubilee*, pp. 46–47; Burgoyne, *Bell*, p. 48; *The Letters of Gertrude Bell*, ed. Lady Bell (London, 1927), II, 510; Report by R. E. A. Hamilton (political agent, Kuwait), December 12, FO 371/3047, p. 406; Ibn

Saud to Viceroy, 20 Safar 1335 [December 16, 1916], FO 371/3044, p. 431.

21. Quoted in Cox to GI, November 26, 1916, FO 371/2769, E236884/4650/44.

22. Ibn Saud to Viceroy, 20 Safar 1335 [December 16, 1916], FO 371/3044, p. 431.

23. Cox to GI, November 26, FO 371/2769, E236884/4650/44; FO to Treasury, December 26, 1916; Treasury to FO, January 1, 1917, FO 371/3044, p. 366. See also L/P&S/10/635.

24. C. E. Wilson to Husain, October 3, FO 371/2769, E218206/4650/44; FO to Wingate (Khartoum), September 6, FO 371/3047, p. 16; files, L/P&S/10/637–638; Antonius, *Arab Awakening*, p. 213; FO to Wingate, November 25; Wingate to C. E. Wilson, n.d., FO 371/2769, E236884/4650/44; Wingate to Cox, December 2, 1916, L/P&S/10/387, pp. 215–216.

25. Husain to Ibn Saud, 18 Muharram 1335 [November 15, 1916]; Ibn Saud to Cox, n.d., in Cox to Arab Bureau, February 1, FO 371/3044, p. 372; Cox to Ibn Saud, February 10, 1917, L/P&S/10/388, p. 177.

26. FO to Wingate, November 25, 1916, FO 371/2769, E236884/4650/44.

27. Shakespear to Cox, January 19, 1915, L/P&S10/388, pp. 190–193; Ibn Saud to Sharif 'Abdallah, 15 Dhu al-Hijja 1334 [October 13, 1916], L/P&S/10/645, file 889; Cox to Arab Bureau, February 1, 1917, FO 371/3044, p. 372; Philby to Cox, January 5, in Cox to GI, January 14, 1918, FO 371/3383, p. 263.

28. Philby to Cox, January 5; Hogarth to FO, January 8, 1918, FO 371/3383, pp. 263, 282, 288, 289; Philby, *Jubilee*, p. 51; Minute by Shuckburgh (assistant under secretary, IO), July 4, L/P&S/10/388, p. 139; Note by Hamilton on talks with Ibn Saud, November 1917, L/P&S/10/645, file 2891; Philby, "Najd Report"; Alois Musil, *Northern Nejd* (New York, 1928), pp. 288–289.

29. Djemal, *Memories*, pp. 152, 165; Antonius, *Arab Awakening*, chs. 8, 10.

30. Djemal, *Memories*, p. 165; Ibn Saud to Cox, 16 Rabi' al-Awwal 1335 [February 8, 1917], L/P&S/10/388, p. 162.

31. Cox to GI, January 3; Wingate (Cairo) to Cox, January 9; IO to Viceroy, January 9; FO to IO, January 20, 1917, FO 371/3046, E7097, E8400/4541/44; Ibn Saud to Cox, n.d., L/P&S/10/388, p. 254; Philby, "Najd Report."

32. Philby, *Jubilee*, p. 56; Cox to Ibn Saud, February 10, 1917, L/P&S/10/388, p. 175.

33. Wingate to General Command (Basra), March 20, in Cox to GI, December 28, FO 371/3383, p. 240; Sykes to Cox, May 10; Cox to Ibn Saud, May 21, 1917, FO 371/3059.

34. Sa'ud Ibn Rashid to Ibn Saud, 14 Rajab [May 7]; Ibn Saud to Cox, 19 Rajab [May 12]; Ibn Saud to Ibn Rashid, 22 Rajab [May 15]; Ibn Rashid to Ibn Saud, 27 Rajab [May 20], FO 371/3057, E178232/113500/44; Ibn Saud to Cox, 12 Sha'ban 1335 [June 3, 1917], FO 371/3059.

35. Cox to GI, May 14, in Cox to GI, December 28, FO 371/3380, p. 240; Hamilton to Cox, June 10, FO 371/3057; Hamilton's diary, June 13, 1917, FO 371/3059; Storrs, *Orientations* (London, 1937), pp. 244–248.

36. Sykes to Cox, May 22, in Cox to IO, May 24; Cox to IO, June 2, 1917, FO 371/3054, E104269, E119702/86526/44.

37. Hamilton's diary, June 11, 28, 1917, FO 371/3059.

38. Ibn Saud to Cox, 12 Sha'ban 1335 [June 3, 1917], FO 371/3057, E178232/113500/44.

39. Cox to GI, October 21, 1917, FO 371/3057; L/P&S/10/390, pp. 141–144.

40. Husain to T. E. Lawrence and C. E. Wilson, July 28, in Lawrence to Arab Bureau, July 29, FO 371/3054; Wingate to Cox, November 2, 1917, FO 371/3061, E210178/191347/44.

41. Hamilton to Cox, July 3, FO 371/3059; Cox to GI, September 30, 1917, FO 371/3061.

42. Paul W. Harrison, *The Arab at Home* (London, 1924); Harrison, *Doctor in Arabia* (New York, 1940); Cox to GI, September 28, FO 371/3061; Report by Harrison, September 1, 1917, R/15/2/33, pp. 179–181.

43. Note by Wingate, December 23, FO 371/3380, p. 422; Wingate to FO, October 5, 1917, FO 371/3061, E192213/191347/44.

44. Cox to GI, September 28, October 30, FO 371/3061; Elizabeth Monroe, *Philby of Arabia* (London, 1973), pp. 58–61; Lord Belhaven, *The Uneven Road* (London, 1955), pp. 22–26; IO to FO, October 11, FO to IO, October 18; Wingate to FO, October 5, 1917, FO 371/3061, E196624, E192213/191347/44.

45. Wingate to FO, November 9, 21; Wingate to Cox, November 2, 12; Minutes of FO, November 22, FO 371/3061, E214717, E222650, E210178, E216252/191347/44; Note by Residency (Cairo), December 23, 1917, FO 371/3380, p. 422.

46. Note by Residency (Cairo), December 23, FO 371/3380, p. 422; Cox to Wingate, December 15, 1917, FO 371/3061.

47. Philby, *Jubilee*, p. 54; Monroe, *Philby*, pp. 66–70; Philby, "Najd Report"; Daniel Silverfarb, "The Philby Mission to Ibn Sa'ud, 1917–1918," *Journal of Contemporary History* 14 (1979): 269–286.

48. Philby to Cox, December 2, in Cox to Wingate, December 15; IO to Viceroy, December 20, 1917, FO 371/3061.

49. Philby, "Triumph," p. 301.

50. Philby to Cox, January 5, in Cox to GI, January 14; Reports by Hogarth to Cairo, January 8, 15, 1918, FO 371/3383, pp. 263, 280–291.

51. Wingate to FO, December 28, 1917, FO 371/3056, E244770/99430/44; C. E. Wilson to Wingate, July 1918, FO 371/3381, p. 126.

52. Wingate to FO, January 10, FO 371/3383, E6696/675/44; Viceroy to IO, January 5, 1918, FO 371/3389, E4279/2240/44; Cox to GI, December 23, 1917, FO 371/3061.

53. Cunliffe-Owen (Riyadh) to Cox, February 5, in Cox to GI, February 15, 1918, FO 371/3383, p. 296; Philby, *Jubilee*, pp. 58–59.

54. Troeller, *Saudi Arabia*, ch. 4.
55. Report by Hamilton, November 1917, L/P&S/10/645, file 2891.

7. Patterns of Saudi Foreign Policy

1. Reports by Shakespear to Cox, April 8, 1911, FO 424/227 pp. 52–54; May 15, 1913, FO 424/238, pp. 210–211; Dickson, *Kuwait*, p. 274. Cf. Philby, *Saudi Arabia*, p. 271.

2. Reports by Shakespear to Cox, January 4, 1915, FO 371/2479, p. 338; May 15, 1913, FO 424/238, p. 210; January 19, 1915, L/P&S/10/388, pp. 190–193. An effort was made to conceal the fact that what Ibn Saud sought from the British was protection against the Porte. The Saudi overtures were thus described as "offers of friendship," attempts "to enter into friendly relations," and "a dozen-year effort to achieve a cordial understanding with Britain." *Memorial*, I, 294, 305; Philby, *Jubilee*, p. 47. This concealment was even more striking in the description of two specific overtures. Ibn Saud's urgent request for protection against the Ottoman expedition in May 1904 was described as a "tentative move aimed at reaching an understanding with Britain," a move prompted by the appointment of a British political agent at Kuwait. Ibid., pp. 33–34. Similarly, Ibn Saud's request for British protection so as to pre-empt Ottoman retaliation following his occupation of Hasa was described as "tentative advances to Britain with a view to an alliance against the Ottomans." Philby, "Triumph," p. 301. It was further asserted that, after the occupation of Hasa, Ibn Saud found that "he had many interests in common with the British," so "he at once established friendly relations with them." Wahba, *Arabian Days*, p. 166.

3. Reports by Shakespear to Cox, May 15, 1913, FO 424/238, p. 210; April 8, 1911, FO 424/227, pp. 52–54.

4. Cf. Helms, *Saudi Arabia*, pp. 277, 117; Report by Shakespear to Cox, April 8, 1911, January 4, 1915, FO 424/227, pp. 52–54; FO 371/2479, pp. 338–340; Ibn Saud to Shakespear, 15 Dhu al-Hijja 1332 [November 4, 1914], FO 371/2479, p. 256.

5. Ibn Saud to Dickson (political agent, Bahrain), 16 Jumada al-Awwal 1338 [February 6, 1920], L/P&S/10/391, p. 369; Philby, "Najd Report," L/P&S/10/390, p. 149; Ibn Saud to Cox, 1 Dhu al-Hijja 1333 [October 10, 1915] R/15/1/480, pp. 40–41; Cox, "Comments," p. 40.

6. W. C. Smith, *Islam in Modern History* (Princeton, 1957), pp. 41–44; Winder, *Saudi Arabia*, pp. 8–15.

7. Cox, "Comments," p. 40; Wahba, *Arabian Days*, p. 170.

8. Cf. Helms, *Saudi Arabia*, pp. 25, 181, 19, 109, 22–23.

9. Winder, *Saudi Arabia*, p. 15.

10. Shakespear to Cox, April 8, 1911, FO 424/227, pp. 52–54.

11. Report by Shakespear to Trevor, March 9, 1910, FO 424/223, pp. 88–89; Reports by Shakespear to Cox, April 8, 1911, FO 424/227, pp. 52–54; May 15, 1913, FO 424/238, pp. 210–211.

12. Arnold T. Wilson, *Mesopotamia, 1917–1920: A Clash of Loyalties* (London, 1931), p. 192; Eyewitness account by Cox, in Bell, *Letters*, II, 510; Van der Meulen, *Ibn Saud*, p. 41.

13. Dickson, *Kuwait*, p. 249; Ameen Rihani, *Ibn Sa'oud of Arabia: His People and His Land* (London, 1928), pp. 55, 212; IO, "Note on the Akhwan," May 1919, L/P&S/10/645.

14. Troeller, *Saudi Arabia*, pp. 142–143.

15. Troeller, *Saudi Arabia*, pp. 216–227.

16. Ibn Saud to Mubarak, n.d. (October 1914), R/15/5/25, p. 186; Report by Hamilton to Cox, November 1917, L/P&S/10/645, file 289; Keyes to Cox, March 2, 1916, R/15/2/32 pp. 279–280.

17. Philby, *Jubilee*, pp. 184–193; Troeller, *Saudi Arabia*, pp. 227–230. Paradoxically, the independence of the Hejaz brought about its doom, while the Mandatory status of Iraq and Transjordan were responsible for their survival.

18. Cf. Helms, *Saudi Arabia*, p. 81.

19. Philby, *Jubilee*, pp. 170–171; Lacey, *Kingdom*, pp. 240–241; Irvine H. Anderson, *ARAMCO, the United States, and Saudi Arabia: A Study of the Dynamics of Foreign Policy, 1933–1950* (Princeton, 1981); Lukasz Hirszowicz, *The Third Reich and the Arab East* (London, 1966), p. 52; Lacey, *Kingdom*, pp. 256–258.

20. Ibn Saud to Shakespear, November 28, 1914, FO 371/2479, p. 292.

21. *Memorial*, I, 377.

22. Report by Shakespear to Cox, January 4, 1915, FO 371/2479, pp. 338–340; Keyes to Cox, March 2, 1916, R/15/2/32, pp. 279–280; Report by Hamilton to Cox, November 1917, L/P&S/11/140, file 4836. Cf. Helms, *Saudi Arabia*, pp. 172, 77.

23. Cf. Helms, *Saudi Arabia*, ch. 6.

24. Holden, *House of Saud*, ch. 25.

25. James Piscatori, "Islamic Values and National Interest: The Foreign Policy of Saudi Arabia," in *Islam in Foreign Policy*, ed. Adeed Dawisha (London, 1983), pp. 33–53.

26. Philby, "Triumph," p. 295.

27. Holden, *House of Saud*, p. 21.

Index

'Abd al-'Aziz al-Sulaimi, 64
'Abd al-'Aziz ibn Muhammad (al-Saud), 8, 9, 12
'Abd al-'Aziz ibn Mut'ib (al-Rashid), 27, 41
'Abdallah al-Sabah, 31, 32
'Abdallah ibn 'Ali (al-Rashid), 26, 27
'Abdallah ibn Faisal (al-Saud), 8, 24, 25, 26
'Abdallah ibn Sa'ud (al-Saud), 8, 14, 15
'Abdallah (ibn Sharif Husain), 159, 180
'Abdallah ibn Thunain (al-Saud), 8, 21
'Abd al-Latif ibn 'Abd al-Majid, 30
'Abd al-Rahman ibn Faisal (al-Saud), 5, 8, 174; exile in Kuwait, 30, 31, 33, 41, 42; return to Riyadh, 51; overtures to Ottomans, 59, 63, 64
'Abd al-Wahhab, Muhammad ibn, 7, 8, 48, 175, 184, 188
Abdul Hamid II (Sultan), 34, 45
Abu Dhabi: Saudi expansion, 2, 67, 90, 165, 170; British influence, 46
Abu Lif, 24
Adana, 19, 61
Aden, 45
Afghanistan, 33
Ahmed Faizi Pasha, 62
Ahmed Pasha, 19
'Ajman, 18, 67; revolt against Ibn Saud in 1915, 128, 129, 130, 138; and in 1916, 136–141 passim, 147, 157, 158

Aleppo, 31
'Ali Haidar, 141
'Anaza, 152
Arab Bureau (Cairo), 2, 113, 133, 149, 153, 156
Arab League, 182
Arab Revolt (1916), 125, 134, 137, 139, 160
Armenians, 31
Asir, 14, 19, 70, 132, 134
'Ayaina, 8

Baghdad, 182; and Saudi expansion, 9, 12, 14, 17; and Muhammad 'Ali, 19; as Ottoman center, 25, 31, 73, 85; during World War I, 117, 132, 140, 152, 156
Baghdad Railway, 54, 77, 87
Baha al-Din, 104
Bahra Agreement, 180
Bahrain: Saudi expansion, 2, 170; and first Saudi state, 6, 12; and second Saudi state, 18, 21–25 passim, 28; and British influence, 35, 36, 46; and British political agent, 53, 70–73 passim, 79, 114, 165, 180; after Hasa's conquest, 85–86, 94, 99, 107, 110; during World War I, 123, 155
Balkans, 46, 85, 86, 167
Bani Hajir, 66
Bani Khalid, 17
Basra: and first Saudi state, 9, 10, 12;

Basra (*cont.*)
as Ottoman center against Kuwait,
32, 34–38 *passim;* as Ottoman center
against Ibn Saud, 48, 59, 65, 66, 73,
75, 85, 96, 101, 104, 105, 107, 110;
British conquest of (1914) and British headquarters, 112–118 *passim,*
122, 127, 129, 130, 132, 134, 142; Ibn
Saud's visit, 144–146, 177
Batina, 21, 24
Bell, Gertrude, 113, 145, 177
Berlin-Baghdad Railway, 34
Bisal, 14
Bombay, 31
Boyarim, 53
Britain, 3, 5, 183–184; and first Saudi
state, 12; hegemony in Persian Gulf,
13, 16, 45–46, 53; and second Saudi
state, 18, 20–29 *passim;* rivalry with
Ottomans over Kuwait, 33–41 *passim;* relations with Ottomans until
World War I, 45, 49, 51–57 *passim,*
63, 68, 76, 79, 93–102 *passim,* 105–
106, 109; attitude toward Ibn Saud
(1902–1912), 50–58 *passim,* 62–63,
74–80 *passim;* attitude toward Saudi
expansion in Persian Gulf (1905),
67–70; reaction to Saudi conquest of
Hasa, 82–111 *passim;* conventions
with Ottomans (1913, 1914), 87–88,
90, 98–99, 102, 215n33; outbreak of
World War I, 112–115; negotiations
and conclusions of treaty with Ibn
Saud, 118, 121–135 *passim,* 193–
198; policies during World War I,
137, 139, 142–143, 145, 147–157 *passim,* 160, 161, 163
Bukairiyya, 58, 60
Bulgarians, 85
Buraida, 55, 58, 64–66 *passim,* 73–75
passim
Buraimi, 12, 18, 23, 90, 172
Bushire, 13, 24, 33, 46, 71, 78

Cairo, 12, 19, 20, 182; Arab Bureau,
113, 133, 140, 142, 152, 153, 156,
157, 160
Caliphate, 167, 182
China Sea, 33
Christians, 13, 28, 40–41, 117, 167,
168, 176, 178

Constantinople, 31, 39, 46, 50, 56, 58,
64, 65, 66, 71, 72
Cox, Percy, 47; assessment of Ibn
Saud, 2, 165, 167, 170, 172, 177, 178;
attitude toward Ibn Saud (1904–
1912), 56, 73–74, 76, 78, 79; reaction
to Saudi conquest of Hasa, 83, 87–
94 *passim,* 98; negotiations with Ibn
Saud, 117, 120–131 *passim;* treaty
with Ibn Saud, 133, 191, 196, 198;
attitude toward Ibn Saud during
World War I, 136, 139–148 *passim,*
151–156 *passim,* 159–161 *passim*
Ctesiphon, 129
Cunliffe-Owen, 156
Curzon, Lord, 54
Cyprus, 45

Damascus, 11, 12, 14, 17, 31, 149, 182
Dammam, 23, 24
Dane, Louis, 54
Darin, 129
Dar'iyya, 7, 8, 9, 10, 14, 17
Delhi, 46
Dickson, H.R.P., 178
Dilam, 52
Dubai, 90

Egypt, 6, 10, 11, 27, 45, 181, 183, 187;
destruction of first Saudi state
(1811–1818), 14, 17, 62, 166, 171,
173, 183; Saudi exile in, 15, 16, 21,
29, 30, 42; 1837 expedition to
Arabia, 19–20; during World War I,
112, 116, 120, 129
Enver, 99, 113, 116
Euphrates, 12, 39, 58, 120

Faisal ibn 'Abd al-'Aziz (al-Saud), 181,
187
Faisal (ibn Sharif Husain), 154, 180
Faisal ibn Turki (al-Saud), 8; establish-
ment in Nejd and exile, 18–20 *pas-
sim;* return and confrontation with
Britain, 21–30 *passim,* 42, 70
Fakhri, 59, 61, 62, 149
Faruq (King), 182
Fertile Crescent, 173, 174, 182
Foreign Office: responsibilities in Per-
sian Gulf, 46–47; attitude toward
Ibn Saud (1902–1912), 57, 69, 77, 80;

reaction to Saudi conquest of Hasa,
81, 88–93 *passim*, 97–105 *passim;*
negotiations and conclusion of treaty
with Ibn Saud, 112, 122–124 *passim*,
127, 129, 133, 134; policies during
World War I, 142, 147, 148, 156, 157
France, 33, 34, 35, 46, 183

Gaskin, John, 36, 47, 53
Germany: rivalry with Britain prior to
World War I, 33, 34, 35, 45; World
War I, 112, 114, 134; World War II,
180, 181
Great Britain. *See* Britain
Grey, Edward, 88, 90, 91, 98, 102, 103,
105, 124
Grey, William, 47, 103, 104, 105, 109,
110

Hadda Agreement, 180
Hadramawt, 3, 14
Hail, 26, 48, 58, 130; during World
War I, 136, 139, 141–142, 147, 151–
164 *passim*
Hakki Pasha, 90, 91, 98–99, 105
Hamdan ibn Zayid, 165
Hamilton, R. E. A., 47, 149, 154, 185
Hamza, Fuad, 30
Hanbali, 7
Harb, 155
Hariq, 51
Harrison, Dr. Paul, 155, 178
Hasa, 1, 6, 7, 35, 183; during first
Saudi state, 9, 12, 15, 17; conquest
by second Saudi state, 18, 23; Otto-
man conquest (1871), 25, 26, 28, 31,
34, 54, 166, 168, 183; Ibn Saud
avoids occupying (1903–1912), 49,
68, 70–80 *passim;* disturbances, 53,
55, 67; Ibn Saud's conquest (1913)
and aftermath, 81–111 *passim*, 135,
178–179; during World War I, 115,
118, 120, 122, 126, 128–132 *passim*
Hashemite, 124, 180, 182, 183
Hauran, 12
Hejaz, 4, 6, 45, 70, 73; Saudi conquest
(1924–25), 2, 173, 178–179, 180–181,
224n17; during first Saudi state, 9–
11 *passim*, 14–17 *passim*, 173, 181;
during second Saudi state, 28–29;
under Sharif (King) Husain, 124,

125, 132, 148, 156, 159; in Saudi-
Sharifi rivalry, 137, 138, 157–161
passim
Hejaz Railway, 77
Hirtzel, Arthur, 102
Hitler, 181
Hogarth, David, 2, 133, 149, 159, 160
Hufuf, 10, 85
Husain (grandson of Prophet), 10
Husain (Sharif, King): comparison
with Ibn Saud, 124–126 *passim*,
132–134 *passim*, 183; relations with
Ibn Saud, 136–164 *passim*, 179, 182;
attitude toward Ottomans, 149, 150

Ibn Far'un, 143, 149
Ibn Khalifa, Zaid, 67
Ibn Rashid, 26, 27, 31, 168; battle of
Sarif, 39, 41, 42; struggle against Ibn
Saud over Nejd, 45, 48–67 *passim*,
71–77 *passim*, 82, 84; and aftermath
of Saudi conquest of Hasa, 99, 100;
at outbreak of World War I, 113,
116, 117, 119, 120, 122; Jarab battle
and aftermath, 124, 128–131 *passim;*
rivalry with Ibn Saud during World
War I, 136–146 *passim*, 151–153 *passim*, 158, 161, 218n15
Ibn Saud, 'Abd al-'Aziz ibn 'Abd al-
Rahman: nature of policies, 1, 2, 3,
5, 42, 178–188; exile in Kuwait and
impact, 3–4, 30–33 *passim*, 35, 39–
43 *passim*, 166, 171, 174, 175; age,
30, 209n2; attitude toward Ottomans
(1902–1912), 42, 44, 48–54 *passim*,
59–66 *passim*, 70–76 *passim;* struggle against Ibn Rashid over Nejd,
48, 50, 55; initial overtures to Britain (1902–1912), 50–54 *passim*, 56–
58 *passim*, 62–63, 70–71, 73–74, 75–
76, 78–80, 223n2; relations with domestic groups, 64–65, 109–110, 175–
176; operations on the coast (1905),
66–70; general attitude toward Ottomans and British, 69–70, 108, 110–
111, 166–174, 183–184; conquest of
Hasa, 81–86; relations with Ottomans after conquest of Hasa, 86, 89,
92–93, 101–102; overtures to Britain
after conquest of Hasa, 86–90 *passim*, 93–103 *passim*, 110, 223n2; ne-

Ibn Saud (*cont.*)
  gotiations and treaty with Otto-
    mans, 104–109, 191–192; position at
    outbreak of World War I, 112–114
    passim; attitude toward Britain dur-
    ing war, 114, 116–120 *passim,* 125,
    126, 131, 136–164 *passim;* attitude
    toward Ottomans during war, 115–
    117 *passim,* 120, 125, 126, 128, 131,
    137–141 *passim,* 143, 145, 148–153
    passim, 161–164 *passim;* Jarab bat-
    tle, 124; relations with Sharif Hu-
    sain, 136–164 *passim;* relations with
    Kuwait, 137, 138, 147, 157; personal
    conduct, 176–178
Ibn Taymiyya, 7
Ibrahim (ibn Muhammad 'Ali), 15, 16,
    17
al-Ibrahim, Yusuf, 32, 36
Idrisi (of Asir), 132, 134, 153
Ikhwan, 5, 82, 176, 178, 186, 187, 188
India, 12, 13, 31, 34, 46, 130
India, government of: attitude toward
    second Saudi state, 18, 21–25 *pas-
    sim;* responsibilities over Persian
    Gulf affairs, 46–48; attitude toward
    Ibn Saud (1902–1912), 51, 52, 54,
    56–58 *passim,* 74, 76, 77; attitude to-
    ward Saudi expansion in Persian
    Gulf (1905), 67–69; reaction to Saudi
    conquest of Hasa, 87–91 *passim,* 98,
    103; negotiations for treaty with Ibn
    Saud, 121–124 *passim,* 127–129 *pas-
    sim;* policy toward Ibn Saud in
    World War I, 141–144 *passim,* 147,
    161
Indian Expeditionary Force, 112, 129
India Office: responsibilities in Persian
    Gulf, 46; attitude toward Ibn Saud
    (1902–1913), 69, 80, 81, 88, 93, 94;
    negotiations for treaty with Ibn
    Saud, 112, 113, 122–124, 127, 129;
    policies during World War I, 142,
    145, 151, 156, 158
Iraq, Mesopotamia, 183; Saudi expan-
    sion, 2, 171, 173, 180, 187, 224n17;
    Saudi expansion during first state, 9,
    10, 12, 14; during second Saudi
    state, 20, 28–29; as Ottoman center,
    56, 61, 62, 102; during World War I,
    112, 115, 117, 119–122 *passim,* 127–

130 *passim,* 134–139 *passim,* 146,
    150–157 *passim,* 162
Iran, 183
Islam, 7, 31
Italians, 85

Jabal Druze, 152
Jabal Shammar: rise of Rashidi fam-
    ily, 25, 26, 29; Saudi-Rashidi rivalry,
    48, 55, 83; during World War I, 151,
    152, 164
Jabir ibn Mubarak (al-Sabah), 32, 129,
    147
Jafura, 12
Jarab, battle of, 124–129 *passim*
Jealan, 66
Jemal Pasha, 150, 151
Jews, 31
Jidda, 11, 14, 45, 154, 159
Jones, Captain, 22
Jubail, 132

Kapnist, Count, 37
Karbala, 10, 11, 12
Kemball, C.A., 44, 47, 50, 52, 54
Kemp, Rear-Admiral, 52
Keyes, A.J., 47, 179, 185
Khalid ibn Sa'ud (al-Saud), 8, 19, 21
Kharj, 20, 51
Khaz'al, 115, 147
Khomeini, 183
Khufaisa, 118
Khurma, 163, 179
Knox, S.G.: political agent in Kuwait,
    47, 58, 62–63, 69, 74, 76; acting po-
    litical resident during World War I,
    112–121 *passim,* 134
Koran, 31, 167
Kulakh, 14
Kut, 129, 137
Kuwait: Saudi exile in, 3–4, 30–43
    passim, 166, 171, 174, 175, 176;
    Saudi expansion, 6, 23, 68; British
    influence, 45, 46, 56, 58, 77–81 *pas-
    sim;* support for Ibn Saud, 49–52
    passim, 57; mediation between Otto-
    mans and Ibn Saud, 93, 101–104
    passim, 109, 110; outbreak of World
    War I, 113, 116, 123, 124, 129, 130;
    relations with Ibn Saud during the
    war, 137, 138, 147, 157; the durbar

(1916), 144–146 *passim*, 149; position during the war, 148–150 *passim*, 153, 154, 157, 158

Lansdowne, Lord, 46
Lapwig, 38
Lawrence, 36, 53
Leachman, G.E., 85, 152, 153
Lee-Warner, W., 1
London, 39, 46, 47, 54, 56, 57, 74, 83, 87, 88, 91, 92, 94, 100, 105, 111, 122, 130, 143, 147, 157
Lorimer, J. G., 47, 52, 97

Mahmud II (Sultan), 6, 14
Malah, 103
Mallet, Louis, 102, 114
Mandil, 'Abd al-Latif, 104, 106, 107, 127
Mandil, 'Abd al-Wahhab, 104
McMahon, Henry, 143, 183
Meade, Colonel, 37
Mecca, 6, 45; Saudi conquest (1803), 6, 10–11, 14, 181; Egyptian conquest (1812), 14; Sharifi rule, 134, 140, 148; Saudi conquest (1924), 179, 180; attack on Grand Mosque (1979), 186
Medina, 6, 45; Saudi conquest (1804), 11, 181; Egyptian conquest (1812), 14; Ottoman center in Arabia, 62, 64, 73, 75; Ottoman enclave during World War I, 138, 149–154 *passim*, 159, 160, 163; Saudi conquest (1925), 180
Mediterranean, 34
Mesopotamia. *See* Iraq
Midhat Pasha, 25
Moscow, 181
Mubarak ibn 'Abdallah (al-Sabah): influence on Ibn Saud, 4, 30, 35, 39–41, 166, 167; takeover of Kuwait, 32, 33; mobilizing Britain against Ottomans, 35–39, 134; and Saudi re-establishment in Nejd, 49–52 *passim*, 56–58 *passim*, 62–64 *passim*; and Ibn Saud's operations on the coast (1905), 68, 69; and Saudi overtures to Britain, 74, 76, 77; and Saudi conquest of Hasa, 99–103 *passim*, 109; at outbreak of World War I, 112, 114, 115, 117, 179; death of, 129, 137

Muhammad 'Ali: expedition to Arabia (1810), 6, 14; expedition to Arabia (1837), 19, 20, 28
Muhammad ibn 'Abdallah (al-Rashid), 26, 27, 41, 48
Muhammad ibn 'Abdallah (al-Sabah), 32
Muhammad ibn Sa'ud, 7, 8, 9, 17
Muhammara, 115, 148
Mukhlis, 61, 64
al-Murra, 66, 136, 139
Musa'id ibn Suwailim, 70
Muscat. *See* Oman
Musil, Alois, 149
Muslim Brothers, 182
Mutair, 155
Muwahhidun, 8

Nafud, 7
Najaf, 12
Nasser, Abdul, 182; Nasserism, 164
Nejd, 7, 166, 168, 171, 173, 176, 183; during first Saudi state, 9, 10, 14–17 *passim*; during second Saudi state, 18–20 *passim*, 25, 26, 29; during Saudi exile in Kuwait, 31, 41, 42; conquest by Ibn Saud (1902–1912), 49, 51–78 *passim*; under Ottoman pressure (1913–1914), 85, 87–94 *passim*, 99, 100, 106–111 *passim*; at outbreak of World War I, 115, 118, 122, 126, 127, 132; and Sharif Husain, 137, 143, 144, 147, 150, 155, 157, 160; and Britain, 138, 142, 143, 146, 156, 158, 161; and Ottomans, 150, 162, 163; Mission, 149, 156–160 *passim*
Nicolson, 123
North Africa, 46, 85, 167

O'Conor, 56–58 *passim*, 68, 69, 77
Odessa, 34
Oliphant, Lancelot, 123
Oman, Muscat, 6, 46, 79; Saudi expansion, 1, 2, 170, 172; expansion of first Saudi state, 12, 13; expansion of second Saudi state, 18, 21–25 *passim*, 28, 68; object of struggle among powers, 34–36 *passim*; Ibn Saud's activities on the coast (1905), 66–69 *passim*; and Saudi conquest of Hasa, 90, 107, 110

Ottoman Empire, 3, 5, 6; final removal from Arabia, 4, 5, 161–164 *passim;* reaction to first Saudi state, 10, 11, 14, 15, 85, 183; conquest of Hasa, 25–29 *passim;* pressure on Kuwait, 31–41 *passim;* Ibn Saud's attitude to (1902–1912), 42, 44, 48–54 *passim,* 59–78 *passim;* policy toward Arabia, 45, 55, 56, 61, 63; and Saudi conquest of Hasa, 82–86 *passim;* policy after Saudi conquest of Hasa, 92, 95, 97, 99–103 *passim;* negotiations and conclusion of treaty with Ibn Saud, 104–109 *passim,* 191–192; outbreak of World War I, 113, 117, 124, 128, 129; policies during the war, 137, 141, 148–151 *passim*

Palestine, 150, 160
Palmerston, 20
Parker, Alwyn, 90, 91, 98
Pelly, Lewis, 23, 24, 28, 177
Perseus, 39
Persia, 11, 13, 33, 34, 77
Persian Gulf: Ottoman rule, 6, 45; Saudi expansion, 12, 14, 18; British presence, 13, 16, 25, 27, 45–46, 50, 52, 53, 208n28; and struggle over Kuwait, 31, 33, 34, 36, 37, 40; impact of Ibn Saud's conquest of Nejd, 66, 74, 76, 80; impact of Saudi conquest of Hasa, 82, 84, 86, 87, 88, 94, 99, 106; at outbreak of World War I, 112, 113, 115, 120, 121, 123, 129, 133, 135; Ibn Saud's assessment of balance of power in, 166, 167, 169, 170, 173, 180
Philby, St. John, 2, 15, 187; in Nejd Mission, 149, 152, 156, 158, 159
Pirate Coast, 12, 13, 208n28
Prideaux, Francis, 47, 70, 75

Qasim (Nejd), 15, 17, 20, 29, 31; Saudi-Ottoman confrontation over, 55, 58–66 *passim,* 71–77 *passim;* Saudi-Sharifi rivalry over, 137, 138; in World War I, 129, 146, 150, 151, 154
Qasim al-Thani, 71, 73, 75, 77
Qasr Ibn Uqail, 59
Qatar: Saudi expansion, 1, 2, 170; during first Saudi state, 12; during second Saudi state, 18, 21, 22; and Ibn Saud's activities on the coast (1905), 66, 67; and Saudi overtures to Britain, 71, 73, 75, 79; and Saudi conquest of Hasa, 89, 91, 93, 95, 96, 97, 104, 107; during World War I, 123
Qatif, 35, 49, 70, 183; Egyptian expedition (1837), 19, 24; Saudi conquest, 85, 102, 105; during World War I, 115, 118, 122, 126, 132
Qawasim, 13
Qur'an. *See* Koran

Ras al-Hadd, 23
Ras al-Khaima, 13, 28
Rawdat al-Muhanna, 73
Red Sea, 6, 14, 19, 112
Riyadh, 7, 175; selection as new capital, 17; during Egyptian expedition (1837), 20, 21; Pelly's visit (1865), 23, 177; and second Saudi state, 24, 25, 26, 28; and Saudi exile, 30, 31, 32, 41–44 *passim;* Saudi re-establishment (1902), 48, 84; center of Ibn Saud's activities, 49, 51, 52, 54, 58–64 *passim,* 73, 76, 85, 100, 105, 107–111 *passim;* at outbreak of World War I, 121; during World War I, 140, 147–151 *passim,* 155, 162; and Nejd Mission, 152, 157
Rub' al-Khali, 7, 30
Russia: struggle with Britain in Persian Gulf, 33–37 *passim,* 40, 45, 46; overtures to Ibn Saud, 51, 52, 53, 56, 57
Ruwala, 152

al-Sabah (Kuwait), 32
Sa'd ibn 'Abd al-Rahman (al-Saud), 128, 137
Sadlier, Captain, 16
Safwan, 63, 64
Salih ibn Hasan, 64, 73
Salim ibn Mubarak (al-Sabah), 32, 155
Samawa, 12, 58
Sami Pasha, 64, 73, 74, 104
Saratow, 99
Sarif, 39
Sa'ud ibn 'Abd al-'Aziz (al-Saud), the Great, 6, 8, 11, 12, 13, 18, 21
Sa'ud ibn 'Abd al-'Aziz (al-Saud), 187
Sa'ud ibn Faisal (al-Saud), 8, 25, 26, 166

Sa'ud ibn Muhammad, 7
Saudi Memorial, 184, 223n2
Sayyid Talib, 55, 101, 104, 117
Selim I (Sultan), 6
Selim III (Sultan), 6, 11
Serbs, 85
Shakespear, W.H.I., 47; first meetings with Ibn Saud, 44, 78, 79, 176; meeting of March 1913, 81–85; and Saudi conquest of Hasa, 88, 89, 94–97 passim, 100, 110; mission to Ibn Saud at outbreak of World War I, 114–117, 175; negotiations for treaty, 118–120, 125, 165, 167; death of, 124, 126; assessment of Ibn Saud, 177–178, 185
Sha'lan, Nuri, 152
Shaqra, 66
Shari'a, 118, 170
Sharja, 13, 18
al-Sheikh. See 'Abd al-Wahhab, Muhammad Ibn
Shi'ites, 10, 11, 12, 170
Shinana, 59
Shinas, 13
Sinai, 150
Sphinx, 52
Soviet Union, 181
Stalin, 181
Storrs, Ronald, 153, 156, 157, 159
Subaihiyya, 104, 107
al-Subhan Ibn Rashid, 27, 151
Sudair, 51, 64
Suez Canal, 34, 44, 45
Sulaiman Shafiq Ibn Ali Kamali, 107, 191, 192
Suleiman, the Magnificent (Sultan), 6
Suleiman Pasha, 9, 10
Sunnis, 11
Sur, 23
Sykes, Mark, 152, 154
Syria, 61, 182, 183; Saudi expansion, 2, 11, 12, 14, 19, 28, 29; during World War I, 12, 138, 143, 146, 150, 151; Greater Syria, 182

Taif, 11, 14, 179
Tal'at Bey, 102
Tallal ibn 'Abdallah (al-Rashid), 27, 48
Tarut, 18, 129
Tawfiq Pasha, 57
Tehran, 31

Transjordan, 2, 171, 180, 187, 224n17
Treasury, 147
Trevor, Arthur, 47, 94–97 passim, 100–102 passim, 110
Tripoli (Lebanon), 34
Tripoli (Libya), 85
Troeller, Gary, 124
Trucial Coast, 1, 165; expansion of first two Saudi states, 13, 21, 22, 24; impact of Ibn Saud's activities on (1905), 76–79 passim; impact of Saudi conquest of Hasa on, 95–97 passim, 104; at outbreak of World War I, 123. See also Pirate Coast
Turkey, 134, 180
Turki ibn 'Abd al-'Aziz (al-Saud), 154
Turki ibn 'Abdallah (al-Saud), 8, 17, 18, 28
Turks, 31, 51, 80, 113, 134, 136, 141, 149, 155, 164, 167, 168, 180
Tusun, 14

Ulama, 110, 117, 175
'Umar Fawzi, 99, 104
'Unaiza, 55, 64, 66, 74, 75
United States, 181
Uqair, 24, 85, 94, 105, 143
'Utaiba, 137, 155

Viceroy (India), 46, 127, 128, 131, 133, 147
Vladivostok, 33

Wahhabism: movement, 1, 5, 48, 186, 187; doctrine, 2, 5, 8, 170, 175, 181, 184, 185, 188; expansionism, 165, 170
War Office, 129
Washm, 55, 64
Whyte, J.F., 36
Wilson, A.T., 177
Wilson, C.E., 147, 152, 157
Winder, Bayly, 173
Wingate, Reginald, 157, 160

Yemen: Saudi expansion, 2, 3, 171, 180; Ottoman policies, 6, 45, 70, 73; Egyptian expeditions, 14, 19; revolution (1962), 183
Young Turks, 46

Zubair, 12, 113
Zuhaf, 39

Harvard Middle Eastern Studies

Out-of-print titles are omitted

3. *The Idea of the Jewish State*. By Ben Halpern. 1961. (Second edition, 1969).

5. *Egypt in Search of Political Community: An Analysis of the Intellectual and Political Evolution of Egypt, 1804–1952*. By Nadav Safran. 1961 (also a Harvard Political Study).

6. *The Economy of Cyprus*, By A. J. Meyer, with Simos Vassiliou. 1962.*

12. *Tripoli: A Modern Arab City*. By John Gulick. 1967.

13. *Pioneers East: The Early American Experience in the Middle East*. By David H. Finnie. 1967.

15. *Between Old and New: The Ottoman Empire under Sultan Selim III, 1789–1807*. By Stanford J. Shaw. 1971.

16. *The Patricians of Nishapur: A Study in Medieval Islamic Social History*. By Richard W. Bulliet. 1972.

17. *A Sufi Rule for Novices: Kitāb Ādāb al-Murīdīn*. By Menahem Milson. 1975.

18. *Merchants and Migrants in Nineteenth-Century Beirut*. By Leila Tarazi Fawaz. 1983.

19. *The Foreign Policy of Saudi Arabia: The Formative Years, 1902–1918*. By Jacob Goldberg. 1986.

*Published jointly by the Center for International Affairs and the Center for Middle Eastern Studies.